The Journey Is Home

The Journey Is Home

NELLE MORTON

Beacon Press Boston

Beacon Press books are published under the auspices
of the Unitarian Universalist Association of
Congregations in North America,
25 Beacon Street, Boston, Massachusetts 02108
Published simultaneously in Canada by
Fitzhenry and Whiteside Limited, Toronto

Printed in the United States of America

(hardcover) 9 8 7 6 5 4 3 2 1

Library of Congress Cataloging in Publication Data

Morton, Nelle.
    The journey is home.

    Includes index.
    1. Woman (Christian theology)—Addresses, essays,
lectures.   2. Feminism—Religious aspects—Christianity
—Addresses, essays, lectures.   3. Morton, Nelle—
Addresses, essays, lectures.   I. Title.
BT704.M67   1985   261.8′344   84-45716
ISBN 0-8070-1128-2

*To
my grandmother,
Mary Ellen Longacre O'Dell,
1847–1906,
who was called Nelle*

*To
my mother,
Mary Katharine O'Dell Morton,
1878–1945,
who in more ways than one made my journey inevitable*

*To
my contemporary fore-sister,
Thelma Stevens,
1902–
who was making the road when I first*

*To
my goddess daug
Nancy Lynn Ne
1958–
who has "miles to go*

The Journey Is Home

NELLE MORTON

Beacon Press Boston

Beacon Press books are published under the auspices
of the Unitarian Universalist Association of
Congregations in North America,
25 Beacon Street, Boston, Massachusetts 02108
Published simultaneously in Canada by
Fitzhenry and Whiteside Limited, Toronto

Printed in the United States of America

(hardcover) 9 8 7 6 5 4 3 2 1

Library of Congress Cataloging in Publication Data

Morton, Nelle.
    The journey is home.

    Includes index.
    1. Woman (Christian theology)—Addresses, essays,
lectures.   2. Feminism—Religious aspects—Christianity
—Addresses, essays, lectures.   3. Morton, Nelle—
Addresses, essays, lectures.   I. Title.
BT704.M67 1985   261.8′344   84-45716
ISBN 0-8070-1128-2

To
my grandmother,
Mary Ellen Longacre O'Dell,
1847–1906,
who was called Nelle

To
my mother,
Mary Katharine O'Dell Morton,
1878–1945,
who in more ways than one made my journey inevitable

To
my contemporary fore-sister,
Thelma Stevens,
1902–
who was making the road when I first knew her

To
my goddess daughter,
Nancy Lynn Nestingen,
1958–
who has "miles to go . . ." thank goodness!

Grateful acknowledgment is made to the following for permission to reprint: "A Part of Me Is Missing" from *Women in a Strange Land* by Anne McGrew Bennett, copyright © 1975 by Fortress Press, reprinted by permission of the author and publisher; the lines from "Commentary" by W. H. Auden, reprinted from *The Collected Poetry of W. H. Auden*, copyright © 1929 and renewed 1967 by W. H. Auden and Christopher Isherwood, by permission of Random House, Inc.; the lines from "Anger and Tenderness" from *A Wild Patience Has Taken Me This Far: Poems 1978-81* by Adrienne Rich, copyright © 1981 by Adrienne Rich, by permission of W. W. Norton and Company, Inc. and the author; "We find our stories through the hallows of time" by Rev. Kathi Wolfe, reprinted by permission of the author; "The Walls Do Not Fall" (no. 33 only) by H. D., from *Collected Poems 1912-1944*, copyright © 1982 by the Estate of Hilda Doolittle, reprinted by permission of New Directions Publishing Corporation; "Margo" by Denise Levertov, from *Footprints*, copyright © 1972 by Denise Levertov, reprinted by permission of New Directions Publishing Corporation; "Woman" by Catherine Leahy, reprinted from *Desert Gumbo*, Grail Communications Newsletter, Volume II, Issue 7, August, 1984, used by permission of the author; the lines from "A Prayer for Old Age" by W. B. Yeats are from *The Poems of W. B. Yeats*, edited by Richard J. Finneran, copyright © 1934 by Macmillan Publishing Company, Inc., and renewed 1962 by Bertha Georgie Yeats, reprinted by permission of Macmillan Publishing Company, Michael B. Yeats, and Macmillan London, Ltd.

The author would like to thank the following books and journals, in which several of the essays collected here first appeared: "Women—on the March" appeared in *Tempo*, October 1970, and in *Drew Magazine*, Winter 1970, and appears here courtesy of Drew University. "The Rising Woman Consciousness in a Male Language Structure" was published in the *Andover Newton Quarterly*, March 1972, and also in an abbreviated form in *Woman-Spirit*, Vol. 1, No. 2. "How Images Function" appeared in abbreviated form in *Quest* 3, Fall 1976. "Preaching the Word" appeared in *Sexist Religion and Women of the Church—No More Silence*, edited by Alice Hageman (New York: Association Press, 1974). "Toward a Whole Theology" appeared in abbreviated form in *Lutheran World*, January 1975, and in *Frau und Religion*, edited by Elisabeth Moltmann-Wendel (Germany: Fischer Taschenbuch Verlag, 1983). "A Word We Cannot Yet Speak" appeared in condensed form in *New Conversations 2*, Winter 1977. "Beloved Image" was published in *La Sfida del femminismo alla teologia*, edited by Mary Hunt and Rosino Gibellini (Editrice Queriniana Brescia, via Piamarta, 6, 1980). "The Goddess as Metaphoric Image" appeared in abbreviated form in *WomanSpirit* Spring 1984 and in *Presbyterian Survey*, November 1984.

CONTENTS

Acknowledgments

I must acknowledge, first of all, that I did not have to start at the beginning. I was born with a rich heritage. My grandmother was of a people whom one historian referred to as a little band of Presbyterians from the Scottish Highlands seeking freedom and justice. They traveled south until reaching the mountains of east Tennessee, which reminded them of Scotland and Ireland. My grandmother used to rock before an open fire in her white starched apron, reminding me before I was old enough to understand that I had her name—Ellen. Ellen spelled backward is Nelle. Her nickname was Nelle. The family called her Ma.

Looking over my shoulder on every page of this manuscript has been my mother—a strong Appalachian Amazon—a woman in her own strength and before her time—no stranger to hard work, hard thinking; unhesitant to take a forthright stand on political and social issues; a faithful church woman and a loyal member of the Women's Christian Temperance Union. In many ways I give her back her own pages. When young, she wrote a prize-winning oration, "The Woman I Want to Be." It anticipated the woman movement today. When I was in my teens, she gave it to me to use in an oration contest. I, too, won a prize with it.

Thelma Stevens, born in Mississippi, was an early inspiration for me. While she was with the Methodist Episcopal Church South, before the union of the three churches into the United Methodist Church, Thelma was boldly involving Southern women in issues of social, political, and international justice. Recently, in her eighties, after sixteen years of retirement, she addressed by published letter the United Methodist Church. Attending her thirteenth consecutive

General Conference, which meets every four years, she called the church to account for "celebrating a glorious past but no future." They had ignored urgent current issues, she pointed out, by establishing "no action plans and program priorities...to guide toward peace...by walling out...all homosexuals in God's household of faith...and by leaving the prophetic role hanging 'fruitless.'"

I am indebted to Claire Randall, who directed the Commission on Women and Religion and who, with Thelma Stevens, involved me directly in the woman movement. In a true sense all of these essays grew out of that early movement.

In 1974, Erika Wisselinck questioned me at length in Berlin about my essay "Toward a Whole Theology." She invited me back to Germany the following year to discuss the essay's theology with German women theologians. Since that time, she has continued to be a constant encouragement as friend and critic. In 1972, when I was lecturing to the Graduate Theological Union community in Berkeley, California, and to its first course on women and theology—coordinated by Sally Gearhart—Sally had probed me in the same way Erika did later. She asked repeatedly: "Do you know what you said? Do you know what you are saying?" To back up her excitement Sally had Jean Mountaingrove publish the entire text of my lecture in the first volume of *WomanSpirit*. I have felt the support of these women since those days.

Others who read all or some of the essays during the selection for this book were Bernadette Brooten, Anne Bennett, Barbara Martyn, Ana Mahoney, Judith Plaskow, Miki Bratt, Charlotte Ellen, Catherine Keller, Sheila Briggs, and Harriet Ellenberger. Harriet came all the way from Vermont to California to help me with the first editing. She gave me confidence while asking most penetrating questions. For her I am grateful.

A number of sisters were always ready from a distance to assist with a knotty question I was at the moment struggling with: Linda Barufaldi, Rita Brock, Peggy Billings, Beverly Harrison, Emily Culpepper, Adrienne Rich, and Mary Daly. Jan Raymond's influence can be seen reflected in many of these pages. I sometimes felt I was imposing on Charlotte Ellen, a close friend and ardent feminist—always there with a freshness that was empowering. She and Howard Clinebell were the first to suggest, then urge, that I publish a collection of my essays.

Friend, mentor, and critic, Peggy Cleveland has been an inspiration for many years. We are both Southern: she from North Carolina, I from Tennessee. We went to the same small woman's college in the heart of the Scottish Presbyterian sandhill section of North Carolina. We belonged to the same denomination (Presbyterian Church U.S.) and both worked on its national board. Our similar heritage, education, religion, and social and political commitment have led us into a common world view so that we bring something of the same criteria and critical analyses to our deepening feminism and our connectedness of feminism with political, social, and ecological issues. Peggy has been almost an alter ego, helping me know what I think, deepen what I believe, and become more courageous in where I choose to take my stand.

Betty Thompson's ecumenical experience and knowledge were an invaluable help in correcting errors, fleshing out history, and providing me with all sorts of extra research data. In addition she continues to support and inspire my work.

Though Jean Fairfax has not contributed specifically to the preparation of this particular manuscript, I cannot omit acknowledging her influence on many of these pages. I have known her since she was dean at Tuskegee Institute. We traveled together in Southern communities before the Supreme Court decision of 1954, and from time to time she has involved me in projects such as her work with the community schools for black children in Prince Edward County, Virginia, when the white public schools closed and opened again as exclusive private schools rather than integrate.

A brief stint as a visiting fellow at the Institute of Policy Studies in Washington, D.C., brought important feedback to my early work on images, and continuing help from Judy Davis.

Burnice Fjellman, a companion in world travel since we met in 1962 in Geneva, has kept me informed on official feminist activities in the area of religion and women in ministry.

From the early days of the Commission on Women and Religion (interdenominational and interfaith), Charlotte Bunch, a charter member, has been a steady and supportive sister, a friend who has kept me in touch with spiraling global feminism.

The Reverend Mr. Roddey Reid, when an Episcopal rector in Bristol, Virginia, helped to involve me in teaching mentally retarded children. Although my teaching experience was brief, these children and their families provided me with an education in another kind of language and knowing that has illumined my participation in the woman movement and my work in theology and language. (See Appendix.)

I shall never cease to be motivated by the almost all night conversation in 1963 with Madeline Barot of France, who became the first official advocate for women in the World Council of Churches. We drank as many tears together from our soup as we had soup in a small dark restaurant in the oldest section of Geneva. Our hearts were heavy over the slowness of the church to enter the modern world when we both had chosen the church for our life's vocation.

Brigalia Bam from South Africa has been an inspiration (more than she realizes) since 1973. She was primarily responsible for structuring the World Council of Churches Conference on Sexism in the 1970s. (See "Toward a Whole Theology.")

Closer to home, I am indebted to my dear friend, faithful supporter, and severe critic, Anne Bennett, a member of my community in Claremont. I respect her judgment. I take seriously her questions and comments. She has listened to me read almost every page of this book, intuiting what I tried to say when I had not been clear. Many times I have stopped on some paragraph to say, "Anne, I can't let that come out in print. I won't have a friend or family left." Back came Anne in her usual soft and gentle but snappy way, "But you know it's true!"

Two groups to which I have belonged have helped me in many ways. Sister Circle has been invaluable to me since coming to Claremont, invaluable for its friendships, its woman rituals, its intimate exchanges, its bold experimentation. On another level and in another way, Thiasos, a group of graduate women in feminism and religion, has nurtured many close friendships. It was organized to explore feminist theory and the unique process of doing theology out of our common woman experiences.

I would like to acknowledge help and inspiration from Professor Robert Funk in the new horizons his work opened to me on parable, metaphor, and presence. My thanks also to Ed Nestingen, and a former colleague, Professor George Kelsey, for support and encouragement stretching over many years.

Mary Daly, one of my earliest sisters in women and religion, has supported me, shocked me, stimulated me, made me laugh, made me weep, but she has never been dull. I learned that when I became angry with Mary the anger was more often in me and was me. It appeared to come when false images were threatened and I feared to stand the testing. I learned early that Mary's shocks are a means of shattering worn out nostalgic forms that prevent the new reality from making its appearance. Those that were not worn out did not shatter. I may not agree with all that Mary says, but I have discovered that the times I was open to hearing her are times my world enlarged and I was nurtured by a deep spirit. I predict that Mary will be heard long after the rest of us are forgotten.

I would like to mention many of my former students from Drew, both women and men, with whom I remain in touch, who have continued "on the way," but they are too numerous to recall by name. Many nurture me to this day. I see their journeys continuing the "unfinished business" toward a full humanity for all peoples of the earth.

I am grateful to Jackie Melvin for her careful typing of the entire manuscript, to Dawn Peters for retyping illegible pages after the editor and I had written all over them, and to Carol Johnston for helping to check references.

I have been fortunate in having Joanne Wyckoff of Beacon Press as my official editor: comprehensive in her understanding, clear in her directives, and gentle in her manner.

A Note on the Jacket

It is not possible to question fundamentals of life or to face the abyss without a supportive community. This I have had—all that one might desire—in a feminist group in the Claremont, California, area. I received as a gift a tangible expression from the women who form this group—a friendship quilt made in great secrecy by some thirty or so women and presented as a surprise.

The symbols embroidered or appliquéd on the pieces that make up the quilt appear endless in their possible interpretation. The love and caring sewed into the pieces reflect a community sharing experience—phoning, planning, creating, stitching their lives together as they stitched the quilt together.

With no room of their own as workspace, they stretched the quilt out on the living room floor of Nancy Webster and bent over the work while sitting on the floor—sometimes several of them together, sometimes only two or three at a time.

With no symbol of her own on the quilt Nancy drew out the filament of ideas from the women, helping them weave their ideas into a powerful statement.

It is not surprising that quiltmaking, as a woman's art form, is partially replacing the early consciousness-raising groups. Aside from its very personal nature of weaving the quilters' lives together, quilting is recovering woman history and also making a political statement. It represents the powerful bonding of women and fierce tenderness of woman friendship. My quilt is intergenerational. The children of no fewer than four women made their own stitches along with their mothers. The age of the women gathered spans from a child to a woman in her eighties. Some of the symbols were traditional, such as a dove for peace. Although in my quilt the dove symbolism is reversed, from the dove descending to the dove ascending—up out of a human community. Another piece was of a womb—promise of a new day, a new order, a new birth. Another piece carried a labrys recalling the Amazon women bent on justice and equality. One woman created an opening flower with the words of a ritual often used in one of our groups—"earth and air and fire and water." Another, having done her doctoral dissertation on an Indian culture in New Mexico, embroidered in Indian design a rainbow wheel with a jewel at the very center of the circles within circles leading to the deepest core of existence. At the top and bottom and the sides of the outer circle were four bird feathers, standing for courage to fly, to extend one's horizon. In other pieces there were: a star, a single cup of coffee, a wise woman owl, a rising butterfly, a triple goddess, a spice of humor in the embroidered words "beware of spinsters," and a many-colored cycle rising suggested cyclical rather than linear thinking.

One of these symbols, created by Joella Mahoney, appears on the jacket of this book. At first glance it appears to be solid, strong, and stationary—a contradiction to the title. Then, one is drawn to the straight, green shoot in the center—alive, moving, unfolding from deep-rooted fingers drinking from unseen springs. A seed husk broken open to start the green shoot on its journey, a repetition throughout centuries. The great disk, sun and moon together, surrounds the shoot with warmth and luminous energy. The horns of Hathor as great tuning forks provide direction, nourishment, and protection along the way. The red of blood flows up and down, forever enabling the flower to unfold and ripening the fruit, dropping other seeds along the way to join the great journey, as if forever.

I've given up a large, loved, and fine oil painting to create a space on my living room wall for the quilt—a daily reminder of communal bonding and a commitment to love and justice.

Nelle Morton
Claremont, California
September 1984

Prelude

These essays, written over the '70s—a ten-year period—mark some of the most radical changes that have taken place in my life. Yet, since working on the essays to collect them in this book, I see that these changes have really been taking place all my life. It has been important for me to put the essays in chronological order, introduce each with the context out of which it grew, to discover for myself first, and then to reveal publicly, what these changes have been. At the time of the first essay in 1970 I was standing squarely in the church, still employed by the church. But the questions I was asking the church and its patriarchal religion never evoked a satisfying answer to me as a woman. In time I began to hear clearly that so much of what the church is saying is not for women. Finally, the pain of participation became greater than I could bear.

One day in the late '70s a copy of a feminist hymn, "Lead on, O Cloud of Yahweh," was placed under my door by Elmer Hostatler, a resident in Pilgrim Place, the retirement community in which I live. I had already left the warrior male God behind, but the last phrase of the second stanza intrigued me and seemed to describe what was happening to me: "we are still God's people, the journey is our home."[1] It named what I was beginning to grope for. Then, when invited by the Women's Center of Drew University to the initiation of a series of lectures on "Women and Religion" established in my honor, much to my surprise the above hymn was sung. I wept. It came to me forcefully that in my journey I may be more faithful to my tradition than many who cling to the unexamined patriarchal symbols that keep us all in bondage.

Even then, I began to ponder the meaning of *journey*. Ordinarily a journey takes us over roads that have been well laid out and well traveled, moving steadily toward a destination. But somehow involvement in the woman movement appears to have reversed that process and road-building becomes inseparable from the journey itself. "There is no road ahead. We make the road as we go,"[2] was the title of the 1976 Women's Seminary Quarter booklet. And sometimes, as has been the case of women in this decade, the clue of the beginning is more often than not discovered until near the end— entirely too late to back up and start over again. My living experience has taught me that my end reveals my beginning. Once accepted, one can see that the end has been there all along—even in the beginning.

A journey actually begins at one's first home. It moves out from there into adventures or into work or preparation for work and then into what has come to be called vocation. One establishes one's home in this place or that. At one time the whole pattern of vocation for women was defined by society in terms of nurturing family and children and in keeping the hearth. Society was ready with all kinds of built-in punishments for those who did not follow this private pattern. Such a determinism has been challenged. We feminists now claim ourselves as sacred gifts and not cogs in an economic or social machine. The departure found few beaten footpaths on which to travel. Now, women listening to another voice and to one another have been able to define our vocation as a sacred trust to be obeyed by holy choice. Perhaps in another generation women all over can begin without compulsory pressures their "letter to the world,"[3] which every women has a right to write and to send out as her own.

A difficult aspect of journey, especially to feminists, is a nostalgic longing to return home. To return to one's birthplace, one's relatives, after living many decades "on the road," is to take off, as it were, one's skin. So much of what one has become includes "gatherings" along the way that have helped to create one: the loving involvements, the commitments, the unbreakable connections beyond blood ties, first loyalties, intimacies across color, class, nationality, and age. One can return to one's birthplace for a short time only—no matter how much love evidences itself on both sides. There is always the implication of betrayal once one asserts herself, breaks the cultural pattern, and refuses to participate in the indoctrination of the clan. This has been particularly painful to those who have chosen a distinctly different life-style.

One may return yearly to one's roots to find at the same time they are the roots of others also. But soon one is forced to recognize that the branches—the trees—may resemble each other but seem no longer to belong together in the same orchard.

A yearly clan ceremonial, for one whose home is "on the road" may hide feelings and tears too deep to shed. To affirm one's roots with those who have the same roots is to embrace with love one's whole life and one's kin. But to return to one's early ways, to one's child faith, to one's baby language, is never to have left. In that sense, going home would deny connectedness with the world as one people and the earth as a home for us all.

To want one's ashes returned to one's native soil when the journey is no longer visible is to make a statement to the river, the mountain, the hills, the meadow (that pervasive wisdom in all things),[4] the people left even though they may not remember: "You have helped to make me what I have become. I am now the husk of that seed you once sent forth!"

From the time I experienced myself as woman and a stranger in a strange land or in exodus toward new time and new space, I came to know home was not a place. Home is a movement, a quality of relationship, a state where people seek to be "their own," and increasingly responsible for the world.

Perhaps the very irregularity, unevenness, lack of unity in form and content of these essays reflects the shape of journey. The short introduction to each essay recalls time, place, variety of experience of audiences who may have different backgrounds and different ways of hearing. The introductions in no way attempt to describe the history of women and religion but only indicate some points of my involvement in that history so that the essays can be better understood. The choice and arrangement of the essays reflects a movement away from the purely academic toward increasing "connection with," involving and supportive of women.

I have been concerned about the repetitive stories, references, and quotations. In trying to delete many of them, I began to see each one saying something different, though the words were the same, as it moved to a different level or another context. Finally it became evident that what I thought was needless repetition may be a cyclical way of thinking, movement, and writing. In the next round upward, in a different context, the "hearing" had something else again to say.

When I follow the cycle year after year for the ten years this book covers, I see now the shape of my own enlarging consciousness. From 1968 when I taught my first course on women, theology, and language in the Theological School of Drew University, I have moved from being a victim to finding new grace in both painful and positive experiences. When I first saw the theological implication of discrimination against women and the religious language that led to it, I victimized myself by wondering how we could survive in a world in which all the cards are stacked against us. What good to teach when women are sent out into a world in which they cannot possibly win! At that time I saw the entire profession, my own colleagues included, inadvertently confounding the issue. There seemed no place to begin. It was during the course—my first on feminism—that thirty students, women and men, rallied around me and began to identify the problems and deal simply with each in turn.[5] As we perceived what was at stake, we became angry—angry that women have been asleep so long, that men could not see. But the anger, expressed and dealt with, in time became healthy.

By the time I had retired, I was sorting events and experiences into those which had been liberating on one hand and those which had been binding and destructive on the other. The former I held on to. The latter I tried to shut out of my life and out of my memory. Only since working on these essays have I begun to arrive at the astounding insight that all of them are a part of me—and I am compelled to deal with what I have let them do to me. In this process I am experiencing a gentle forgiveness which I did not know I had the potential for, and which in itself is healing. I am also experiencing a new creative power (not power over) that I trust. I hope in some way I can channel this power toward liberating my sisters everywhere. This is what I mean finally by owning all of me—even that little girl who went "barefooted and took off winter underwear every spring."

In the process of working through that which cripples me as well as that which heals, I have been surprised again and again with the way I have respected the power of images and the importance I have given language itself. Already I knew from a study of structuralism how an image or symbol could spin itself out into a social and political shape and direction. It took little more work to see how much of the liturgy of patriarchal religion, with it unexamined images and symbols, helped create, shape, and perpetuate the social, political, and economic systems of which we are a part. I had been writing on theology, women, and language with a view to publication. A year after moving to California I had ten chapters finished, but by that time I had unearthed so many facets of the subject I had neither the time nor the ability to do the research demanded and the disciplined writing necessary to make my discoveries clear to the everyday women and the masses of people in whom I now see our final hope. Also, I discovered I had moved far beyond much of my early writing. I trust this collection may substitute for the book on language and theology I have promised for many years.

All these years, I thought I was working on theology, but in the process of preparing these essays for publication I find I have moved closer and ever closer to images and the way they function—images projected especially by theological language. Perhaps I should say "unexamined language." I think this shift has come about since my retirement from teaching in a theological school, as I have moved out of the purely academic and identified myself more closely with the common woman. Everyday women and masses of people the world around are hearing from the theologians and religious institutions that which the theologians are little aware of sending forth. Following the early emphasis on Christian art and iconography, images and theology have been largely separated in the public view—especially in the American scene. Images have been allowed to go underground primarily into the unconscious, into the private unconscious or into the community unconscious or both. Such a separation has injected a deep confusion not only in the religious world but also in the secular world. Theology has come to be related primarily to reason. When we speak of the theological task we refer to a certain way of thinking about ultimate values and ultimate longings, most often related to a specific historical tradition. But image, once in the subconscious, may act on its own quite apart from reason or conceptualization. This lack of understanding of the function of images has led not only to an "in" group in theological circles but also to a dangerously irresponsible use of theological knowledge and language.[6]

Technically speaking then, these essays could not be classed as theology. But one cannot deal with images as I have done without powerful theological implication. More properly they could be viewed as a critique of the images and symbols that patriarchal religion has foisted on the world. I have taken my stance among the masses and listened with the common woman's ear to that which patriarchal religious institutions must begin to accept responsibility for. No longer can they hide behind: "But the intention is . . ."; "In the original language it says . . ."; "The real truth is . . ." when the world is hearing something else again as it continues to bow hopelessly under poverty, threat of nuclear war, and discrimination. Not accepting responsibility for how what one says is heard is only a step from the refusal to care about and accept responsibility for the world.

Once old images are shattered more positive images that allow for new forms of response to ever-changing conditions may come into play. Images have to do with the senses. They are rooted in feelings. The stimulation of any sense may trigger the functioning of most unreasonable images that have never been brought to consciousness or have never been put to rest. Once the mind is cleared of accumulated blocks, it is free to embrace new images—positive images in all sorts of fresh new ways.

The theologians and the religious institutions say how necessary it is to examine faith again and again in each generation, in each new phase of our social order, to remain faithful to that with which they have been entrusted. But where are they doing it? The new order has become so radically changed that the meaning of many of the old symbols does not hold. The potential of nuclear disaster makes old images obsolete since they do not, they cannot, mean the same thing they meant in an agrarian culture or even in the developing urban culture. The presence of women in today's world is now changing and will increasingly change the entire configuration of community. But nostalgically the patriarchal religions evoke the old community in which woman was and is invisible. Those women who engage in goddess liturgy and participate in goddess energy may be doing more for us all in loosening the hold of the old symbols (objects of worship in themselves), so that fundamental change and growth can take place in the human scene.

But most male theologians are not expected to hear women. They have bought too deeply into the patriarchal system to be attracted by what feminists are saying. These essays then, are primarily for feminists. First, I address those feminists who have washed their hands of religion because they have experienced exclusion, male domination, and violence from the patriarchal religions and their institutions and theologians. This includes women who have been publicly kicked out. I hope such feminists will back up and take another look at theology and the images it projects. It is not enough to walk away. We must make it our business to know step by step how religious images create political and social structures. It is equally important to work from the other direction, to see how customs, etiquette, manners, structures, and other forms of social and political ritual provide compulsory external norms that lead to internalized assent, commitment, and feelings. Trace these outer forms to their images and symbols and see how their origin was designed to keep women in line. Until we understand the imagery and symbolism of the whole patriarchal theological system from both directions, we cannot understand our own bondage or know where or how to begin to break that which binds us, or even know how the Goddess herself, or even the God, for that matter, is bound.

Secondly, these essays are for those feminists who are enrolling in great numbers in seminaries and theological schools and those already in ministry. Many feminists within religious structures are becoming powerful critics of the theology undergirding their community life. This would mean a bold look at the faith of the community and the structures that bind one to another and the degree to which all exist, or do not exist, for love, liberation, and freedom for all people.

With increasing courage, many such women are examining themselves as women to determine how they can bring their uniqueness to ministry; how they engage the oldest and youngest in ministry with no hierarchical standards of values; how they engage both women and men equally. If women cannot bring something of unique value because they are women—as opposed to copying an exclusive male pattern of living, of thinking, of ministry—they had better get out. It would be well for ministers, rabbis, and priests who are women to keep before them Audre Lorde's admonition that one cannot dismantle the master's house with the master's tools. I do not believe that reform or revision (stifling pigeon-holes) are the answer. But it may be possible that removal of one patriarchal stone, then another, and another, and another, can finally weaken the whole patriarchal system until only "that which *is* will remain," or "that what cannot be shaken will remain."[7]

Those many institutional religious communicants and attenders who are women—commonly called lay women[8]—will be closely related in positions of potential power. I am trying to hear with their ears and the ears of their neighbors and their neighbors' neighbors. I would hope the most ordinary woman would have the chance, in the presence of other ordinary women, to tell her story and to consider what it means to be a woman-identified-woman in the political and social situations of the communities of which she is a part.

The third feminist group I can see reading these essays is lesbian. Of course, lesbians are hardly a group distinct from either of the first two, since many, perhaps most, of the first are lesbian and far more than one would suspect of the latter are lesbian. I have listed lesbian because the current persecution of the lesbian and gay life-style is one way patriarchal religious groups betray their faith, quaking with fear when anyone varies from their commitment to compulsory heterosexuality. Such an attitude has created one of the most obscene and dishonest situations within religious institutions as one woman after the other has been fired from top church boards or teaching positions for being lesbian and the reason attributed to other causes. Such an institution whose "professed faith" claims to be based on love, openness, and liberation in actuality seeks to control and define sexuality by legislating and domesticating love itself.

Compulsory heterosexuality permeates the patriarchal religious system. It is one of the powerful weapons used to keep women, especially, in line. Well I remember when the movement against racism was the cutting edge of social issues. Later people involved in the struggle against anti-Semitism and the struggles for labor organizing, for peace, and for women's liberation had the same experience. They met the same fears, the same hesitancy, the same arguments against, and the same slowness to pick up the meaning of faith in relation to them. All of them in turn, after much human sacrifice, experience today a modicum or token of tolerance. Now compulsory heterosexuality or homophobia (that breeds deceptions, lies, and mystifies all other social and personal issues) appears to find in patriarchal religion its foremost stronghold.

I hope this book will be read by many women who are not in any of the groups mentioned above—just women, ordinary women, poor, rich, of whatever color or country. In a profound sense we are all sisters—by virtue of our creation. We are sisters again by virtue of our differences. We are sisters a third time by virtue of our similarities. We are more alike than different. I'd like to hand this manuscript to you— wherever you are, whoever you are—and say, "This is how it is with me; how is it with you?"

I see this book for two groups of men especially. The first are those men who know that patriarchy is as crippling for them as for women. They are men who know also that patriarchy must be attacked by them at points in their lives where they have been most vulnerable to its violence; who know that their way of attack must be different from that of women— and at this point in history, separate. These are not men who have jumped on the feminist bandwagon or expect feminists in any way to save them. They are men who, with other men, seek to touch the pain in their own lives and to break the false images they have learned since childhood to live. I find inspiration in and rapport with their struggles.

The second group of men for whom I see this book carry pain also, much pain. But in a different place and in a different way. They live in some way close to feminists or with a feminist—in the same family, perhaps, or as a close friend, colleague, or as people drawn together by common interests. They care enough for the women and believe in them enough to know that women are concerned with something of vital and cosmic importance. At the same time they cannot understand fully what it is. What women are after has been for so many centuries programmed out of these men's lives that their hearing is diminished. They support in silence but in suffering. Many of these men are my friends—some are relatives—whom I care for deeply, but I cannot allow them to deplete further my limited energy. The personal nature of these essays just may be chance begin to enlarge their perspective of the world and its people so that they may begin to perceive more *humanly* and less *partially*. Having said all this I trust these essays into the hands of both women and men that they may in some way bring us ultimately into one another's presence. I am arguing, at this point in history, for separateness. But as Charlotte Bunch reminds us separateness is a tactic, and not the end goal.

Before deciding to proceed with this project I sent copies of several essays to persons of different traditions and commitments, such as Jewish, humanist, Catholic, radical feminist, Marxist, goddess women, and Protestants, to get a broad opinion on whether to attempt a collection for publication.

Harriet Ellenberger, co-founder of *Sinister Wisdom*, answered: "I don't know who you have in mind as readers . . . or if in fact you visualize a reading audience in at all specific terms. But I personally would love for the introduction to be done in such a way as to signal radical feminists who read it that the following essays are about their lives whether or not they ever associated the movement with Christian religion or not. I have in mind everybody I know who is Jewish or who (like me) spent a long time thinking they were Marxist or who came out of the anti-church left or who knows what else—everybody, that is, whose first inclination is that they will not read *anything* that quotes with approval *anything* that purportedly was said by *anybody* named Jesus (unless Jesus is spelled Jesús, in which case he's an Hispanic male, that is what his mama called him. He can't help it, and you're an anti-Hispanic cultural chauvinist if it sets your teeth on edge) . . . I just don't want this book to be pigeon-holed and dismissed by dykes I want to give it to or loan it to once it gets published."

After reading that letter, I turned to the essays again and was surprised that I had said so little about Jesus. I remembered that in "Preaching the Word" I had deleted a paragraph on Jesus as the Word, at the suggestion of a theologian who said it did not belong in the place I had used it. In the Berlin essay, "Toward a Whole Theology," I asked some straightforward and piercing questions about the theme of the upcoming World Council of Churches meeting scheduled for Nairobi. The theme "Jesus Christ Frees and Unites" raised such questions in my mind that I could not at that time commit myself, beyond urging women to examine what such a theme could possibly mean for them as women. I referred to the resurrection spirit and later to Jesus' reference to spirit in his Sermon on the Mount as I developed "A Word We Cannot Yet Speak" and again in the Dublin essay, "Educating for Wholeness." As I examined one after the other reference, it came to me with full force: since I had been moving increasingly from theology per se to dealing with the images projected by patriarchal religion—particularly the male image posited over the centuries in the word *God*—that must continue to be my first order of business. I felt we could not do feminist theology until that block was removed. And until it was, anything I might say or want to say about Jesus would be heard the wrong way, that is, as an effort to shore up the ontological maleness of the old God . . . and continue to hold Jesus up as an idol, and a male idol at that.

Another question asked me primarily by radical feminists is why I have used so many male references. Again I had to examine myself and the essays for, at first, I simply did not know. It was too easy, and not the entire truth, to say that men have been about the theological task far longer than women, and I was well indoctrinated in male resources and even a male way of theologizing before women began to take theology seriously out of woman experience. But now that I read all I can get my hands on by feminist writers and theologians I still use many male references and read much male theology.

I must make it my business to know what in the male way of thinking and theologizing projected as the whole may prove good for women and what jars our sensibility and denies our humanity. What is it that does not even begin to touch my experience and the experiences of those women hungry for spiritual nourishment? I must know where and how patriarchal religion violates women and I cannot know for myself and in behalf of my sisters until I recognize the full violation. On the other hand, for sheer nourishment, to isolate our own experiences and images, and for exploration into new ways of being present to one another and visible in the world my primary support at this stage is in all-women's groups.

An important second reason for my necessity to keep in touch with men and use what they offer that may be relevant for my purposes is that men by and large have done more work on a theoretical understanding of philosophy, no matter how biased it may prove to be. Metaphor is a prime example. Few women have probed metaphor in its functioning or examined what a bonanza it offers for the liberation of and a new language for women. And the ones who have have taken their cue from linguistics rather than language, philosophy, or interdisciplinary studies. I find most of my examples of good metaphor in women's writings, especially in their poetry, songs, and novels, and draw nearly all of my understandings of process from the way women and even children "make" metaphor. But women have not seen the need to develop a theoretical understanding of metaphor that would help other women find new words for the new experiences we are having that can find no expression in the masculine English language. (See Appendix.)

Before the final draft of this manuscript had gone to the editor, several feminists who had read all or part of it had marked the phrase "woman movement" for correction to "women's movement." Two asked me what I meant. One, Charlotte Ellen, had made a list covering an entire page of that and similar expressions, such as "woman sensibility," "woman perspective," "woman work," "woman word," "woman space," "woman time," "woman history," "woman spirit," and "woman sensitivity." She felt I was trying to express something by using "woman" as an adjective and she wanted to know what it was. I did not know. I only knew that something powerful was missing when I made the change. "The women's movement" implied something tangible and more organizational, such as NOW, or a woman's club, or a woman's auxiliary. To say "the woman movement" and use "woman" as a modifier is not necessarily talking about gender but opens up a whole, moving, pervasive way of perceiving—an emerging, accelerating, enlarging, powerful, growing potential that cannot be contained by the use of the possessive "woman's." When I say "woman movement," "woman word," "woman space," or "woman sensibility," I imply something in constant ferment. It would include those who are not yet aware, or not yet aware of being aware. In using this term there is no pigeonholing or labeling or categorizing of self or another as "radical feminist," a "real feminist," or a "militant feminist." I guess I am too much of a teacher to be influenced by such terms. The student I was always ready to give extra time to was that student who was "on the way," the one who was open to change, who revealed possibility for growth. The most discouraging student to have in a class is that student who thinks she has arrived when she has not started; or a rigid, dogmatic student who is so narrowly committed she will not hear anything but that which shores up what she already believes; or that pious student, the do-gooder who wears the stereotyped image, who can neither change nor relate. There are women who say, "Of course I am a feminist," and add, "but I am not militant." All of us are getting the benefits of feminism and are a part of the movement in ways none of us is aware.

Compare the expression the "American Revolution" to the "Americans' Revolution." How its meaning is reduced! The former includes not only people who were living at that time but all generations since, and those yet unborn. It includes structures of history and is dynamic.

I am not urging this on anyone else. I am merely explaining why I use the expressions "woman movement," and so on, and "women's movement" in different ways.

I do not pretend that these essays deal with images and symbols in other languages, though I think patriarchy has permeated the globe. I only know how my native language has limited the woman vision in my own country and the way we see and relate to the world. Yet, I believe that the woman vision is global—not only from English-speaking women but from other women around the world. I have spoken often in these essays about the earth as a common home for us all, cosmic space, new time and new connectednesses, inclusive love which is bonding and binding. But I can speak only from my own soil, and speak only those words my language has given me, and be alert for those words we cannot yet speak until a genuine global vision becomes a reality. But that will come only when all women know where we come from, attend to the many languages given us, and know other women of the world who work out their freedom from where they are. But women do have some common experiences and the two times I have spoken at world conferences, I experienced women stretching to be in intimate touch with one another, knowing we are more alike than different. And it is the alikenesses that are already stirring new words within us. In our differences shared are those words yet to come.

1970:

Women—on the March

I have chosen to begin this collection with the text of comments I made at a mass meeting at the Interchurch Center in New York City on August 26, 1970. The occasion commemorated the fiftieth anniversary of the ratifying of the Nineteenth Amendment, granting women the right to vote. It marked publicly renewed commitment to the equality and liberation of women. The essay does not pretend new insights but it allows for connections and observations that provide context for my journey through the '70s. Embarrassingly, it exposes my own theology still cast in male categories and out of male experience.

The essay reveals where I was coming from at that time, and while I have not reworded the content of my position I would never speak in this fashion today. I have come a long way in fifteen years—but as a matter of record, so have my sisters in religion.

The ad hoc women's caucus of the Interchurch Center in New York City called the noon meeting and invited all who worked within the building—executives, secretaries, receptionists, janitors—to join in the march at 5:30 down Fifth Avenue and in the rally at 7:30 in Bryant Park. The Interchurch Center houses boards of the mainline denominations of the United States, the Church Women United, the American Committee of the World Council of Churches, the Commission on Religion and the Arts, the Missionary Education Movement, and others.

1

A long list of prestigious women's organizations—educational, cultural, professional, political—participated in calling and sponsoring the observance of the Women's March, but at the beginning *not a single religious or church group was on the list.*

This is indeed a contrast to the Women's Suffrage Movement, motivated primarily by women in religion, which held its first national meeting in a church (Methodist Episcopal in Seneca Falls, New York) and spoke boldly to the part the church played in discrimination against women. In contrast, this new phase, which constituted itself publicly on August 26, 1970, as a national movement, was organized and inspired outside institutional religions and mainly by younger women of the New Left.

What had caused this shift away from the mature women of the last century who were ministers, translators of the Bible, and church historians? Elizabeth Cady Stanton had sought to correct the overt sexism in the Bible; she gathered women scholars and produced what is known today as *The Women's Bible*.[1] Susan B. Anthony, an intimate friend of Stanton and a companion leader in the movement, was a committed Quaker. Matilda Joslyn Gage, author of *Woman, Church and State* in 1893;[2] Sojourner Truth, itinerant minister; Anna Howard Shaw, Methodist minister; Harriet Tubman, and the Grimké sisters were devoutly religious but maintained a deeply critical attitude toward institutional religion. They saw a vital connection between black oppression and oppression of women. Not many, if any, saw the interrelation between these and oppression of the poor. They were essentially middle-class Americans speaking so boldly and bravely that both the church and press sought to discredit them. When the second feminist wave crested, many women of religion dissociated themselves from the earlier movement or ignored the writings entirely. It is possible that the church women were preoccupied with a struggle for identity within their own denominations.

It took women in secular education to resurrect the history of these feminists and connect us vitally with the last century, to make it clear that we in the twentieth century have a history—women such as Eleanor Flexner (*A Century of Struggle*, 1959), Aileen Kraditor (*Up from the Pedestal*, 1968), Alice Rossi (*The Feminist Papers*, 1973), and Gerda Lerner (*The Grimké Sisters from South Carolina*, 1971),[3] and others. The achievement of the vote in 1920 was followed by a period of enticement by consumerism before women began to move into the work place—to stay. The vision embracing lesbians, working women, women of color, and Third World women is now developing a global connection and consciousness.[4] The field is far from covered, as Adrienne Rich pointed out in her Clark Lecture at Scripps College in Claremont, "Resisting Amnesia: History and Personal Life," while Stanford male faculty was fighting a deadly battle to keep Estelle Friedman, a brilliant historian, from tenure on the ground that women's history is not a valid field for historical pursuit. How little the men in control are aware that history is not whole until the whole people become a subject for research.

In many ways Simone de Beauvoir (*The Second Sex*, 1953) and Betty Friedan (*The Feminine Mystique*, 1963)[5] bridged the two phases of the same movement. But the tinder that sparked the current phase came directly out of the New Left and for the first time pinpointed class and the crippling economic system as important factors that were keeping women oppressed. Many women in religion read liberation material halfheartedly, assuming that liberation was what religion was committed to in the first place.

True, in 1960 Valerie Saiving Goldstein wrote an essay, "The Human Situation,"[6] in which she challenged Reinhold Niebuhr's position that "man's" greatest sin is pride and lack of obedience. She argued well the point that they may be sins of men, but could only be virtues for women. Most of us dismissed the essay as having no particular relevance for us, and continued reading Niebuhr. But in 1968 Goldstein's essay was picked up again, photocopied, and distributed widely among women in theological schools and departments of religion in universities. Judith Plaskow,[7] a graduate of Yale, pushed Valerie's theme further in a doctoral dissertation. She implied that anyone who developed an ethic out of the experience of one sex and applied it to both, or out of one people and applied it to all human beings, can only relate to the other/others, paternalistically.

Thousands of women responded to the march down Fifth Avenue with thousands down other avenues in other cities in every state in the union. Long after the headlines had faded they established unmistakably that women are a power to be reckoned with.[8]

★

FIFTY YEARS AGO today, on August 26, 1920, the United States ratified the Nineteenth Amendment, giving women the right to vote. I remember my mother gathering women on her street to take them to the polls that day.

As you have been informed by your invitation to this noon meeting and your invitation to participate in the Women's March down Fifth Avenue this afternoon, the march here in New York City and in many other cities of the various states of our Union is to commemorate a historic occasion and to dramatize for all America the unfinished business of equality. I find it difficult to realize that this right to vote had to be granted to more than half the citizens of a nation that claimed to be founded on equality and freedom.

That this national act took place in the lifetime of many of us present, who have spent many of these years working professionally in the church, leads us to take a long look at our ecclesiastical experience. Why is no church officially on the long sponsoring list for this celebration, along with educational, professional, civic, and political organizations? What does this march of church women, along with secular women, women of other religions, women of no religion, and men who are sympathizers, have to say to the church at large and those church bodies whose executive offices are housed in this building?

How is our participation a theological act? To what degree is membership in the church now—full participating membership I mean—as much a matter of sex privilege as the vote was fifty years ago. And why?

We have learned much about the church in these fifty years.

We have learned to give up the illusion that freedom can come through individual struggle. We have learned, through heartbreaking disappointments and dehumanizing work inequities, that competence, commitment, creativity, and efficiency are not enough to deal with a male supremacy that has become a pervasive, structured force in our church.

We have learned that men in control of our church tend to consider it a threat to their virility (and resistance against God-created subservience) when women make any great effort to participate in top decision making. Further, these men tend to dismiss such women, usually with politeness, by dragging all sorts of red herrings across the issue.

With the words "her voice is too rasping," a nationally prominent church executive clouded some truly prophetic statements broadcast by Betty Friedan. A seminary professor's "she just doesn't turn me on" was enough to stymie further consideration of a woman candidate for a faculty post. The old Freudian cliché takes countless forms: "They don't like being women." "They want to be men." "They have a hang-up on men." "They are men haters." "All they need is a good man in bed." It would be interesting to examine the psychology behind such sayings or analyze the way paternalism and ridicule become so cutting and reduce creativity in work.

Not the least of our learnings is that the majority of women like the church and society the way they are. These "Aunt Janes" want to continue to be protected and supported. They want to be without sustained community and political responsibility. They like to be thought of, and treated as, the children they have become.

After serious research we are now learning that the struggle is far deeper than getting the vote, or equalizing salaries, getting ordained, or demanding mutuality in marriage—important as each of these goals is. We are learning that the roots of the subservient-master patriarchy sink deep within the psyche, shape styles of life, set relationships, and determine destinies long before conscious awareness.

We have learned, to our shame, that one of the worst perpetrators of the deadening stereotype is that body calling itself the Church of Jesus Christ.

Where is this body today?

Witness the few men taking advantage of the open invitation to attend this noon mass meeting. One would expect a sizable number, if not to support, at least to find out how women employed here feel about their work with the church.

What does this say to us in the church?

Male ownership of the church has existed so long that it is responded to by both men and women as absolute—revelatory—with no alternatives. Women, therefore, cannot be damned for liking it as it is, nor men dismissed when threatened by new possibilities. False images have distorted our authentic hearing so that we are not attuned to be open to another voice, to consider another dimension in the life of the church.

The church has made sexism a sacred right by supporting the double standard in its offices, ministries, functions, and discriminatory quality of membership. The double standard will persist so long as women do not have control over their own bodies and over their basic welfare. It will persist so long as men make decisions about women's place in the church, women's jobs in general, women's time and the place they spend it, and about women's names and the way they give identity. Try reversing some of the labels to see what I mean: "househusband," "call boy," or "our mother God." Substitute the opposite in the dehumanizing *New York Times* headlines reporting Cynthia Wedel preaching at Riverside—"A Grandma Preaches at Riverside" (May 18, 1968); or Lynn Morrison's pastorate at New Providence, N.J.—"Blonde Minister." Sexist references simply rob Christian service of its human dignity.

The church has supported commercialization of motherhood as the norm for the true existence of all women. Through its sentimental madonnas, bland advent sermons, insipid "baby Jesus" stories, it has made of Christmas not Incarnation (God with us), but alienation (God separated from common life). Thus, it has put woman on a pedestal to be adored—the goddess of heaven—or in a kitchen, or at a typewriter, to be used.

The church has published material that molds little children into these stereotyped roles while they are still in preschool. Before most church children can utter the word *God* they have started to listen to culture tell them who they are. Not long ago a task force of the United Methodist Board of Social Concerns presented a documented analysis of stereotyping in certain nursery material.[9] They called for a similar examination of all church school material published by that denomination. Though the motion passed, it would be embarrassing here to record some of the responses the task force received.

How could all of this have come about and continue still in the church's life and practice?

Perhaps the church's most blatant error lies somehow in the way "he" has preached, taught, and "used" the Bible.

No theologically aware person looks to the Biblical document for scientific explanations! Yet, the best church executives, preachers, curriculum writers, and teachers (to say nothing of seminary professors) fall into a trap when they get to the story of creation, particularly the creation of man.

Written long after the early Biblical writers had come to name their God as one who had made himself known in their history, the creation stories served to affirm that God was one and the same Creator-God of the cosmos and all that lives and breathes in it.

Note the fantastic turn the Biblical writers give the pagan sources providing imagery for their confession. The Babylon-

ian myth, for instance, makes their first god, Marduk, the
creative energy produced as male and female principles—
Apsu and Tiamat merge.[10] In contrast, without explanation or
detail, the Hebrews posit the astounding, simple confession,
"in the beginning God"!

Yet, when the Hebrews came to record their confession
they had available only word symbols from the patriarchal
culture they inherited when they settled in Canaan. No
wonder that for centuries the image of God lost the central
unity, the androgynous dimension the Hebrews confessed
with "in the beginning God," and became partisan—a great,
white, male, authoritarian father! No wonder the church
came to be known as "she" and God's special dispenser of his
love and grace as "he." This sort of blasphemy gave rise to most
spurious interpretations of sin as rebellion, disobedience,
wandering, pride—all male-conceived theological terms. No
wonder the status of woman became subordinate when she
had to look to man for her identity rather than to God![11]

I believe the early Biblical writers were confessing something far more profound than a cultural pattern. Yet it is the
cultural pattern that came through—and still comes through
today in ecclesiastical behavior.

If this movement says nothing else to us, as church people, it can call us to question the source of our identity.

When Krister Stendahl points to Galatians 3:26–29 as the
breakthrough on identity for both men and women, he insists
the English translations miss the powerful interruption in the
last correlative rendered in the Greek:

> "For in Christ Jesus you are all sons of God, through
> faith. For as many of you as were baptized into Christ
> have put on Christ. There is neither Jew nor Greek,
> there is neither slave nor free, *there is no 'male and
> female'*; for you are all one in Christ Jesus." In the
> Greek text, *arsen kai thelu* ("male and female") is more
> of an interruption than English translations (KJV,
> RSV, NEB) would indicate.

These verses, set in the context of transcending the law, make obvious reference to the law of male-female polarity. "... The most primary division of God's Creation is overcome, that between male and female—the terminology points directly back to Genesis 1:27 and in the direction of man and the image of God, beyond the division into male and female."[12]

"Male and female" would reckon faith by gender and create hierarchies, specialized privileges, discriminations in salaries, rank, position, and control. It would put sex in things and roles rather than in persons. Abolishment of the male-female dichotomy would define the Christian Community eschatologically with a kind of radical openness that would prohibit any possibility of determinism and causality. As Christ is one, as there is one baptism, there can be only one membership, one ministry. To distort it into either a male or female one is idolatry.

This insight from the church's faith will not allow people of the church to settle for mere equality. It demands a far more radical response. It calls the church to enter into its true heritage. It calls all its members to have done with cheap identities. It calls for new interpretations of sin, new understandings of repentance, and new experiences of salvation.

The Women's Liberation Movement on this day presents the imperative to slough off culturally contrived, stereotyped images of maleness and femaleness and allow the faith that our documents and pronouncements confess so eloquently to lead us into a new humanity.

Is it possible that the spontaneous mass movement gathering momentum in parts near and far suggests that the whole human race may be growing ripe for change?

Is it possible that the youth, the blacks, the women, the poor, those men who sense they, too, live out of stereotypes, and all the disinherited everywhere are bringing us to the verge of experiencing for the first time what it really means to be human?

We know that the whole creation has been groaning

in travail together until now; and not only the creation, but we ourselves, who have the first fruits of the Spirit, groan inwardly as we wait for . . . the redemption of our bodies. For in this hope we were saved.[13]

That the church is offered a chance to forge a new lifestyle—even without a clear vision of its shape—is cause for great rejoicing. "It doth not yet appear what we shall be." But herein lies the faith: that we venture and experiment with many new models, with new forms, with the new women and men we are called to be. That we are given by God this new song is celebration, indeed.

1971:

The Rising Woman Consciousness in a Male Language Structure

In the tradition of the suffragists came Thelma Stevens of the Women's Division òf the Board of Global Ministries of the United Methodist Church. Long before the Methodist churches united in 1939, Thelma, a member of the Methodist Episcopal Church South, was involving Southern women in issues of social justice and political action. With the union, Thelma's work merely enlarged to cover the entire nation.

It was not surprising that on her retirement in 1968 she committed the entire $10,000 retirement gift from her board to the cause of women's liberation in the church. She designated $5,000 of the money to be spent through the Church Women United Program Division and a newly formed Commission on Women under Claire Randall as administrator of the funds.

A first task of the Commission on Women established regional experimental workshops/retreats during the fall of 1970 and the spring of 1971 to discover and create, if possible, a model for churches to help women become aware of their liberating potential. Tillie (Mrs. Harvey) Winn of Trenton, N.J., and I were employed to give direction to these workshops.

In the spring of 1971 the commission cooperated with Sisters Margaret Early and Mary Austin Doughty, professors of Alverno College in Milwaukee and founders of the

Women's Center at Alverno, in setting up the first consultation on Women and Theology. This two-week event
brought together women—some of whom later organized
the women's caucus in the American Academy of Religion,
set up women's centers in theological schools, and
introduced courses on women and religion in seminaries
and universities.

The Alverno consultation was significant in its effort
to break free from the purely male theological hermeneutic, only to realize finally how deeply we had internalized
patriarchal structures and concepts. It was not until the
following year at Grailville, a Catholic lay women's community in Loveland, Ohio, that more communal methods and structures were experimented with. These two
conferences became a watershed for women of religion to
critique boldly the traditional male-oriented theology as
partial (not including woman experience) and examine our
own experiences for sources of theological reflection. The
1972 conference was funded by a $5,000 grant from the
women's division at the suggestion of Peggy Billings,
Thelma Stevens's successor. From it came the Seminary
Quarter for Women, offering academic credit to women
enrolled in theological schools. As an ecumenist, Thelma
Stevens earmarked the last $5,000 of her gift to fund a
special course in an accredited institution on "Women in
Global Perspective."

Centers on women and religion were established in
such schools as Graduate Theological Union in Berkeley,
Boston Theological Institute, Yale Divinity School in New
Haven, Union Theological Seminary in New York, Candler
in Atlanta, and the Women's Ecumenical Center in
Chicago.

Data for "The Rising Woman Consciousness" came
from such activities as the Women's Commission; the
regional experimental workshops; courses on women,
theology, and language taught at Drew Theological School,
Union Seminary, Perkins School of Theology; an experi-

mental study of suburban women supported by a grant from the Auburn Foundation; and diaries, correspondence, interviews, tapes, research, and evaluations connected with these.[1]

★

IN THIS ESSAY I seek to inquire into the nature of the rising woman consciousness and if possible to describe it as a phenomenon in the process of shaping itself. An analysis of the data mentioned above would indicate that in spite of the input of reading, study, and reports on the one hand, and various forms of corporate action on the other, the core of what is taking place in the woman movement is revealed most vividly and poignantly in small intimate groups—sometimes structured, more often clustered spontaneously and informally. I do not claim universal application of my findings, however, to date, I have discovered no radical contradiction in other groups with which I have been in touch in this and other countries. Nor do I claim that what I describe here happened in just this way to all women attending the groups listed. What I do claim is that this was the experience of enough women to allow some generalizations on my part and to provide an insight into the shaping of the consciousness itself. Many women participants who have read these findings, while denying that they may have expressed themselves so extremely as some of the women quoted, affirm that the description is accurate in what happened to them: "That is just the way I felt." "She said it before I got around to it." "When things get intolerable you explode, I mean literally."

Consciousness, phenomenologically speaking, is not a vague abstraction. To be conscious is always to be conscious of something. In the case of the new woman it is the coming to awareness of herself, her identity as a human person with the rights, responsibilities, and potentials thereof in light of her unexamined, traditionally accepted position in present and historical social situations. From data in hand, this *consciousness can best be identified in the new language of the sister-*

hood as compared to the language one can now hear being spoken on the street.

Woman Consciousness as Phenomenon

The first indication of a stirring consciousness appears to be defensiveness. Since women find it difficult to admit they are searching for liberation, perhaps they are not even aware of the need. Women seem to go to great length to make clear to other women that even though life may be tough on them at times, in the long run all is well. They have been conditioned to be loyal at all costs to father, husband, children, boss, and colleagues. Irrelevant claims are exchanged: "I love my husband." "It is my choice to keep house." "I have never really known discrimination. I have learned how to get along with my boss." "Any woman can make it if she has what it takes." "Some women need help. For them there should be equal pay for equal work."

Round after round of defense finally winds down to a vague hurt—a diffused hurt that most often cannot be isolated or located. As a woman seeks to get in touch with the pain, she begins to admit a sense of boredom, of being caught and trapped. Broken articulation opens up more of the same hurt until it finally focuses to a point of despair. The hurt becomes intolerable. Now the only alternative to despair is hope. But where, at such a time, can women turn for hope? Women who have lost all hope are too numerous to mention. They rarely show up in such groups as described above. They are the ones who become suicides or resigned to sacrificial martyrdom. They are the ones who turn to a kind of therapy that forces them back into the cultural syndrome that produced the bind in the first place. Their usual escapes, such as volunteer activities, child-possessiveness, the perfect hostess, sex indulgence, drugs and alcohol, no longer promise a way out. This point, just short of despair, marks a basic aspect of the new woman consciousness, which, as already indicated, does not evidence itself easily or quickly. Usually it takes a group of women hours of work together before change becomes describably visible. Even then, the turning point in the reported experiences occurred at different times for different women. Later in recalling her moment of insight no woman was able to attribute its timing to any particular happening or to anything that was said. One woman referred to her moment as "a volcano erupting," another as a "dam breaking loose." Visible and audible gestures have been anything from choking, to holding the stomach "as if touching the bottom of a pit," "the very center of one's being." Pounding on the floor or table, shaking fists at the heavens, holding the sides of the chair, and shaking one's head all signified that something cataclysmic was taking place. Sometimes nothing was more visible than a face drawn and contorted. Other times no change was visible at all. Sometimes incoherent and inarticulate sounds became audible. Once I saw a woman's throat open with a cry so great the cry could not come to sound—as in an old person who dies.

The explosive moment served to unstop all sorts of angers, complaints, pent-up negativisms never before uttered by "nice" women and in many cases never consciously thought and certainly never owned. Always these were specific, directed toward members of the family—parents, husbands, children—toward relatives, colleagues, bosses, friends, and neighbors. Sometimes anger lay so deep and was so long suppressed it took days or even months to get in touch with it enough to deal with it. One woman, frightened at the enormous extent of her anger, was known to hang on to her group for a year before moving to a deeper level. Rarer is that woman who because of the constituency of the group or because of former experiences with members of the group is never accepted by the group and is forced to seek another for her own health.

Groups that have continued and maintained a wholesomeness are those which have been able to get their experiences early into a larger perspective through study, research, strategizing, and politicizing. Calling into question hierarchical structures and acting against oppressive social practices have contributed in every case to deepening and actualizing the new consciousness.

Reflection

In reflecting on the experience thus far, one is struck with expressions as mentioned above, "a dam breaking," "erupting of a volcano," "volatile heat," "belched venom," "ripped up from the bottom," "a burst from inside," accompanied by gestures that may be characterized as spontaneous—far from calculated risk. It would seem no speaker cared who, if anyone, heard her; or what her movement might do or mean to relationships or reputation. Obviously the cries of the women were not uttered in order to communicate, with the expectation of being heard, or with any hope for relief. Indeed, just the opposite. They came forth because they could not be controlled. All that can be said of these cries and gestures is that they indicated that the women were alive—that they had not given over utterly to despair.

It is evident by this time that the experience takes on Biblical overtones. Words such as "abyss," "despairing," "hopeless," "last extremity" converge in a cry that might well carry the content of "Who will deliver me from this body of death?"[2] It is doubtful the Biblical cry was directed or that it anticipated any form of deliverance any more than did the women. It is clear, however, that both came up from the deep. The women never saw themselves as having gone consciously into this depth—this descent into hell, into death. They felt they had been put there. They saw themselves as having been forced into the predicament in which they now found themselves. It was as vivid as the cry of Jonah who saw himself "cast...into the deep, into the heart of the seas, the flood... waves...passed over...waters closed in...deep...round about...weeds wrapped about...at the roots of the mountains...down to the land whose bars closed...forever."[3]

The initial experience of incoherent sound and gesture uttered out of such an intolerable situation did not return. There was no need to stay on that level. The sound reached an ear, an ear that was there before the sound was uttered. The hearing of the agony behind the cry opened the way to the intentionality of that which followed in the form of speech. Authentic communication thus became established for the stories that followed. It is questionable that any of the women had arrived at a sense of trust before they began to tell their stories to one another. Perhaps the nearer truth is that trust came because they were heard and not the other way around.

A new kind of seeing and hearing was beginning to be experienced by one group of women after the other. Once they recognized in themselves a common oppression, they could hear from one another that which many, more astute and intellectual than they, could not hear. They could hear that which men, particularly, find it difficult to hear—not because men are incapable of hearing. But because the kind of thing that has been going on in and among women has been so long programmed out of the male experience little or no equipment is left with which to receive it. Women standing in need of one another with a lifetime of re-education before them found themselves in a peculiar position to be the recipients of mercy from the least among them. Experiencing grace in this manner has become one of the most powerful liberating forces in the lives of women.

It is important that the data that these women shared was out of their living, historical experience. Yet, the new words and the new way old words came to expression, while in the context of history, were not evoked by history. Neither oppression nor suffering shaped their speech. Women came to new speech simply because they were being heard. Hearing became an act of receiving the woman as well as the words she was speaking. The speaker, stripped of every old prop, of every necessary measure to shore up the old ego, was able to go in all her agony directly to the other women present. In receiving the speaker (who had touched the quick of their own existence) the women heard the speaker speak for them to the extent that they, in turn, were able to receive themselves. They were able to relate to one another out of their whole selves rather than partially through the mind alone, or through the emotions alone.

A communal process of theologizing was experienced by the many groups of women partly because no expertise was present to supply the proper word and no authority had been paid to keep them on the track, to tell them what they think and what they see and what they hear and where they must come out. Women were thrown back onto their own resources and on one another. They made it possible for the least one present to be heard and heard her own way. She may be wrong. She may be sick. She may be confused. She did not have to be agreed with but *she had to be heard*. Often, it was a comment or question from the least liberated or the most ignorant which illumined the whole.

Experiences such as these have brought women to a new joy when they discover themselves and others for the first time; and to renewed conviction that it is no longer appropriate to allow men to define their lives and to do their theological thinking even though the men are the women's own pastors or their own professors; nor is it any longer appropriate to allow men to provide their identity even though the men are their own fathers, husbands, their bosses, their colleagues, or the leaders of their community. These women have come to see that the gift of themselves is precious, sacred, with unique potential. Tasting a liberation they had never known before, they found it good. They began to appropriate a new kind of courage to explore the future with no known history to inform and a new ability to articulate that which has never before come to speech. They began to know themselves as persons of worth who would pick up their own lives and be responsible for them. They covenanted together that never again would they allow themselves to become isolated from one another.

From a study of the women's recorded testimony it may be concluded that neither protests nor political action of the

most radical sort marks the rising of the woman consciousness but *the new language on the lips of those experiencing
liberation.* Yet the new language both reflects and creates
protests and political action.

The Jar of Words

It was the male pronouns and nouns used generically that
stirred the women first as they moved about their community.
A teacher referred to "a student doing *his* homework" to a
mother who had only girls in that school. A League of Women
Voters member was startled by a visiting politician's remark
that "every voter must follow *his* conscience in the stance
he takes on the transportation bond issue." The prevalence of
male terminology in the common speech appeared insignificant
and even funny at first. Everybody knew that everybody did
not mean literally male and that was that. *Then there came a
time when it ceased to be funny.* Women began hearing themselves shut out of their own traditions; alienated from church,
synagogue, and other religious groups; "I couldn't believe it
when my priest referred to 'each member in relation to *his*
own baptism.' Has this been going on all along and I never
heard it before?" "I had to turn off my TV when that wonderful
Dr. R— kept referring to 'grace that was available to *every
man.*' " "Even God was *He.* Christ, *He,* the Perfect One, had a
bride who was *'she'* the unfaithful church-ess. How blasphe-
mous can we get!" "The old rabbinical prayer, 'Thank thee,
Lord, that thou has not created me a woman,' is still prayed in
my synagogue, only more subtly now, 'Thank you God that we
are *men* who can shape the destinies of all *mankind.*' " "I
cannot find a hymn in our hymnbook that does not exalt the
male ego. And all my life I thought I was giving praise to God."
And so it went.

As women questioned the generic use of male words, they
were put down repeatedly with ridicule. Finally it became
quite evident to them that male and not the generic in the

male terminology was meant. Once women began to be aware of what language had done to them as little girls and was now doing to their own little girls, they experienced as dehumanizing the pervasive male character of the entire language system. In spite of the report that members of the Harvard linguistics faculty denied that language is sexist,[4] their world-famous Otto Jesperson declared as far back as 1923 that English is "positively and expressly masculine . . . it is the language of a grown-up man and has very little childish or feminine about it."[5] He admitted it was "not at first meant to express any parallelism with characteristics of the two sexes . . . but the designations are not entirely devoid of symbolic significance."[6]

There is no longer doubt in the minds of liberated women that the common speech of the American people presents an image of male control in pulpit, politics, education, industry, and family. It has become obvious that this language of the people reflects their history, their world view, their understanding of one another, and the value placed on their lives together. It has come clear, also, how the language itself perpetuates and even creates for children a view of humanity in which women are considered of minor importance in shaping history and participating in politics.

The Jar of Images

Words do more than signify. They conjure images. Images refer to that entity which rises out of conscious and unconscious lives individually and in community that may shape styles of life long before conceptualization takes place. Images, therefore, are infinitely more powerful than concepts. Concepts can be learned. Concepts can be corrected and can be made precise. Concepts can be formulated, enclosed, and controlled. Concepts are linear. Images, on the other hand, cannot be so controlled. They are not so easy to identify or to describe. They have a life of their own. Often they function when persons are most unaware of their functioning. A common example of image is the interchangeable use of words such as: black, dark, foreboding, shadowy, sin, evil on the one hand, and white, pure, sinless, chaste, snow on the other.

A woman theologian who read a paper at the Society of Biblical Literature meetings in Atlanta in the fall of 1970 wrote: "One can be present and still not be part of what is going on 'man to man.'...When I spoke on the telephone to one of the professors organizing the show he asked me what my job was to be at the meeting—typing?" One wonders about the image out of which this professor of a leading seminary operates.

Recently came the report of a bishop at an ordination service tweaking the hair of a person in the front seat. With no more information than this, what image would you guess functions here? A thoughtful bishop noticing a little child during a solemn ceremony? As a matter of explanation, the person whose hair had been tweaked had received her theological degree from an established seminary, had passed her ordination exams, and was waiting in the front pew to be called up for her own ordination. What kind of image is communicated here of the bishop? Of the church he serves? Of the woman in particular? Of women in general?

A group of women who work at the Interchurch Center, 475 Riverside Drive, New York, communicated their concern for the language spoken and the images evoked by the building and its decorations.[7] The nineteen-story office building, "the result of an effort to demonstrate growing Christian unity," houses the National Council of Churches, the U.S. Conference for the World Council of Churches, and various boards and liaison offices of Protestant and Orthodox denominations and related agencies. The angular building of solid granite utilizes an entire block on Riverside Drive. White slabs rise logically and precisely one upon another to the top with no wasted space and no deviating line. On the wall inside the Claremont entrance there is a large linden wood sculpture in plain view so that all entering may be reminded of who they are as employees in the building and as members of the Christian church. A picture post card sold at the entrance describes it as

> one of the largest carvings of this kind in the Metropolitan area (11' x 16'), the mural shows thirty individual forms representing nineteen kinds of work. A family group is at the base of the formalized tree shape. The theme of sacredness of vocation is taken from I Corinthians 10:31.

Seven of the thirty figures are women, represented as nursing a baby, on knees scrubbing a floor, serving a man seated at a table, assisting a male doctor, feeding chickens, pounding a typewriter, and teaching children. Over a year has passed since women employed in the Interchurch Center registered their feelings about the humiliating effect of the imagery communicated daily through this work of art. Yet the sculpture still stands. How great its esteemed value when reckoned in terms of the personhood of human beings!

The imagery comes through so strongly and in so many forms that children do not fail to get the message early. A group of Princeton women studying the sixth-grade readers used over the country produced conclusive evidence that sexual stereotypes reflect themselves in picture and story.[8] The Central New York Conference Task Force studying United Methodist Church nursery curriculum materials discovered all the stereotypes listed in the Princeton study with the added implication that "God made it to be this way."[9]

Angry women, while vowing that it will never be so for their children, become aware daily of new ways they condition their own children through their speech, through imagery, and through gesture. Researchers Dr. Jean Berko Gleason and Dr. Elliot G. Mishler of the Laboratory in Social Psychiatry of the Harvard Medical School observed that parents speak in a different tone of voice to boys and girls.[10] A hail-baby-well-met style for little boys and a gentler dealing with little girls were owned by a group of parents who admitted calling their daughters Sweetie, Pudding, Doll-Baby, Daddy's Pet, Daddy's Little Sweetheart, and boys Bronco, Cowboy, Polar Bear, Little Nut! What is said here and said so clearly that most children hear is that *this is the way it is, and any deviations* will be considered abnormal and will either be punished or treated as sickness. So deep is the male character of language and culture that Germaine Greer terms it "sex of the mind."[11] Women now see it as a split in the psyche itself to the extent that they experience alienation in a world that does not receive them as human beings.

The Jar of Male Structures

Many of these women make a good case for the relationship of logic and reason to the hierarchical, authoritarian order structures that have controlled and closed social and political life and have programmed out the authentically communal, imaginative, and parabolic except as they are dealt with cerebrally and offer no threat to the system. Acceptable words and images perpetuate the structures and become paradigms of them. Structures, on the other hand, reflect themselves in common speech and serve to keep the words and images alive. "It begins to make good sense," insisted a participant of one of the groups, "that as long as life together is structured on an authoritarian, hierarchical pattern, we will have competition between nations in the form of wars and rumors of wars; racism between peoples of such dimension that the dominant group simply cannot see, or change, or break the racist syndrome. Costs of such a system may be reckoned in a perennial number of its citizens at substandard or poverty existence." In time the writer may be proven correct in her assumption that institutional sins of war, poverty, pollution, colonialization, and racism are direct projections of sexist words and images out of a predominantly male-oriented language system. And so long as present structures remain inviolate these sins will continue to be programmed into national and personal life.

Women experience themselves at the mercy of structures that deny them their humanness.

In his treatment of structuralism, Jean Piaget, genetic epistemologist at the Sorbonne and the University of Geneva, postulates that structure is preserved by an interplay of its transformation laws that never yields results beyond the system and never tends to employ elements external to the system.[12] Only when that which is without comes into the mainstream can any basic alteration come about. Since women experience themselves outside history-shaping, government-making, and theology-writing processes, it may be that until they are welcomed within, wars, poverty, and racism will continue. So long as the partial usurps the whole, and parades as the whole, a new speech expressive of a full humanity cannot come about.

Toward an Interpretation

For a more objective way of examining the woman consciousness as announced by the new language, I have not turned to the linguists, the language philosophers or to the speech theologians. I could not evade the suspicion that their speculative categories logically and cerebrally conceived might overlook the basic inquiry at hand. Automatically, I turned to Piaget's work[13] on word formation and beginning speech in small children but soon dismissed him as not helpful at this point because his findings, recorded often by formula, tend to bypass much of the power of what he is about. However, his organic approach, refusing to separate the mind from the body and the individual from the world (environment), is worth noting. Piaget dedicated his life to discovering the origins of human intelligence and the dimensions of human knowledge. Not surprisingly, he began with children when they first began to speak (in the beginning was the word, he assumed). After observing first sounds, gestures, and thought schemata, he realized that something was going on long before words formed on the child's lips. He was compelled to push back to discover roots of intelligence in sensory-motor perception.[14]

Antonin Artaud, French dramatist and poet, in describing his own approach could well have been referring to Piaget:

> "I call organic . . . [that which is] based on the mind in relation to the organs, and responding to each of them at the same time."[15]

Artaud[16] and later Samuel Beckett[17] emerged for me as most adequate to inform the shape of the woman consciousness and to suggest an important step in the process of language formation, since both concerned themselves with primordial sound and gesture. Artaud took a long and maddening journey to the place where he sensed words took shape. Both he and Beckett, repudiating clichéd language, the traditional literary forms, and the didactic in modern theater, committed their lives to a search for what they called an authentic language.[18]

At first Artaud sought some primitive tribe near the primordial state in order to learn the secret of sounds and gestures still unseparated from the makers of the sounds and gestures. A long trip to Mexican Indians and other early societies left him discouraged. He then turned inward and entered what Bettina Knapp calls "his own inferno."[19] His journey to the core of his own life images and archetypes provided the guide and the data of his struggle. So long as he was able to transform the images into the visual and audible symbol of poetry and the theater, he avoided the despair of madness. In the process he was able to get a vision of a new theater, undreamed-of knowledge of himself, but along with it all, untold suffering. Artaud worked simultaneously on two fronts. He sought to repress the rational, logical processes in favor of the potent images appearing to him, which when once dealt with rechanneled his rational thinking processes. The other front had to do with encountering people with punctured words and phrases in common usage that had stereotyped and atrophied vitality and reality. He evoked much hostility by his shock method. As Artaud learned to think out of his senses, he became convinced that elemental sound and gesture were ritual closely akin to worship.[20] The office of these sounds, he perceived, was not originally for signification, or to make anything, or to do anything to anyone. They merely affirmed life itself—given and received. The imagery emanating from the sounds and gestures invited metaphoric and symbolic participation rather than a literalistic response.

Samuel Beckett achieved the symbolic in his archetypal characters whose conversation is reduced to the barest economy of words.

> Amos Wilder gives Samuel Beckett credit for probing more deeply than any modern dramatist into elemental gesture and word to the very root meaning of what traditional language sought to say. In Beckett's plays the audience is led to a point of confrontation where direction lies only one way. How sparing the words in *Krapp's Last Tape!* A man's whole ingrown, stagnant history unwinds through an interplay of timing in a limited time; darkness sharply broken; scarcely audible sound clinging to the tongue, reaching into memory, then left hanging; and minute gestures recalling a constellation of associations. In *Endgame* so carefully does Beckett employ words and gestures a whole host of lost images is summoned. Shuttling from a past which helps to expose and inform a present, he gingerly hints at a confused hope for any sort of future. The garbage cans themselves speak what words cannot speak of a personal anguish that is social because everyone in one's aloneness shares it.[21]

And so Samuel Beckett, as well as Artaud, negated common reality structured by a language that had become worn out in order for a new reality to make its appearance through the use of a more authentic language. While Beckett's approach has not been labeled organic, he insists that language that is authentic participates in reality through the speaker's whole person—not just the intellect, not just the feeling—so that in speaking, hearing, and gesture one is close to the primordial movement or act that in faith terms has come to be interpreted as word.

Conclusion

As was observed in the first part of this essay, the turning point in the woman consciousness lay in our movement in and out of *the Abyss.* Unlike women, the artists moved into the depth deliberately, but with unflinching courage through violence, confusion, contradiction, suffering, and a maze of artificiality seeking to trace the springs of life to their source. Beckett's story is told repeatedly in his own novels and plays and in such studies of him and his works as "Descent into Self," *Into the Silence, Journey to Chaos.*[22] The artists stretched toward elemental sound and gesture sensing in them an expression of wholeness, of authenticity, of honesty. They saw these sparse expressions shorn of efforts to control, to impress, and to manipulate. They saw in them the most pure form in which one human being comes into presence with another human being. With great creativity the artists worked what they found into art forms.

The women, on the other hand, felt themselves plunged into the depth by forces not of their doing. However, once they were able to lay bare hands on that which placed them where they were—their oppression—to kiss its ugliness, they experienced the power of deliverance without being able to articulate its nature or reflect on the profundity of the process.

Beckett and Artaud, from the beginning, were more conscious of what they were about. Otherwise they could not have begun at their point of weakness—for Artaud worked out of his disease,[23] Beckett out of his "impotence and ignorance."[24] ("I have no voice and I must speak. That is all I know."[25]) The women in the groups discussed earlier, hurting, were not aware of working out from the oppression that precipitated the hurt in the first place. Nor did they know what freedom was or what had happened to them when they first tasted its exhilaration. Yet, almost overnight, in a most miraculous way, they became bold, articulate, and strangely aware—on the way toward achieving a sense of personal worth and exhibiting a self-confidence. "I'm going home feeling good about myself for the first time since I can remember."

Those of us who helped to plan for and structure the groups in the first place were not fully aware of what was taking place, nor were we prepared for what happened. Witness the cerebral nature of our evaluation instrument! The first response asked for was a reaction to the total workshop/retreat experience: was it "mindblowing," "enlightening," or "not worth the time spent"?

Not until evaluations were in and studied did we become aware that women were telling us something we had not had the vision to ask for. When a sizable number crossed out "mindblowing" and wrote in "explosive," "bomb dropped," "the whole earth shook," "I was snatched out of my complacency," or ignored the instrument altogether and wrote on the back page, then another and another page, we had to take another look at what had happened. Letters that followed, and an avalanche of Christmas cards with further information of a most profound nature, forced us to admit that the woman experience had dimensions beyond our most far-reaching anticipations, or understanding.

Observe the organic—the gut-level—response of the women. They spoke out of the totality of their beings. It was far from a purely intellectual exercise nor was it feeling out of relation to the mind. Actually it was mind and body at one with their words and gestures. Women can be heard and understood only if they are heard out of their new stance. No longer do they strain to speak a male speech. Without presumption one can call the new creation of the woman an art form that is equally as organic and integral as that of Artaud and Beckett.

But the women experienced a community Artaud was never able to appropriate fully. They discovered they could not live without the support of one another. They came to know both the pleasure in sharing their new self-knowledge and the necessity of the sisterhood for maintaining their life. They came to know they were called into being because someone heard and the hearing drew forth their speech.

A spasmodic ear here and there during Artaud's lifetime sensed what he was about. The lack of a consistently listening support destroyed him as a person and made him "alienated from his society, divided within himself, a victim of inner and outer forces beyond his control."[26] The legacy he has left, however, has changed the language and style of modern theater,[27] and perhaps affected our language far more than we realize. Beckett, on the other hand, is alive and is being heard. His works are published and produced in many world theaters. Not all his readers know what he is about but even those who do not seek to understand and respect what he does. A *Festschrift* by twenty-four scholars published in 1967 became a tribute that the artistic world has not let go of this man.[28]

The dedication of the two artists moved them steadily on their journey. Artaud "died" rather than betray that which he had come to seek and to know as truth. Beckett's trail of novels, plays, and poems traces the shape of his commitment. If any validity lies in comparing them with the women, one may conclude that the commitment in the rising woman consciousness can be traced to the fact that the women have experienced together a common hell and have been delivered from it. They know themselves as new women. They know they will not easily allow themselves a betrayal of themselves and one another. Every day produces a deeper involvement. As one woman put it: "Nothing that happens to me is unrelated to the woman question."

That which has happened to women in the small consciousness-raising groups is the unique contribution of the movement in the '70s. Individual women of the past have been equally as committed and as courageous, but without the community of commitment that arises out of a common exodus. Individual efforts rarely reach political fruition. The direction from which the women's groups emerge is literally *up from down under*. They rise like mushrooms over the world as if "the whole creation has been groaning" to be born.[29] One may safely predict that the consciousness will accelerate, increase in power, until a new language of the *full human experience* begins to express itself all over.

Already women in touch with a new reality experience the unexamined male language as illusion, and are aware that so long as men protect the hierarchical structures and maintain control over creation they engage in the deepest betrayal of themselves.

To all men who read these words: It is well to heed the new speech of the new woman. Never have her words come from such a stance and from such assurance. They cannot be heard by listening out of "old ears." She is not speaking from that standpoint anymore.

She may come on stumbling and trembling and awkward for some time to come. She may sound strident or downright trite when measured by the going logic. She may come to you as "too simple." But if you can listen out of your wholeness (there is an organic listening as well as an organic speaking), you may be able to hear what is in back of her words, what is around them, and beyond them.

It is killing women not to be heard.

And to women: As a great woman, Margaret Fuller, wrote more than a hundred years ago, may God keep you safe until the word of your life is fully spoken.

1972:

How Images Function

Through many years of teaching and leadership I gave
increasing attention to the place of image and symbol in
the teaching/learning process. I became convinced that we
live out of our images; not out of our concepts or ideas.[1]
Yet education on the whole continues to teach conceptually and religious education is no exception.

My understanding of images deepened during a
sabbatical year (1962–63) spent in Geneva, Switzerland,
studying with Professor Jean Piaget, genetic epistemologist
of the University of Geneva's graduate school and of the
Sorbonne in Paris. His book *Play, Dreams and Imitation in
Childhood*[2] had already suggested a powerful way images
and symbols function in small children. I was particularly
curious to discover how they related to story and especially
to the Biblical story and fairy tales for children. The study
was enhanced by a year-long, city-wide exhibit in Geneva
of Marc Chagall's artworks under the title "La Bible."
Further enrichment derived from the winter session of the
Ecumenical Institute's graduate program on liturgy held at
Céligny, several miles up the lake from Geneva. Exciting
books on worship and liturgy had been borrowed from
leading theological libraries of the world, but the program
itself was more doctrinaire. However, my special research
on baptism, particularly infant baptism, led me to the
heart of the way symbolic ritual comes alive as participated in by an entire community, including children,
before there is comprehension. Combining the work of
Professor Piaget and the artworks of Marc Chagall, I now

understand better the power of myth, symbol, and imagery in liberating a people. At the same time I began to see how they indoctrinate, oppress, and control people in patriarchal religions and the political structures of patriarchy. Much in the freedom movement became clear both in the use of imagery and also in the violent response of whites when the white patriarchal symbols were confronted as phony.

The study of images has been no end of help for me in the woman movement as we have begun to analyze symbols and pursue images that mystify issues of justice and equality and that have been powerful sources for change and growth. Image, as I have pursued it in this essay and in other essays throughout this collection, cannot be approached purely as a linguistic form, although it cannot be separated entirely from language philosophy. Nor is it psychological, though James Hillman's brief work on *Archetypal Psychology*[3] enlightens aspects of my approach. I started out claiming my work as theological. But by the time I had finished this collection I saw myself moving into *theopoetics*, to use the language and approach of Professor Emeritus Amos Wilder of Harvard.[4]

My exploration here provides me with opportunity to pay personal tribute to Professor Piaget. It is not surprising that my work often set me against Ronald Goldman of England and many American educators and psychologists who measured all acceptable material for children by Professor Piaget's intellectual-conceptual scale of development tasks.[5] But image, myth, and symbol could not be measured by such a conceptual scale because they are language of a different nature, and operate often out of the unconscious but always out of the imagination and intuition, as Piaget himself makes clear.

★

It is clear that any problem solving is affected by images that function in ways of perceiving, evoking, and even constructing reality. Nowhere is this more evident than in discussions on abortion.

Since the word *abortion* triggers uncalled-for emotion both in those who favor it and those who oppose it, and apparently in those who claim an objectivity, one is compelled to look for some hidden power functioning at a subliminal level. Such a force that can surface emotion in the best of us, that appears to act on its own, that clouds issues, and that misplaces the focus of discussions may safely be designated as an image operating in the unconscious.

Jean Piaget observed that a child forms an image out of her imitation of that outside which imposes a concrete value, style of life, or perception of reality on the child.[6] In time the image shaped within the child may begin to have a life of its own. If the image becomes conscious, it may be said to have become a part of the child's own self. But if the image remains in the unconscious, which it very often does, it may arise unexpectedly in the life of the child, take control of a situation and even control the child in such a way that the child herself cannot distinguish the self from that which, foreign to the self, dominates. When an image remains an unconscious part of a person's self, the innerness of the self (that which flows innately out of the rhythms of the universe) is denied. Piaget holds that for health an equilibrium between the inner and the outer must be achieved.[7] Since images may set styles of life long before persons reach the age of conceptualization,[8] we may expect many adults to be controlled by images that formed in their psyches when they were children. And since image operates on a different level from an idea or a concept[9] it cannot so easily be corrected or changed or even detected when persons are grown.

In the same manner that image formation has been observed in a child, it may be observed in a culture or society. Over the thousands of years a culture is shaping itself, certain images force themselves into the community's psyche and become set.[10] A consciously aware, questioning, and growing community will reexamine and internalize intentionally some images and exorcise others from its corporate life so that its spirit life retains a dynamic and vibrant ferment, ever renewing itself yet maintaining continuity with its past. On the other hand, if the images have continued over the centuries to operate only in the community's unconscious, they may be said to have frozen the community's growth and the images themselves become stereotyped. Then they become demonic, operating nostalgically rather than dynamically, and with a life of their own, arise within the body politic dominating a political action or affecting (even distorting) the intelligent inquiry into or courageous move on an issue.

As we turn to the abortion issue there appear to be two foci around which images function: 1. the right to control one's own body, and 2. what has come to be called "the right to life." On one hand, women who assert their right to end an unwanted pregnancy (and supporters of this position) do so on the basis of a woman's right and responsibility to own and control her own body.[11] They view both men who oppose this right and also women who have internalized men's definition of them as operating out of a patriarchal perception which claims the right of men to control women's bodies and that within a woman which has not yet made its appearance as viable, visible life. On the other hand, men and women who oppose abortion base their view on the right of the fetus "as person" to have its own chance to life. They view any who oppose them as potential murderers and renunciators of motherhood.

In most discussions one side will be dealing with the right to exercise exclusive responsibility for one's own body, while the other will be arguing for the "right to life." Their difficulty in hearing one another may be laid at the door of an age-old image functioning in the individual and societal psyches— the image of the man as the sole parent. Each side may claim to be profoundly theological. When the control of one's own body is denied, the right to be responsible for the sacred gift of oneself is cut off and the woman is not allowed to respond to the creative forces of her own life. Also, when the "right to life" of the fetus is denied then the prerogative of the creator to bring life into the world or take it from the world is usurped.

If the ancient myth that life and spirit originate in the male is the source of this image, it follows that the male is the sole parent of the child, thus defining the woman as the nurturer of the male's babies (both before and after birth).[12] The myth gives rise to such images of woman as incubator, sex object, breeder, and housewife. The man is then seen as decision maker, provider, owner of the woman and the child, and head of the household. From these images have spun all sorts of laws restricting woman's ownership of property, her freedom of operation in a public sphere, the classification of certain children as illegitimate, the institution of prostitution, and the double standard and the definition of sexuality and legislation governing it.

The church and synagogue have legitimated these images of sexual expression and social consequences in a variety of ways: by observing marriage within their institution as a social function rather than worship (thus in cases of abortion and divorce leaving both parties to face a traumatic experience alone), by passing the bride as property from one man to another, by usurping the "giving birth" functions of women for symbols of the sacraments of baptism and the Eucharist, and by indoctrinating children with concepts of humanity in terms of sexist role definitions.

The history of the myth of the male as sole parent has its roots in earliest patriarchy. With the knowledge of paternity (male participation in conception) the ego consciousness of men began its ascendency. In time it expressed itself as a system in patriarchy, recasting many of the earlier mother myths in order to support men as the superior sex and to establish the priority of the male as the progenitor of life. A function which up to then had been seen as women's alone suddenly was claimed by men alone. The man constructed a myth that life actually originated within himself. In the act of intercourse he came to believe that he placed a minuscule baby into the womb of the woman—reducing her to the nurturer of his babies (nurse of live "seed")[13] and using her for breeding purposes since she was seen as unable to pass on blood strains from her own body. She became "like the earth into which seed was sown." The concept and practice led to the man claiming as his property anything that was born of woman. Therefore, he considered it his right (reflected in early Greek and Roman history[14]) to kill all defective children, any female children he chose, all children who were not of his own loins (illegitimate), and even the woman who secretly had aborted, for if left to natural birth the fetus might have become a male baby.[15]

Even among artists and scientists the myth has had a slow death. In *The Eumenides* Aeschylus has Apollo explain to Orestes that the true life-begetter of the child is not the mother but the one who sowed the life seed into her body. He has Apollo offering proof by pointing to Zeus who gave birth to Athena without the help of a female. In 1677, when Leeuwenhoek put semen under a powerful microscope and saw the spermatozoa wriggling, he claimed to have beheld the male's live babies. Even when de Graaf in 1672 discovered ovarian follicles many scientists refused to believe they had anything to do with procreation. The mammalian ovum (though visible to the naked eye) was not discovered until 1827. Scientists were looking for it at the wrong time—after, not before, intercourse. It was not until 1875, a little over a hundred years ago, that the union of the male and female gametes was observed. Thus came the final blow to the male's illusion that he was the sole parent. However the image of sole parenthood had been so deeply internalized by a patriarchal culture that to this day it has not been shattered.[16]

Biblical and theological support of the myth stem from the patriarchal language in which the Biblical document and early church and synagogue ecclesiastical papers were written. Patriarchy may be defined as any social system in which men are perceived as inherently superior and more powerful than women. Such social systems, creating their own forms of ruling and competition, have pervaded and shaped the entire western civilization. Patriarchy has led to universal oppression on women, the poor, the nonwhite, to domination of the Third World peoples, to world wars, and the exploitation of the earth and its resources.[17]

Once sexism is seen as patriarchy-gone-underground, one may readily observe how the early myth and its many images have not yet been put to rest. Women fighting for the right to end an unwanted pregnancy on one hand, and men fighting equally hard to maintain the right to make the decision regarding it, both appear to be operating out of the ancient myth that the man is the sole parent. Women fighting to free themselves from the control of men in order to make the decision about their own bodies are in reality still fighting the myth of the male as sole parent, operative now in the national body politic. Men fighting to keep the control—whether through church, legislature, the home, or social custom—reflect a reluctance to give up the ancient myth that continues to function in their psyches.

The right to life argument is a bit trickier. But it, too, appears to derive from the same myth. The man does not identify with the dilemma of the woman, but instead with the fetus, which he sees as part of himself. In his identity with the fetus he is forced to go through the woman's body to reach it, morally compelling him to the same concern for the woman as for the fetus (which the woman considers as part of herself). But when the woman can be viewed, even in the remotest sense, as the nurturer of man's minuscule baby, or the egg can be viewed, primarily, as nutrient for the sperm in which real life resides, then the man could logically claim the right to make the decisions regarding the welfare of the fetus. But to be consistent men would have to be equally concerned with all the minuscule babies lost in every ejaculation spilled out on the ground and all ejaculations with prostitutes from whom they walk away. (In this sense the prostitute becomes a symbol for every woman.) The man actually concerned with "right to life" would be compelled to an equal concern for every pregnant woman (or for every human being, for that matter) exposed and even killed in famine, war, prison, etc. As Philip Roth wrote in *Our Gang:*

> CITIZEN: In as much as I feel as you do about the unborn, I am seriously troubled by the possibility that Lieutenant Calley may have committed an abortion. I hate to say this, Mr. President, but I am seriously troubled when I think that one of those twenty-two Vietnamese civilians Lieutenant Calley killed may have been a pregnant woman.
>
> TRICKY: Now just one minute. We have a tradition in the courts of this land that a man is innocent until he is proven guilty. There were babies in that ditch at My Lai, and we know there were women of all ages, but I have not seen a single document that suggests the ditch at My Lai contained a *pregnant* woman.[18]

Theodore of Mopsuestia in the fourth century did not buy into the male minuscule baby idea and yet maintained that physically the male gave the first birth: "We are first born of the male in the form of human semen,"[19] implying that the origin of life resided in the male. Afterward the life took on a physical form and was born of woman (a less significant birth). Here, and in other patristic writings as well as in the New Testament, the image of the sole parent begins to take on cosmic dimensions, for in the potency of the semen the Spirit of Life resides. And the Spirit of Life capitalized can only project the image that the divine spark descended as the Holy Spirit and identified itself as God, Himself. Nowhere is this imaged better than in the birth of the Christ Child when God became the parent of Jesus, and Mary was seen as the instrument through whom God came into the world as His Son, His Only Son, only His Son. The body of Mary was denigrated to the extent she was elevated as Goddess of Heaven (otherwise she would have been an adulteress or prostitute—another persistent image of woman on the pedestal or in the dust) and when her Assumption was declared[20] "she was taken into heaven in bodily form."

When life is absolutized and symbolized in a fetus, one is confronted with yet another knotty point—how does one account for a live egg before it is impregnated? When does life begin? What is the meaning of person? When does one become a person?

Psychologically, the deep anxiety of women over abortion derives from living in a patriarchal society in which guilt is produced by the clandestine way we are forced to get an abortion rather than in the act or event itself. On the other hand, the anxiety of men over abortion derives from the possibility of losing control. In order to gain and maintain control, the man identifies with the fetus (where no mutuality is possible) instead of the woman. He sees the fetus as part of himself (God-come-flesh) further separating himself from the woman who cannot identify with a male God. Here we see not a right to life but the right of the male parent to determine life, who shall live, and when life begins, while women are fighting for our right to be our own persons. But those who control life—so claim the patriarchs—not only have a right to define what life is but where life resides. Thus a myth out of an ancient culture continues to organize us, fix our relationships, determine our actions, and inform our communication to this day.

1973:

Preaching the Word

Having participated in the 1970 exploratory sessions that led to the creation of the Women's Institute of the Boston Theological Institute, I came to know Mary Daly, Emily Culpepper, Brinton Lykes, Jan Raymond, Linda Barufaldi, and some of the graduate women in the theological programs in the institute. Therefore, when the women's caucus of Harvard Divinity School and Boston Theological Institute's related schools were able to secure the Lentz monies for a 1972–73 series of lectures on women and religion and to fund a visiting professor for one year, I was happy to accept the invitation to be one of the lecturers, but I was puzzled then and still am at the topic assigned to me: "Preaching the Word."[1] Knowing many of the women on the planning committee, I was convinced that they did not want a lecture out of the patriarchal theological interpretation of Word. And at that time not enough women had developed a feminist-style hermeneutic to provide data for what I was anxious to do and what I knew was expected of me by the graduate women.

I reviewed the data that had produced my 1971 essay in hopes of getting a clue. Then it came. It was the woman herself—her flesh and blood self. Her body had to be dealt with before she would be allowed to preach or before the word could be heard from her as Word. "This is my body..." Whose body? Which body? What kind of voice is necessary to proclaim the word? What ear to hear it? When is the word Word?" In my preliminary struggle two things came clear. First, certain images had to be shattered or at

40

least recognized as existing on a subliminal level before
the theological meaning of woman and word could be
considered—deeply internalized images of male preaching
versus female preaching. I did not want to approach this
(at least in the beginning) from a rational standpoint. I
wanted to trigger these images where they operate. The
meaning of woman word and woman preaching had been
mystified by the images and could never be heard radically
or described until the images were penetrated and the
depth meaning of word and preaching—beyond gender—
could be bravely faced. Second, once beyond gender, that
is, beyond word as dependent on male, the subject, or first
cause as I wanted to present it, is hearing and not
speaking. The redemptive factor is hearing. Who hears?
Who is heard?

In an introduction to Faust, I remembered the
writer/editor quoting Goethe as saying "In the beginning
was not the Word. In the beginning was the Act." I blurted
aloud, "Ah! No! In the beginning was not the Word. In the
beginning was the hearing." Suddenly the whole patriarchal
interpretation of word and preaching reversed themselves
for me. And I was freed to begin writing the lecture.

If the style of a woman's preaching was not to deliver
(to proclaim) the Word but to place her ear close to the
pulse of the people, then a new kind of pentecost would be
possible. Each tongue would be loosened and each would
be speaking her/his own word and that word would be
herself/himself. A new insight on laity came to me
through this experience. If the Word became the people's
word, then the people, and not the preacher (or, and the
preacher), would become the minister.

My first problem in this lecture became a matter of
how to reverse roles of men and women in the audience.
How could I have the men present try on the cultural and
religious stereotyped images of women, and the women try
on the cultural stereotyped images of men? It became

necessary for hearing to take place on a feeling as well as a cerebral level.

I found what I wanted in Theo Wells's "Woman—Which Includes Man, of Course: An Experience in Awareness."[2] She allowed me to paraphrase it for a divinity school setting. Harvard had opened its doors to women students, but continued as a bastion of male control, history, and atmosphere.

Following my lecture at Harvard a former student from Drew, Ed Mark, then a pastor in Cambridge and teacher of film at Harvard, asked me—rather too loudly for my comfort: "Do you not think the church can be redeemed?" Had I said that in my lecture? Had I implied it? I was stunned for a moment. He was not asking me what I had said, he was asking me to own—to bring up to my own consciousness—that which had become obvious to him behind what I had verbalized. After a moment I answered, "NO!" Ed had heard something that was at work in me, or else he was very sensitive, or both. It came to me later that he helped me to begin hearing myself. As long as the word was in the beginning and a male word there could be no speech of women. Some feminist scholars see in John 1:1 a replacement of wisdom (Sophia) from Proverbs 8. Others indicate that even in wisdom literature, Sophia was controlled.[3]

From that time on I recognized that the deepest source of my community was no longer in the institutional church.

I never walked out of the church as did Mary Daly at her 1971 Harvard sermon, though I admire her courage and her honesty and I support her prophetic exodus. My experience in and with the church cannot be compared to hers. Nor have I been excommunicated as was Sonia Johnson (although I was fired from a church once because of my stance on race—and from a Brooklyn church at that!). Sonia has become a new power since her brave witness. But none of this implies lukewarmness. I work

where I can. I go where I can. I feel my faith is stronger
than it has ever been. The murky smog of patriarchy has
pervaded the universe. The church not excluded. "If we
leave the church, where would we go?" once asked Beverly
Harrison. However, many women no longer find the
church open to them. Many women still in traditional
religion, employees in the church, do not believe the
church can listen or will allow women full membership.
They are my sisters. I support them. Some, however, do
and as a result find themselves dismissed by many
feminists. Some brave and radical feminists are struggling
within the church. They, too, are my sisters. I will not
forsake them.

★

WHAT IMAGE is evoked by this usually-perceived-as-masculine
vocation being dealt with by a woman speaker? To what
extent does this image affect the way you begin to listen to
what I say, and once listening, to the way you hear? Are you
able to get in touch at a feeling level with what is stirring in
you? I invite you to participate in an exercise toward this end.
Are you ready?

Just suppose for a few moments that it is like this in your
entire seminary life...that it is the *usual* thing to hear a
woman's voice...that a male professor in the classroom is the
exception, the *interruption!* How do you begin to feel, if you
are a man? How, if a woman?

Suppose not only the professors but the predominance of
students are women...that Harvard has a history as a woman's institution, with a feminine operational style.

What is evoked in you as you gradually become aware
that the language in such an institution has a distinctly
feminine character...that feminine words function for both
masculine and feminine...that every time a professor says
womankind she means, of course, "all humanity"? When one
enrolls in a seminar on "The Doctrine of Woman" the profes-

sor intends at least to consider men also. When one sings of the Motherhood of God and the Sisterhood of Woman, one breathes a prayer that all men as well as women will come to experience true sisterhood.

Intellectually, you think you know all the time what is meant since this is the way it has been for generations. But what do you begin to know out of your gut?

How do you feel, if you are a man, when you have raised the question about the generic usage and have been dismissed by women who insist it is merely a semantic form? How do you feel, if you are a woman, when the few men around keep hammering on the fact that they experience alienation by such language?

What kind of support do you feel (if you are a woman) or lack of support (if you are a man) when you realize that it is like this in the whole world and that it has been this way since you were a little boy or a little girl; that there has never been a male President of the United States; that all seminaries and most universities have women presidents and deans? It should come as no surprise to you that most seminarians are women, since the seminary's woman recruiter has no particular program to enroll men. It is understandable why all the men students should feel they are on trial—you know, having to prove themselves. Imagine the frustration when a man uses his energy to get a hearing and has little left for creativity!

Once in a while a man gets nerve enough to protest the use of Mother God, saying that it does something to his sense of dignity and integrity. Professor Martha hastens to explain that no one really believes that God is female in a sexual sense. She makes it quite clear that in a matriarchal society the wording of the Scripture, of liturgy and theology, could come out only in matriarchal imagery. The last student who raised such a question, it was discovered later, had just joined a male liberation group and it had gotten him all screwed up. Everyone knows that this man came to the Divinity School in the first place to get married, and eventually to be able to keep house and support his woman in her pastorate.

What images function here? How do they make you feel if you are a man? If you are a woman? What sense of self-worth or value of being human is raised?

Let us follow such a seminarian a step further. It soon becomes obvious that he is denying his masculinity, that he is forgetting his true vocation bestowed upon him by the Creator Herself. No one is wise enough to know why God made female reproductive organs compact and internal so that woman is physically free to move about unencumbered and take her natural place of leadership in the world of womankind. Or why God made the male's organs external and exposed, so that he would demand sheltering and protection from the outside in order that he may be kept for reproducing the race. Any time a male student rejects his own built-in longing to be enfolded by a woman, or give his woman a female child, or to enhance her vocation, he is in trouble. He becomes a fit subject for the best female therapist the Divinity School can secure. Feel into this. Feel for all men in all divinity schools. Feel for women—that is, generically speaking, when one person begins to cut himself off from the community sisterhood by rejecting his own creation.

Needless to add, the young seminarian is led by the therapist back into his childhood where he is able to get in touch with his internalized envy of his sister who could run and dance and climb and ride horseback preparing herself for leadership. Finally he is able to face the long-remembered episodes of her jeering at his organs, which she said "flopped foolishly."

As with most minority students no serious therapy is demanded. In an encounter group with a competent woman trainer and the help of two men and ten women he soon develops a better attitude toward his divinely destined role and looks forward to giving his future wife the support she needs to be a real woman in the world.

In the same spirit, though without the fantasy—but, on second thought, maybe a bit of fantasy at that—let us seek to evoke some of the images surrounding the pulpit, the altar, and the baptismal font where the church claims the Word of God becomes most visible and most audible.

For hundreds of years an aura of holiness has been maintained about the altar. Today it has become the focus of the invisibility of women in the church and symbolic of the church's male supremacy. Relaxation of male control has changed little except in form since 1825 when a Jonesboro, Tennessee, women's society was thanked for raising the enormous sum of $40.25 for missions:

> The lovely and retiring modesty of the female sex, together with their delicate structure, forbids that they shall ever rival the hardy sons of Levi in the gross services of the altar. The Kind Author of our being never designed them [to]...go in search of lost sinners....And yet they may be abundantly useful; yea, they are greatly so. They not only welcome weary pilgrims to their friendly mansions and hospitable cottages but they warm, clothe and feed them.[4]

In order to get at what was going on here and continues to go on in churches, it is necessary to remind ourselves that images function powerfully long after they have been repudiated intellectually. They may continue to function until dealt with at the only level where they can be altered—that is, in the community psyche. I shall seek to evoke some of these images rather than present an argument; to raise questions about them rather than suggest answers.

It is a matter of history that the majority of church bodies in America have one by one opened doors officially to women for ordination. Ordination grants the privilege of *preaching the word.* In barring women from the pulpit, the Catholic Church, the Orthodox communions, the Episcopal Church,* and the Missouri Lutheran synod may have a greater self-

---

*Written prior to the ordination of the women priests in 1974.

understanding than the so-called open churches. Their official pronouncements, while discriminating against women, at least coincide with their practice. At the same time, it may be observed that no "open" church body includes more than a minuscule proportion of ordained women.

Woman candidates in the open churches claim they are discouraged from entering the pulpit through subtle and devious methods. In the spring of 1973 a woman seminary graduate meeting initially with the district committee on ministry was given to understand that if she sought other than a parish ministry—i.e., a ministry in which she would not preach, baptize, marry, or bury—the committee would be more open to receiving her. Not one question was asked of her about her commitment, her understanding of ministry, her theology, or her beliefs. They let her know that they thought that her highest qualification was as a wife and mother. This same woman was featured in a film produced by her denomination. There was resistance at first to inclusion of a scene showing her in the pulpit on the ground that churches would be offended. But her faithful persistence led both to her ordination and the retention of the pulpit scene. Three years ago, another woman graduate of the same seminary, finding it difficult to get ordained in her state, applied to a neighboring one. In an initial interview the pastor of a well-known church opened conversation with her by asking: "How do you handle your sex life?"

In January 1973 I was invited to meet with a group of ministers. I found myself in the presence of angry and puzzled women, all beautiful, competent, and theologically able. They had been moved frequently by the official hierarchy. Some had been sent to remote areas. Some had not been received fully in church courts and church dialogue. A few were on the verge of opting out of the church completely. Some serving in joint pastorates with their husbands reported ministerial committees who viewed skeptically a husband in such an open relationship of mutuality.

The question emerges out of the reality of these and

numerous other situations: What is it about the Word of God that makes it so important for the proclaimer of that Word to be of a certain sex, and that sex male?

Why is it that even when they are robed or gowned, clergymen breaking bread and pouring wine manage to project an image of the authority of maleness, with no suggestion of femaleness?

How is it that the Word of God has become identified with a deep voice? Is God dependent on sex?

What kind of theology is it that requires male hands for a sacrament to have efficacy?

Everywhere women ministers witness that they experience resistance to, and fear of, their ministry, not from local churches but from ministers who ordain them and from whom they must receive approval on their way to a parish. One is forced to question the quality of education these men have received in theological schools that contributes to such continued discrimination. Could it be that theological schools have overlooked the male imagery they have perpetuated in theology, church history, and liturgy, preaching, teaching, and pastoring—not to mention male structure and model of the male professor! Could it be that they have concentrated on conceptual to the exclusion of holistic learning? In what seminary have myth, image, and symbol received more than a cerebral nod? Perhaps modern man, and I do not use that term generically, thinks he is beyond myth!

Have theological professors been unaware of the power of images and the way they concretize themselves sociologically, shaping community and individual life-styles long before persons conceptualize? Or do they not know how sociological structures may manufacture or evoke a myth or image to support and harden the structure? Years ago it was observed how an interchangeable use of images for *black*, such as "dark," "sin," "dirty," "foreboding," "ugly," and for *white*, such as "pure," "sinless," "clean," "light," "truth," tended to produce an inferior self-image in black children and a superior self-image in white children before either arrived at the age of conceptualization. Dr. John Money of the Johns Hopkins Gender Clinic makes a more startling observation from his clinical findings. The sex identity of a child, he says, is established by the time a child is eighteen months old. By the age of three sex identity is set as hard as concrete, so powerfully have the cultural images done their work. It is more difficult, states Dr. Money, to change even so early a mistaken identity than it is to simulate by physical operation sex organs corresponding to the mistaken identity.[5]

But the question persists: Why has preaching the Word become the crux of the place of women in the life of the church?

I believe that women preaching, more than any aspect of the church's ministry, threatens to expose the church and its seminaries as primarily masculine institutions rather than human communities.

Consider what might happen with women in the holy places: behind the pulpit, proclaiming the Word, breaking the bread, consecrating the elements, baptizing, burying, and marrying!

By her very presence a woman would confront the church daily with its own baptism. As preacher she might serve as a catalyst for unleashing the imagination of the people for all kinds of creative lay ministries, new styles of relatedness, of being present to one another, gifts of grace to one another. The entire laity just might come to know itself as ministry—a people of God in the world in the truest and most radical sense. The new language and the new speech emerging out of such common involvement in ministry, listening, and living might furnish a new kind of movement and song for celebration. And then celebration itself could indeed become the work of the people, rising out of the heart of a people rather than structured and controlled from above.

Once the pulpit is de-sexed it can no longer be labeled as the phallic symbol in the sanctuary with the Book on top to give it authority. Women would more than likely carry the Book down among the people, open it, saying, "See...see for yourselves! Read! How do you read? See...see, even here seeds of liberation long ago overlooked by a patriarchal mind-set and culture." Then the most ignorant and timid ones might obtain courage to open their eyes and the self-confidence to begin to think for themselves theologically. Should that happen, most embarrassing questions would inevitably be raised...agonies and lostnesses...alienations and oppressions...would be articulated unashamedly and boldy. In time an entire people might come to know itself as disinherited and open itself for the liberating experience of a new humanity.

Such a movement would inevitably bring to death a certain ecclesiastical hierarchy and allow women—that is, those who wear the skirts all the time—to enter the pulpit in great numbers to preach the Word.

By the same token, breaking bread and pouring wine—once seen as the serving role in which women are cast all the time—might reduce the holiness of the altar. Why should eating of the bread and drinking of the wine be separated from the consumption of the kindly fruits of the earth? Are not both simple acts of faith? Should not all that one eats be valued both physically and spiritually? Is it not time to rescue the powerful symbolism surrounding the sacrament from a preoccupation with things, and restore it to eating and drinking out of the people's common humanness at the deepest source of their existence, where the bread and the wine lead out to the boundary of a new future?

Were women allowed to baptize openly, the uterine waters of baptism might begin to heal the split between physical birth and spiritual birth, since both are ejections out of the great womb. It might even herald the end of "joining a church." More realistically, the newly born would be engrafted into a community of faith—received into its deaths, its births, its life, its struggles, and its joys in the world—sustained by a grace not conditioned by sex. The community of faith would embrace the totality of life's experiences in which God is not absent from any. There would be no point to postponing the new birth ritual to a time when the mind could begin to grasp its mysteries. Inevitably, new birth would shift to that moment from which it was once split off by a patriarchal perception which assigned body to woman and spirit to man. It would affirm that persons are loved before they comprehend, are in the struggle before they choose to be. Indeed it would envision a love that enables understanding; that begets trust; that calls persons to pick up their own lives as sacred gifts, not leaving them to the mercy and pressures of stereotyped images that rob them of their humanness.

What would happen to adults in churches—or to churches themselves, for that matter—if women ministers should receive children as "in ministry," and not objects "to be ministered to"? Undoubtedly Jesus placed a child in the inner midst of his disciples neither as an object lesson nor essentially for the sake of the child, but to confront the entire community with its own faith because the child belongs in ministry. Has the child not been relegated to a place of insignificance in the church to avoid reminding adults of too much unfinished business in their own lives? Is not the child in touch with resources that adults no longer value or have lost the ability to value or even to understand? Removing a child from the church's core ministry simply robs the church of its own faith and reduces its celebrative life to a blandness devoid of the ecstatic and the mysterious. Baptism, no matter at what age, serves as the symbolic act by which a community engrafts a person in ministry. As baptism is one baptism so ministry is one ministry. Therefore, to identify ministry "to children," rather than "children in ministry," becomes another betrayal of the community's faith. It would be a strange phenomenon, indeed, should the church and not the world begin to usher in the next and perhaps the final liberation movement—that of children.

The imagery in male language and structure serves to alienate women and dehumanize men.

Once the alienating male language and imagery in liturgy become inappropriate, it might be possible to celebrate out of the common life of a people rather than out of a superstructure manipulated from above that can come through only as phony to the oppressed. But women do not want the celebrative life of the community to be feminine any more than we want it to continue to be masculine. There is no objection to theologizing out of masculine experience. The basic problem lies in claiming the resulting theology valid for the entire community. Distortion occurs when the part parades for the whole.

Women shun a monopoly of the community's symbolic acts. We do not seek a feminine theology except iconoclastically to show up one kind of idolatry with another. All we want is the elimination of sexism at the core of the church and seminary life so that a new kind of transcendence may be experienced in the human flesh. It was none other than that male chauvinist Luther who said: "The deeper we can fetch Christ into the flesh the better it is for us all."

Given the partisan state of the church, women have hesitated to take those positions of leadership that have been open to us. In the first place, we have been conditioned all our lives not to seek positions of authority; and many who seek such positions are preconditioned to fail even when we have the ability to succeed. Many women are unable to take on the "man's way" without losing our integrity. We feel that the present male structure and tight male control allow for little flexibility. Women experience dehumanization in seminaries and churches by inequity of salaries, promotion, rank, and limited dialogical participation. Women hesitate to recommend one another for a vacancy in a seminary or church, or to become aggressive ourselves in seeking churches and the ministry, teaching, and administrative positions. We feel that by and large men still want token women. And tokenness is no step at all to freedom. Women are convinced that once we are heard and received, a new and as yet unknown way that transcends sexism will emerge. But women are fast losing hope that hearing will or can take place.

The males in control in both seminaries and church courts find it difficult or nearly impossible to hear the preached Word as Word from a woman's lips because of the imagery operating in their own lives which identifies a woman by her sex function.

The following *Windham Journal* report of Maggie Van Cott's appearance in the Hudson Street Methodist Church pulpit in 1869 and the brief newspaper accounts of other incidents indicate how imagery functions so as to screen a woman's words and message.

> The clerical toilet of the Rev. Widow Van Cott, as she stood up before the multitude...and dispensed the Word, is described as having been neat, and that she looked as blooming and blushing as a newly-made bride. Her hair was nicely fixed and frizzed, and her face glowed with a modest but conscious splendor, as she stood before the congregation in her rich but tasteful dress of bombazine. She wore a neat black jet ornament on her throat, and a handsome gold chain peeped from the black belt around her waist. Every word she uttered was delivered with unction and force. There is considerable power and attraction in the manner in which the widow lifts her smooth white hand and nicely rounded fingers to the ceiling, and then brings them down with energy on the wooden shelf of the pulpit. When warmed to her subject her face seems lighted up and full of stirring animation. Her face in happy moments contracts and expands, and her handsomely shaped body sways to and fro with excitement. Her elocution is natural and florid, and her sentences uttered in a bass tone voice.[6]

When a small New Jersey church ordained its first woman minister some of her ministerial colleagues referred to her as "the preacher who wears skirts," except in small intimate circles, where they said, "The new preacher does not wear pants."

"Balloonist's Widow, 77, Joins Seminary to Pursue Long Ambition—Priesthood," said the announcement of Mme. Piccard's enrollment in theological school in the fall of 1972.[7] The same issue of the newspaper headlined the story of another woman pictured with a group of ministers: "Grandmother's Path to Pulpit Is Long."[8]

Identifying and describing any person in the pulpit or classroom by their sex function is immoral.

To summarize: women such as those mentioned above experience a great sense of alienation by this kind of immorality reflected in generic language, in male imagery, in hierarchical structures. But we confess the ultimate alienation lies in the persistent and pervasive masculine character and control of the institution, the ontological maleness of Transcendence with its theological spinoff out of the male rather than out of the full human experience.

While women are constantly up against the limitations of language to express full humanity, we have now available a more adequate language than we are willing to use. Consider how much richer one's speech is in the use of *humankind* rather than *mankind* and *all persons* instead of *all men.*

A fundamental question now insinuates itself: Could the limiting imagery in the word Word—Logos—*derive from a patriarchal way of perceiving and experiencing the universe? Would a more inclusive perceiving allow for persons to be heard into existence rather than spoken into existence?*

Could it be that *Logos* deified reduces communication to a one-way relationship—that of *speak*-ing—and bypasses the far more radical divine aspect of *hearing?* Once such a possibility is entertained, and the Biblical confession read from that perspective, is not one confronted by a pervasive Wisdom in the universe which *Logos,* and its self-extension *technology,* seek to manipulate and control? That the more divine act is *hearing to speech* rather than *speaking to hearing!* That the pervasive Wisdom or Transcendent One hears the human being to speech; and that the word is the human being's word; and that word heard into speech creates and announces new personhood—new consciousness awakened in the human being?

Every liberation movement rises out of its bondage with a new speech on its lips. This has been so with women coming together, seeking to get in touch with our own stories and experiences which we have discovered welling up from within, from underneath, from out of our past, from out of our traditions rather than down from above. But to evoke our story to speech, women experience an imperative—a prior great Listening Ear... an ear that hears without interruption down through our defenses, cliché-filled language, pretensions, evasions, pervasive hurts, angers, frustration, internalized stereotyped images until we experience at the lowest point of our lives that we are sustained. Women are literally hearing one another to speech. But the speech is our speech. It may come on stumblingly or boldly. But it is authentically our own.

Through hearing and speaking, women sense the possibility of doing theology out of our own experiences. We understand better how church dogmas, ecclesiastical practices, liturgies, and language that are oppressive of and exclude women have derived from male experience. Only a patriarchal hierarchical scale of values could project the imagery in order of decreasing value:

GOD

MAN

WOMAN

CHILD

EARTH

Such a hierarchical system, leaving no room for the human, could have toppled long ago had the so-called recipients of the revelation been sensitive to that which happened in their midst and allowed themselves to be heard into a new radical liberating speech.

Let us examine briefly the system out of which theology has emerged for more than two thousand years. Only the child ranked beneath the woman in first-century Palestinian culture. But the girl child was considered of infinitely less value than the boy child. The only human creature lower than the girl child was the boy child who had no father, who had no name, who had no lineage—an illegitimate one, a bastard. The dictionary terms such a one "inferior to or varying from standard." An illegitimate girl, as viewed by patriarchal society, could marry into a name. A bastard boy—never! In such a one—lower than the lowest, cut off from the land of the living—could the most lost or oppressed of the earth find himself or herself. . . God-with-us . . . Emmanuel. But a patriarchy could not bear so radical a source of salvation. Rather than permit the hierarchy to falter, they quickly snatched the child out of his low estate and set him up at the right hand of the Father—thus shoring up the old ontological masculinity of God, interpreting the event with such a theological superstructure as to institutionalize its maleness with built-in protection against women and children. So it has continued to this day—due largely to the powerful functioning of imagery and ritual.

Seminaries keep supplying churches with ministers and universities with religion professors who have never come to terms with the way images go underground, shape life-styles, and set a kind of mentality that is no longer able to perceive wholeness.

The women movement confronts the churches and seminaries with an opportunity to respond in terms of the deepest cleavage in the human experience—that of sex. It cannot be turned off or easily dismissed. Its ferment is stirring in countries around the world, countries unrelated to one another—like mushrooms springing up out of the darkness. It carries a cosmic overtone. The words of Betty Friedan in 1963 and Simone de Beauvoir twenty years earlier and the feminists of the last century did not start the movement. These women merely gave public utterance to the private whisperings that have been heard into expression for generations. Today the movement accelerates as a massive shifting of perceived reality and, in the words of theologian Mary Daly, "a vast reordering of the forces of the universe."[9] A Biblical writer could well have envisioned such a moment:

> We know that the whole creation has been groaning
> in travail together until now; and not only the crea-
> tion, but we ourselves.[10]

Thus we are brought near to the possibility of new revelatory moments that break into the present and open a hopeful future for all humanity.

In the light of all this, what could the church's renewed emphasis on evangelism possibly mean to women at this moment in our history?

What hope does it offer to those women who are already on the rolls of the institutions or, for that matter, to those who are outside—more than half of the human race—the subjugated half?

Of the nearly one hundred on the planning committee of Key '73, an interdenominational cooperative evangelistic effort, I was told by an official that only one woman was included.

A national television series interpreting this new thrust engaged in dialogue each Sunday morning a group of two or three men, in addition to the moderator. The language of the dialogue, out of the male experience, came through to me and many other women as a foreign language: Jesus Christ as the Word for modern *man*; *He* is the Word for all *men*; as *men* hear the gospel..."; "as *men* communicate the gospel..."; "calling *men* to repentance and renewal of life, difficult in our culture...but still good news to *men*"; "good news to poor *men* ...liberation to bound *men*"; "*men* need what the church has to give." One minister ventured: "But if news is good to the poor...liberation for the oppressed...it may be bad news to the top dogs." He was not heard, even though he repeated his remark.

In no plans that I have seen or heard has the current brand of evangelism promised to herald the end of sexism and usher in a new human community in which all persons could receive the gift of their uniqueness, stand up, and be responsible because they are so enabled by the inclusiveness of community which ever examines itself in light of its confessed faith. Therefore I see neither local churches—as the TV panel indicated—nor the ghettoes as the new field for mission work today, but the seminaries and the ministers they produce. It is *they* who continue to proclaim a Word that comes through as a male word from a male God.

Ecclesiastical institutions continue to operate out of a prophetic rather than out of an apocalyptic model. The prophetic relies on the expert, the insightful and powerful leaders, the stars and the superstars who read the signs of the times, pronounce the word of the hour, and command obedient but individualistic followers. Since the prophetic model depends on a hierarchical ordering of values, its best expression can never fully transcend the status quo. The apocalyptic, on the other hand, takes with dead seriousness the reality of community, recognizing the infinite and unique value of the "least one" within it. It cannot afford to listen only to the expert and the star. It relies more on faithfulness in the humanizing and politicizing process. Its ear is tuned to transcendence at the heart of the body politic, thus allowing for the appearance of a new reality that cannot be predetermined or manipulated or controlled by any one mind. Since the apocalyptic hopes for a new humanity, the dynamic of its daily life contributes to its actualization.

What this implies for theological curricular development and for the church's ministry in terms of method, content, and structure is unlimited. Many seminaries are still under the illusion that the involvement/reflection model has eliminated the old dichotomy between theory and practice, when as a matter of fact it has merely reordered the pieces.

Liberation derives not from individuation *per se* but from the humanness of an authentic community in which identity can be defined in terms of person and not in terms of anatomy or grade. Self-actualization becomes a misleading term when thought of only as "forever moving toward one's full potential." I am speaking of a liberation that emerges out of one's true beginning...one's deepest roots.

"Humanizing the hierarchical structures in churches" is one stated goal of the newly established Commission on the Status and Role of Women in the United Methodist Church. Many church women support the commission's effort, but just as many are beginning to take a dim view as to whether the church can be saved—or will change. "The coming of woman will be the final humanization of the species," wrote Betty Farians when she was chairwoman of NOW's (National Organization of Women) National Task Force on Religion.[11]

Many women have gotten their first glimmer of liberation in the community of faith. They say that in spite of the male control something came through to them, for they do not believe God is intimidated by maleness. But they are now coming to see that what came to them was not what the church was saying...not what men in the pulpit are saying, or mean, today. Women are hearing in the churches not a word that liberates, but language that alienates, that drives us to one another, and to the Spirit of all, which has enabled us to survive and which literally brought us from death to life.

Women, as indicated earlier, are not concerned to open up churches and seminaries in order that more women be received into a sexist order. But women are concerned to be heard. We believe that once men begin to hear—can hear, really hear and see—a new order and a new language free from sexism could emerge.

By her conditioned nature woman finds it hard to rebel—even from a sexist institution of which she is the victim. She has been led to believe that rebellion violates her femininity. Yet there may come a time, and soon, when rebellion becomes her only positive response to that great source of life with which she is now in touch and from which she receives nourishment. When the chips are down and women have to choose between what heard us to speech and the hierarchical voices that maintain control, we have no choice, for we know we are in touch with the life sources of our humanness. Women are not about to let go of the thing that has brought us to life. And all over, women are experiencing God as a great hearing one, one who heard us to speech, rather than one who has spoken us to hearing.

God has often been interpreted as inept in the films of Ingmar Bergman—especially when his characters hopelessly face the meaninglessness and absurdity of existence. But suppose this logic is reversed and God's silence is perceived as hearing persons to response! There is a moment in every Bergman film when human response and human communication at its deepest level become the most crucial part of the film. Otherwise the communicator is dead. And it is at that moment, when the communicator is freed from the authoritarian hang-up, that love looms as a most poignant reality.

As Bergman asserts in his film *Cries and Whispers*, a stronger metaphor for loving than *touch* or *word* is that guttural cry out of the extremity of one's existence. As one becomes aware early in the film that the deepest pain is dying in life and not dying in death, one expects the cries of Agnes, one of the three sisters, to be primarily physical pain from her terminal cancer. Maria, a second sister, cries out at Agnes's clinging corpse, which confronts her with her own death—with the end of her constant touching and using of others. Her dismissal of the faithful service of Anna with the afterthought of a bill thrust into her hand becomes the final symbol of her shallowness. Only Karin, the third sister, is left. Karin, the stern, tall, beautiful, tender one hidden beneath layer after layer of stiff, corseted brocade. Only Karin backs up against the wall and cries out from the bowels of her earth. Only Karin has courage to lacerate her own body as primordial witness to an already dead marriage. Only Karin rebuffs Maria with "Don't touch me...Don't touch me...Don't touch me," as she senses the sister's touch as possessive and not loving.

Authentic word begins with the guttural cry at the extremity of one's own self-seeking, one's well-ordered, stereotyped life. It informs the film of the ineffectuality of ordinary communicative techniques, of mechanical devices that attempt to tick off and control time. It confesses the limits of contrived groups, encounters, and instruments that claim health and intimacy when there is only triteness and counterfeit. A guttural cry in one brief moment marks the end of the phony and reverses the ordinary.

And in that reversal the self is freed from its boundness and participates in a transcendent spiritual identification with others appropriating a kind of grace that enables praise.

1974:

Toward a Whole Theology

This address[1] was delivered in plenary session of the
World Council of Churches' first world conference on
discrimination against women, held in Germany. The
consultation, composed predominantly of women, was
called officially to deal head-on with the structures of
injustice and discrimination against women within the
World Church Body. In presenting the theme, "Sexism in
the 1970s," the planning committee sought to be aware of
the varied cultural and political patterns in the countries
from which the delegates came. It sought to make clear
that women were not representing their countries primarily, while not overlooking that "the place they were
coming from" would affect the color and the kind of
struggle the church waged. The planners wisely chose
the historic city of Berlin, torn apart by war, politics,
and ideologies (with the dividing wall still visible) yet
easily available to East Berlin women who could participate.

Long before the World Council was constituted in
Amsterdam in 1948 the preparatory commissions (Faith
and Order, and Life and Work) were confronted at every
session by women insisting they were an integral part of
the World Body. As Betty Thompson, formerly of the
World Council staff, so perceptively observed, the "persistent pressure over the years originated out of the reality of
local churches on every continent. It is no longer a 'for
women only' issue."[2]

As early as 1927 (twenty years before the council proper was formed) the first meeting of the Faith and Order Commission at Lausanne included only seven women among hundreds of men, but they made their voices heard: "...The right place of women in the church is a question of grave moment and should be in the hearts and minds of all." Philip Potter, a Jamaican and recent executive secretary of the World Council of Churches, referred to this as "polite language of the time."[3] When the commissions met at Oxford and Edinburgh in 1937, of the 425 attending the Life and Work Commission at Oxford only 23 women were delegates and none were on the program. When the World Council was officially constituted in Amsterdam in 1948 the entire assembly declared "that the church as the Body of Christ consists of men and women created as responsible persons to glorify God and to do his will." But the statement went on to add, "This truth, accepted in theory, is too often ignored in practice." "For years the World Council went no further."[4] Potter paid tribute to the women who "through years of heartbreaking work kept the council confronted with the rightful place of women in the church." While he mentioned Kathleen Bliss, a brilliant Anglican woman, and Madeline Barot of France, who were involved from the beginning, others rightfully expand the roster: Susanne de Deitrich and Francine Dumas of France, Rena Karefa-Smart of Sierra Leone, Brigalia Bam of South Africa, Justice Jiagge of Ghana, Sarah Chakko of India, Dr. Kiyoko Takeda Cho of Japan, the Reverend Janet Crawford of New Zealand, Pauline Webb of England, and the Reverend Connie Parvey of the United States.

But somehow the "polite demands" and theological affirmation of unity were not enough to bring about action. Not until a working section on Structures of Injustice and Struggles for Liberation was officially set up did there appear to be any overt movement toward an analysis of the injustice of sexism. The working section combined with continuous pressure from women and bold radical questions on issues of power, domination, oppression, and racism raised by students, finally led to the 1974 conference in Berlin.[5]

It was not surprising that the combined pressures building up over the years exploded into anger, frustration, and confusion in the Berlin consultation. The political language of the countries varied greatly and demanded hard listening, patience, and questioning before the conference was able to zero in on the most volatile and intimate aspects of the lives of women—sexism and religion, and the interconnectedness of the two: (1) the racial and political implications of sexism; and (2) the degree to which revered and ancient symbols of faith were inadequate to deal with modern technology and a scientific society. It became obvious, then, to the leaders of the conference and the delegates (often months after returning home) that the sexist issue could no longer be glossed over.

Potter himself expressed deep appreciation for what Berlin opened up, and for the new study materials made urgent by the Berlin consultation and commissioned by the Fifth International Assembly of the World Council at Nairobi, Kenya. Together they led to the Sheffield Conference of 1981. These experiences, he admitted, had opened his eyes to the issues involved in sexism and to the fact that the World Church delay no longer its work in areas of authority of Scripture, a new conception of ministry, a new understanding of tradition, and new understanding of sexuality and what it means to be human.[6]

Connie Parvey, responsible for the Sheffield preconference study material, added that her own deep interest began when she attended the 1974 Berlin Conference on sexism. "Many of us," she said, "had been at world gatherings before but had never been at a meeting of all women who were our peers—women from many continents, churches, professions—women in education, law, medicine, theology, politics, the social sciences, etc. For many, the Berlin experience was a turning point."[7]

structure, are opening the way for us to question some of the hierarchical structures of the church that perpetuate sexism in its life and in the life of society and the world. Perhaps the World Council already senses that a sexist structure of reality is a theological issue, that any theology developed by one sex, out of the experience of one sex, and taught predominantly by one sex, cannot possibly be lived out as if it were whole theology. For whole theology is possible only when the whole people become a part of its process, and that includes women. And in time, wholeness may be approximated when men can begin to hear women, and to listen to women, and when men and women together can participate fully and equally and joyfully in bringing faith to expression.

I appreciate particularly the fact that I have been asked to speak on "Toward a Whole Theology." *Toward* immediately gives us the right, and presents us with the urgency of entering the process with our own experiences and with our own stories. It saves us from pretensions of easy rationalization and linear logic and opens us to responsible participation on our terms in a community whose chief claim to uniqueness lies in its transcending dimension and its inclusive offer of freedom. *Toward* suggests that we are on the way, on a journey—growing, groping, reaching. Creating the path by the journeying, moving in the assurance that the journey is of infinite worth. Certain that something of great value is sought as the woman, renovating her whole household, searched for the lost coin. *Toward* affirms God as verb—out ahead—known in liberating, moving, changing, healing, breaking down, and building up.

Whole in the topic goes far beyond *toward*. *Whole* reminds us not to repeat another's speech, given to us to speak as if it were our speech, leaving our speech unspoken, and leaving the church poorer without us. But *whole* means something else again—a oneness of body and mind, a oneness with one another in our helplessness, in our powerlessness, and in our great pain. Help me say it. Many of you know the language better than I know it for you are from cultures close to the inside of nature. Some of you know how to be at home in your bodies. You have a theology of the birthing process—of Creation itself. Some of you must teach the rest of us how to plant our feet in the earth and feel the surge of energy from a great source that comes up from down under. *Whole* means putting back together history and nature, split apart by a patriarchy that assigned history to men as prized, and nature to women as denigrated.

Whole means reclaiming the body as good. Male theologians have said that, also. But when, as is their tendency, they have said it out of orderly reason rather than out of the viscera, it allows sex to be relegated to the genitals, and that has given rise to the male priesthood since, they claim, ministry is a generative, seminal office.[11] The liturgy affirms that the Creator embraces and transcends both sexes and blesses physical union. On the other hand, it hastens to provide opportunity for women to confess to male priests and male ministers the inevitable guilt engendered by its own contradictions. *Whole* theology would anticipate the elimination of the split so that guilt would no longer be inevitable.

Wholeness would exorcise a sexist mind-set so that freedom could become a viable option for all living people. *Whole* concerns itself with the whole of life where it is being lived out, not maintaining a dichotomy by application of some ultimate doctrine to issues such as population, birth control, abortion, ecology, energy, conservation. It would confront these issues head-on and with institutional sins such as war, racism, poverty, and the kind of national and international structures that perpetuate them. *Whole* envisions the time when there can be honesty and mutuality in human relationships—no more of the games now supported by religious and social rituals. *Whole* means survival within systems until footholds for a new space and new time are gained enough to deal with the system itself.

Whole theology cannot come through the Western world alone, nor the Eastern, nor from any control group speaking out of their experience as if it were the experience of all people. *Whole theology*—as full human experience—is possible only when all the oppressed peoples of the world can speak freely out of their own experiences, be heard and touch one another to heal and be healed.

Out of Our Common Experiences
We Can Begin to Anticipate Wholeness

If talking about human experience is a way of talking about God, and talking about God a way of talking about our life together, we have already begun to do theology in this consultation. Even the multimedia presentation, presented earlier on this stage at this consultation, announced as coming from outside the church, raised a profound theological question and reflected the images and questions that come to us out of our cultures, namely: Who is the creator of your existence? To whom do you listen for your identity and for the shaping of your destiny? When we deal with economic and political issues, and examine the systems critically, we are also raising the theological question: Are we allowing the kind of economic systems we have to shape our human destinies, or are we moving in to reshape these systems?

Let us now identify some common experiences that may have surfaced here or that we have shared previously, unknown to one another. The power experienced when women come together, as *women*, is termed by theologian Mary Daly[12] as "power of presence." What a miracle that we have come from distant places into one another's lives here, in this place—now, in this decade! We bring into our own and others' consciousness our stories, our traditions, the point at which our struggle to become human is most acute. We offer ourselves as God's grace one to the other. The power of presence opens a new aspect of future for us all.

We do not gather as an auxiliary of any institution, the WCC, or even our own churches. We come in our own right, as women, to claim our share of an inheritance promised long ago. And this pentecostal power of presence calls into question any system, whether in church or in society, that tends to control and manipulate that inheritance and our human destinies rather than to liberate them.

We Share a Common Work Experience

We know the making of bread and the serving of it. We know the weight of a baby before it is born and afterward and again when it is fed to a war or economic machine. We have been to the fields together. We know the clicking of a typewriter, the nurturing of the young, the attending of the ill. We have talked over back fences, at market, on assembly lines, in office and school, in the cooking place and cleaning place, and on the street—but our talk, often under our breath, was never recorded. We come into one another's presence out of work into which we have been locked—or locked out, even taken for granted, nothing paid or paid a pittance. We know not the hour our work begins or the time of its ending but its rhythms have brought us into a kinship that a common language could not create.

We Have a Common Nonhistory

The world's understanding of itself and its development, if we take historians at face value, has not included women. Nor have church historians included us. A history that is not objective and does not embrace all its people must be seen as a partial history. Our partial history has provided us with male models only. Without historical memory one has no future and a limited present. But all over, we are beginning to get in touch with our stories and to create our history. As mushrooms, they spring from whisperings of centuries. They form a new kind of history—not of great men, or great events, or even great women but a history of the most common masses of people—our aspirations, our pain, our hopes, our frustrations, our revolutions, our deaths, and hopefully our resurrections.

*By Virtue of Our Being
Women We Share a Common Pain*

I speak not of the physical pain of childbirth, though that is a tie that transcends our differences in speech. I speak of the pain of forever being "the other"—of not being considered worthy or capable of participating in the mainstream of political and community life; of not being allowed to share in policy making; of being so culturally imprisoned into stereotyped roles and images as to prevent genuine human involvement. Once a woman achieves some sense of her own power for social change, the tendency is to maintain her as "the other," the token, while deftly channeling her efforts into the system. The pain of being isolated as "the other" approximates the scapegoat or the witch burnings or gas chambers. Perhaps the greatest pain women bear from the church is the verbal offer of liberation while being pushed to the periphery of the church's life and ministry. This brand of sexism is enemy to both men and women. It has robbed the church of its vitality. It has rendered the male-control-group deaf to what is basically amiss in society. Sexism is one message of the church the world has not failed to hear.

*We Share a Common Tradition That Claims
Liberation as Its Chief Business*

What in our Judeo-Christian tradition have you experienced as liberating? What has enabled women to hear a liberating gospel? Wherein lies hope that freedom is possible—possible for you? For all? In spite of male control of church and its seminaries, has God, unintimidated by sexism, reached through to us? Have we heard what the church has not really said? What the church cannot afford to say? Has our becoming aware of ourselves as women derived out of the church or in spite of the church?

The next World Council of Churches meeting will be in Nairobi. Its theme: "Jesus Christ Frees and Unites." Many of

you will be attending. What does that theme mean to women?
Is it a kind of shibboleth that we repeat? What meaning are
you going to give it, out of this consultation? What questions
do you have about it in relation to women? What recommendations can speak to its meaning in terms of women?

What has led women of every nation, race, class, culture
to begin to sense our being bound together into a sexual caste,
within which we have been conditioned to protectiveness and
dependency? We have been confined primarily to menial
labor. Contrary to the gospel message, the totality of our being
has been defined by our anatomy. We gather from separate
nations in which we are struggling for survival. We are of
separate classes, the structures of which we have not yet
transcended. We are of separate races. I ask myself: Does my
prior identity lie in my being white or my being woman? Both
are accidents of my birth. I am more aware of being woman
because of the discriminations I have suffered as a woman.
Am I too close to racism to feel the cut of its thrust? My sister
has been made to suffer because she is black...maybe in
some places even more than because she is woman. I do not
want, nor will I allow myself to be pitted against her. Yet I
ponder: How can I, I as a woman, how can we afford to
hesitate, to lack courage, to lack commitment, to fail to move
radically into a future opening to women for the first time in
history? How does my tradition support me? I do not know the
next step which I must, and will, take—and I hope take boldly.
Because of an opening future into which I know I shall enter, I
am impelled to probe my past—my tradition—for many of the
answers to my questions and for many questions my tradition
asks my present and my future. I know that the degree to
which I can come to terms with my past determines my
openness to my future and the distance into my future I am
able to move.

I believe that the patriarchal conditioning of my tradition
is not the last word. I believe that seeds of liberation are
hidden in our common tradition. I believe that many gems not
perceived by the patriarchal mind-set of writers, translators,
and teachers of religion are embedded in the Biblical docu-

ment and await the insights of women to discover and bring to expression. Calling presuppositions into question and forming the questions precede seeking the answers.

What name for God is free from sexist imagery? Elohim, an early name for a supreme deity in the Biblical document, signals the emergence of Hebrew monotheism. Literally translated, it refers to the whole council of heaven—goddesses and gods. It resists, therefore, reduction to one gender.[13] What community transcends sexism? The New Testament envisions a community in which there is neither Jew nor Greek, neither slave nor free, and no male and female (note the change in the form of modifiers for the last phrase: neither/nor changed to no). No one in the new community will be identified by her/his sex.[14]

I am still seeking Elohim and the fulfillment of that Galatian promise, that Spirit which heard me to speech, spoke me to being, and which brought me to this point in history and to this place in my world.

Women Are Already Celebrating That Power Which We Are Experiencing But Cannot Yet Name

There is yet no language that embraces the full human experience. There is no God-language free from sexist imagery. Elohim, as suggested above, conceptually transcended sexism but in its interchangeable use with masculine names for God has been filled with masculine imagery. Yahweh, derived from the name of a Sumerian goddess, is another.[15] Lord, King of the Universe, Mighty One, Everlasting Father, Prince of Peace, Man for Others, Son—with accompanying masculine pronouns and attributes—project images of domination and sex partiality. To include the feminine opposites for the purpose of equality and balance falls short of the dream of women. Feminine names and pronouns for God, as masculine, draw from stereotyped cultural images. Two crippled parts make only a crippled whole.

The dilemma is not only that of women. The entire religious community is at an impasse since no new symbols have emerged to carry the agony, the mystery, and the ecstasy of what has been happening.[16] Old symbols and imagery root too deeply in a patriarchal culture to function adequately in the new context.

What are women to do? What are they doing? Many continue with the old language while raising the fundamental questions at every opportunity. Others have formed exodus communities or rely on intermittent "exodus services" during these wilderness days. Still others have opted out entirely for the time being—even wondering whether we have moved beyond the symbol system (viewed as a patriarchal construct).[17]

But celebrative ingredients are inherent in our experiences; that creative event that brought us to life, the greatness of our freedom, the new support community, and even the pain that has made us aware of our oppression. We ask forgiveness of one another and all the oppressed of the world for our poverty of language to embrace the full human experience and our slowness to throw off our oppression. We give praise for what is not yet, but which *really is*—for that promise of liberation for all people of the world which does not let us go. Since the context for experiencing the power of presence is promise of a new heaven and a new earth, we begin to live it out and in the living it becomes an actuality.

When We Look for Our Cardinal Sin—The Roots of Our Oppression— We Are Confronted with Patriarchy as a System of Organizing Society

We cannot move further toward the promised liberation until we deal with the source of the obstacle to its fulfillment. How can we know freedom as long as the tentacles of sexism are sunk into our psyches? As long as the traditions of which we are a part are not able to allow the hierarchical structures to topple? I propose this section as part of a grand yes, but a yes that begins with an unmistakable no. The no is not to the whole of our tradition and the whole order of things. It is to those images, symbols, and structures that blind us to the yes. We are saying no to a system that legitimates these images and symbols through cosmic myths and daily ceremonial rituals that shore up the system.

A brief look at the ancient patriarchal culture in which our tradition is cradled can provide distance and perspective for understanding and dealing with the subtle and demonic way sexism has pervaded the cultures of the world, our relationships, our political life, and our minds.

With the advent of patriarchy, culture departed from its harmony with creation and its oneness with the transcendent Creator,[18] which is another way of referring to the split between history and nature, the body and mind, reason and emotion. Patriarchy emerged with the male's knowledge of paternity, out of an earlier matriarchal or matrilinear culture.[19] It took the form of male ego-ascendency (dominance and control) and a race to beat death (immortality). In neither of these was the agenda to keep women in an inferior position. But in both of them, reducing woman to a secondary place became inevitable and in time overt. In other words, women were not the primary enemy. The primary enemy was anything that kept men from control of the earth and from gaining immortality. If a man could control his woman, assuring himself her child was his, and if he could pass property on to his son, he would live forever.

Patriarchy has been described as a way of structuring reality in terms of good/evil, redemption/guilt, authority/obedience, reward/punishment, power/powerless, haves/have-nots, master/slave. The first in each opposite was assigned to the patriarchal father, or the patriarch's Father God, frequently indistinguishable from one another, the second to women as "the other" and in time to all "others" who could be exploited. The father did the naming, the owning, the controlling, the ordering, the forgiving, the giving, considering himself capable of making the best decisions for all.

Patriarchy polarized human beings by gender and endowed each gender with certain roles and properties so that neither could experience full humanness.

Patriarchy structured society by sexual stratifications, hierarchically ordering human beings according to assigned value (man, woman, child).

Patriarchy evoked cosmic myths to support the structures. With gender-stereotyped images it created a master/servant mentality which in time spawned racisms, sexisms, nationalisms, colonialisms, classes, and castes.

Patriarchy maintained the structure by retaining the power or sharing it with a favored few, leaving the majority powerless—that is, women, children, and outcasts, who are actually "the woman." Patriarchy could not exist without a powerless majority.

Patriarchy bestowed the identity on those controlled and offered no future except that given by the father (Father).

Patriarchy assumed the right of ordering by divine right and, by the same, demanded obedient response.

Patriarchy was maintained by outer, and not inner, authority. Inner authority became a threat to the patriarchal system.

Patriarchy created the way of remembering history and recording it through the "fathers" and not through the people: Father Abraham, Father Isaac, Father Jacob.[20]

Patriarchy did not originate with the Judeo-Christian tradition. It was the prevailing culture long before the Hebrews settled in Canaan.[21] But it provided the Biblical writers with the only language in which to record their salvation history. Let the Bible itself speak of the function of language in its story of Moses and the burning bush. Note Moses' extended argument with the voice from the bush as he demanded its name. "...they will ask me. What is his name? What shall I say?" The voice answered, "I AM WHO I AM.... Say this to the people of Israel, I AM has sent me to you." Moses was hearing that the voice was above naming but if a name was necessary it must come from the language of the people. And indeed it did, no less than six names.[22] The word *God* in this story, like *Elohim* and *Yahweh*, attributes no gender to God. The gender lies in the limiting language and the male images out of the prevailing culture that projected an ontological masculinity on the deity. Perhaps the burning bush, the pillar of cloud and fire, the Spirit out of the wilderness, the Wisdom who "was before anything that was made,"[23] the descending dove and the pentecostal tongues of fire reach for the androgynous symbolization of the presence and activity of God in human community. All correspond to some radical social change,[24] as "The spirit is upon me...good news to poor...release of captives...sight to blind...liberty to oppressed."[25] Logos and its self-extension in technology may be seen as an effort to manipulate the Spirit, Wisdom *(Sophia)*, domesticate it, and bring it under control. Today patriarchy is a passé word marking an ancient culture. Not so easily recognized, however, is the way it functions as a system in sexism. As a system it functions politically and socially by pointing to and sacralizing personal, family, and community values while its subtle chief end continues as a form of ruling, and a habit of controlling. Sexism, as the sophisticated modern form of patriarchy expressing itself in different styles and forms in various countries of the world, continues to achieve the same old patriarchal ends. The visibility of patriarchy in our history helps us to understand the invisible nature and depth of sexism in our lives.

Sexism, Then, No Less Than Patriarchy, Is a System and Not Simply Some Unwritten Innocuous Rules of Etiquette to Guide Us in Behavior One Toward the Other

Its most subtle expressions are those in which we inadvertently engage daily. Language, ceremonial rituals, and discriminating acts work together to keep their larger political and national spin-offs intact. Examine the commonly-perceived-as-innocent gesture of a man holding the door open for a woman. It could be analyzed as a male/female approach to a major social obstruction with the shape of political participation of each.[26] The "weaker one" in obedience to the unwritten drama waits while the "protector" attacks the barrier, overcomes it, steps aside for the "weak one" to pass safely through. Myths such as dragon-slaying support the ritual. Politically the male rulers, those "capable of deciding on the welfare of a nation," and those who have in one way or another accumulated power to control, manfully shoulder the voting responsibilities for an entire people, as is still the case at the time of this conference in six major countries where women do not yet have the vote.[27] They make decisions for the country on behalf of the "weaker sex" but always out of a male definition of what is good for the "weaker." The majority is kept inept, ignorant, and away from responsible participation.

Rituals practiced in many countries function similarly: a woman walking behind her husband, a woman covering her face in public; or from another angle, a woman not eating at the table with her husband, or serving him, while he takes the service and deference for granted. The full implication of sexism can be understood only when seen as patriarchy in modern form. Sexism, too, is a system ordered by gender in which one sex has come to be considered superior to another sex on the basis of creation (anatomy). The cosmic dimension locates discrimination as an act of the Creator, leaving no hope for those discriminated against. Thus sexism becomes a major theological issue. Yet religious forces blessing the sexist culture are rendered unable to see it as such. Women, children, illegitimates, homosexuals, prostitutes, the poor, ethnic or racial groups who could help the control group see are kept outside the mainstream of the church's life and work. We can argue endlessly that the gospel itself is not sexist. We can argue on a conceptual level without touching the sexist imagery projected in its common language, liturgy, practice, and structures that shape and set life-styles long before the age of conceptualization.

The sexist ethic works itself out socially and politically when the haves take on authoritarian power, paternalistic properties, relegating to women and the weaker, less powerful, controlled groups the properties of women. In any sexist culture those at the top keep their position inviolate as long as a certain percentage remain pacified and programmed to accept few national benefits. In spite of elaborate welfare aids of some institutions (in which women are more often than not used in a volunteer capacity) a certain percentage remain poor—for only then can the system survive. Finally, when the poor lose hope, or achieve no conscious awareness that they might better themselves, or organize, they remain isolated and powerless. Women unaware of the extent of their own exploitation become subtle instruments used to keep other oppressed groups in the position of "the other."

Racism modeled also from patriarchy assumes a hidden dimension of sexism. Starting with explorers from Europe and the West, colonized nonwhite people were treated as "the other." The pattern followed in the subjugation of women was transferred to race as racial groups were by force of persuasion kept in their place, dependent and comparatively docile. The sexist ethic operated under the disguise of color. As far back as 1944 Lillian Smith[28] insisted that racism and sexism were interrelated that neither could be dealt with radically when isolated from the other. White men considered blacks to possess greater sexual virility than themselves. They reacted by raping black women. When some white women related to black men, white men responded savagely by protecting "their women" and corporally punishing the black men. It became common practice in courts to let all white men go scot-free and imprison, lynch, or sentence to death the black men for the same act the whites performed as their right of ownership, so that both "their women" and "their blacks (male and female)" became objects of sexual exploitation. The whites assumed the masculine properties of a great white God, seeking to own, control, and subjugate the nonwhites. The black male had the same kind of myopia as white males, unable to see or understand their own victimization by sex.

With the spread of technology, sexism supplied the model for relations of nations and even multinational networks. The sexist ethic showed up in multinational corporations, in which capital was exported to countries where cheap labor was available. The people of developing countries, not protected by laws, received limited benefits from their labors. Not having developed the power or skills for sophisticated bargaining with the corporations, they tended to become helpless in holding corporations to responsible action. Some countries struggling for autonomy discovered a corporation paying taxes to the colonizer rather than to their country. Without proper controls the multinational corporations stand to become the most powerful instruments in the world—dominating the resources of the earth, controlling people, operating as world courts, and setting international policies.[29]

Sexism functions through them in two ways. One, as a model for increasing power and expansion in order to maximize its own profits, regardless of the human factor. The other is the use of women by conning them into a role that is necessary and exceedingly important for the economic interest.

> Were the economist's preoccupation with the individual pursued, in fact to the individual, there would again be grave danger that the role of women would attract interest...women are kept on political leash primarily by their commitment to the family...their service in making possible the indefinite expansion...is justified and even sanctified as a service to the family. The service is then submerged in the concept of the household—and is thus kept out of view ...what is now seen as a moral compulsion is, in fact, a service to economic interest.[30]

The total development of all people can hardly come

about until sexism, recognized as a system, is exorcised at its roots—in the system itself. The church, especially in the West, has found itself in a double bind by being partially supported by the profits of multinational corporations and in turn supporting them. As long as the sources of profits are kept invisible from women, and women kept invisible in pulpit and decision-making leadership, the sexist system will go unchallenged.

Sexism, ideologically and theologically, keeps postponing freedom in the hope of finding a great deliverer, rather than hoping in, by, and through a consciously aware community of people.

Liberation movements of the poor, the Third World, and peace shore up the worldwide sexist system so long as their teaching materials and methods evoke the unexamined symbols of patriarchal religion, which in the end support political systems that keep us all in bondage.

*Women Doing Theology Becomes Top Agenda for
Such a Consultation as This!*

I should like to summarize what may be considered the beginning of a theological process for women. All over the world women, rather than reaching up, have begun to reach down, to reach back and to reach ahead. We have begun to articulate our stories, to own our pain and to confront the stereotyped images out of which we have been conditioned to live out our lives. It has required full knowledge of the subtlety and power of sexism. It has involved breaking the images from within by shock, exorcism, and radical repentance—for the change of an image is an infinitely more difficult matter than the correction of a concept.[31]

Reaching back into our tradition, we can begin to appropriate what is already ours—*so great a ministry.* How timidly women have said, "I am minister!" How apologetically, "I am theologian!" Yet by virtue of baptism, every one of us is minis-

ter. And by virtue of being minister, compelled into the theological task. We may not be technical, systematic, or academic theologians. But we are in ministry and in the theological
process and have much to do and to say. It may prove dangerous,
for it will open ministry to the entire laity. And should that
happen, something, somewhere will have to give.

We are saying no to all that is alien to ourselves and our
ministry. We no longer can tolerate confessing sins we feel we
have not committed—sins defined by male experience out of
the control group. We can now begin to confess those sins we
feel we have committed. The suppression of our own anger,
not recognizing it as a way of fighting through to a place where
love can express itself; the lack of confidence and boldness,
the lack of pride, the unquestioned obedience, and the false-
ness of our humility.

We can celebrate that which is most really real, that
which transcends sexism and exclusivity, that which breaks
in through our celebration and comes known to us in the
liberating process at work in "the wretched of the earth."

We begin to experience theologizing as a process—
organic, communal, and holistic. Organic because it comes up
out of the deepest abyss of our being—at the point of our
deepest cleavage from the male. Organic, also, because body,
mind, spirit come up as one. We have not come into this
astounding new thing through our minds alone. We have
lived it into our own existence. Compelled by our pain, our
being trapped, our extremity, we did only what we could do. We
were drawn into one another's presence. We began hearing one
another to speech. We experienced God, as Spirit, hearing
human beings to speech—to new creation. The Word came as
human word, the human expression to humanness. The creative act of the Spirit was not Word speaking, but hearing—
hearing the created one to speech. The communal process
maintained openness to the power of the Spirit experienced as
community rather than dependent on the star, the expert, the
individualistic competitiveness inherent in a hierarchical
structure.

Holism gathers up the totality of living experiences—eating, talking, dancing, waking, discovering, discussing, studying, worshipping into a new environmental space and a new kind of time. It may be seen as a unified focus of all the faculties of one's being, each feeding on the others and many of them surfacing simultaneously. Holistic recovers gesture and movement as essential to theologizing. Learning to listen with one's whole body. Learning to hear with the eye and see with the ear and speak with the hearing. Knowing the Spirit in movement and not in stasis.

Such a process makes us aware of the way some of our bodily and work-role functions were usurped for the rituals of the church over which women were forbidden to officiate as celebrants. New birth, symbolized by the uterine waters of baptism, was separated from physical birth. The Eucharist took the serving role in which women are cast all the time and adapted it as a seminal experience that only men could perform. The healing, caring, and nurturing functions of women were caught up in the Word preached by the male. Claiming our visibility and ministry equips us for re-entry into the theological process, as does the rediscovery of the power of the Spirit who, like women, has been relegated to the boundary of the church's doctrine and made a stranger to the core of the church's life. The pentecostal tongues of fire may symbolize our coming to new speech and the boldness with which we now make ourselves known.

At This Point One Can Only Fantasize or
Speculate on the Shape of a Whole Theology!

But of one thing we may be sure. It cannot come out of one group or one sex speaking for the whole. Women cannot speak for the whole any more than men have been able to speak for the whole. A whole theology would envision all of the people speaking out of their own experiences into the process and toward full humanness.

We are safe to begin with mutuality in which both men and women can come into the process hearing and speaking openly with one another. Perhaps by the time women begin to be truly liberated, men can begin to hear women speak their speech and define their own needs. But the process itself anticipates the crumbling of the patriarchal system now experienced as sexism. Mutuality invites a totally new way that cannot now be described but can only be anticipated; it will not be a way known or dominated only by men, or known and dominated only by women. Long ago the Judeo-Christian tradition envisioned a new history, inclusive of all people, and at home with the natural universe; peace to replace warring, justice and love to govern human relationships, and a new heaven and a new earth to replace the present competitive, exploitative one. Those historical moments when the vision came nearest to actuality were times when the feminine surfaced in Wisdom, Spirit, Movement, Tongues of Fire, Dove, and approximated a balance—a mutuality. Messianic passages of the Biblical document described a coming one who would flesh out or fill out in wholeness that which the patriarchal community had rejected. They affirmed a future that would bring a new beginning of history when God's image (male and female) in humanity would be actual and apparent.

Simultaneous with mutuality would be accent on a new humanizing process in the community, with the release of a new Spirit movement transcending sex, in which social structures would support the process. Doubtless there would be less Word of God and more speech of people. God, as Spirit, would move in the human and world community, hearing people to their fullest expression. And people would be able to recover their healing relatedness one with the other.

But this vision is not new. It is part of our faith tradition. What is new—might be new—is the possibility of its being taken with all seriousness, to be lived out of as if it were the reality which it is. It would issue in a new kind of power—a shared, responsible power, beginning in the community of faith where no distance would ever be allowed again between power and the people. Power primarily concentrated in one person, be that person clergy, king, or pope, robs the many of growth. Any dominance of authority creates obedient subjects shorn of initiative and responsibility.

Were the human community taken with dead seriousness in our theologizing, there would be no more temple—for God would be in the midst of the people.[32] The personal could be recognized for the political it is and the political the personal. A new heaven and a new earth would indeed appear...for the old patriarchal heaven and earth are already disappearing.

1975:

A Word We Cannot Yet Speak

I developed this essay[1] when Jaunita Weaver was collecting essays under the title *Companions of the Way.* Her essays intended to describe various adventures of women in search of a distinctly feminine dimension of spirituality. My essay turned out to be entirely too long and ended in a different vein than I had intended. There was something I felt I had to clear out of my way before I could begin what Jaunita had asked of me.

At the time I was a part of a small nurturing, healing, deeply supportive group of women; we created our own rituals out of our common life together—but when anyone referred to us as spiritual the word seemed to jar. Finally came the question: Are women taking an ancient word—spiritual/spirit out of a patriarchal culture and mentality—a word already filled with patriarchal concepts and images that "came down from above" and trying to make our new transcending, up-from-down-under experiences and emotions fit into the ancient outdated symbol? There was no doubt among these women about avoiding the use of the word *religion.* Religion at that time connoted an "institutional" reality of which women increasingly have become suspicious.

As the essay reveals, I explored the history and origin of the word *spiritual/spirit* and found that it predates patriarchy. But the question persists: Has it been so domesticated and controlled there is no hope for recovery? We live in a new age with new scientific/religious knowledge. Is there a brave new word waiting to embrace the nurturing experiences women are now having that cannot be fully described because of a patriarchal language structure?

Sally Gearhart once gave me the phrase "a word we cannot yet speak." While we were not at the time thinking in terms of spirit or spiritual, we agreed that women are having emotions, visions, experiences that no words in the patriarchal language can describe. I want to posit the possibility that there is a word, that there are many words, awaiting woman speech. And perhaps there is a word that has not yet come to sound—a word that once we begin to speak will round out and create deeper experiences for us and put us in touch with sources of power, energy of which we are just beginning to be aware.

★

A NEW PHENOMENON is making its appearance in the woman world. We name it, at least for the present, "spirituality," or refer to it as a new dimension of the spirit. It is not yet clear whether the name is a deliberate choice or whether it happens to be the only one available; whether it evokes the effort to redeem the history of a once-proud prepatriarchal experience or whether it is temporary—awaiting the emergence of a new transcending organic word we cannot yet speak. On the surface it appears to be taken over without change from the patriarchal vocabulary in which spirit has been domesticated and brought under control of a hierarchical way of thinking. It is the purpose of this essay to explore briefly some of these possibilities so that women involved in the spiritual quest will be more aware of the ways our language affects the quest itself and ourselves. Language, in this context, includes images, symbols, gestures, even structures, as well as bare words and constellations of words.

Once the rise of spiritual interest is sensed as a possible rebellion against patriarchy (even when patriarchal politicians resort to use of spiritual symbols for political purposes) and as a search for alternative life sources, it is not surprising that we in the woman movement and feminists in general should attempt to create new forms of spirituality out of our own experiences, especially since the ongoing interpretation of spirit derives from male experience. What is surprising is the uncritical use of the patriarchal term to canopy the range of women exploring and creating the new reality. I contend that something totally new is struggling to be born at this point in history and will require new word symbolization and new imagery to bring it to fullest expression.

Some thirty-five years ago Susanne Langer[2] drew no little attention to what she termed the "formative" or "generative power" in word symbolization. That means that words have a power potential far greater than as a means of communication or a means to record past events. Brave new words and old words used in fresh ways actually create new realities. More frequently, even when they are not fully articulated, they expose old forms as no longer able to express what may be obviously struggling to come to new expression—to be born. And could be born except for the old restrictive forms that speakers cannot or will not let go.

Both Albert Einstein and Niels Bohr[3] working separately on their respective theories claimed that the old language symbolization of physics had become irrelevant for their work. They turned to creating new forms of language rather than attempting to introduce new physical content into previous symbols. Einstein explained:

> Thus room was made for thinking...that allowed a new kind of description of space and time as mutually related and dependent on general physical conditions, such as velocity, acceleration, gravitational fields, etc.

> In like manner Bohr perceived "... the uselessness of the efforts to change only the content of ... classical laws."

In this essay I might well question whether women's use of the patriarchal term *spiritual* is adequate to shape what we are coming to know or whether we can redeem an earlier prepatriarchal history inclusive of women and the oppressed of the earth. Either effort may, at the moment, be unintentional but no less real. One or the other, however, appears inevitable.

Spirit Is an Old, Old Word

The earliest meaning of spirit that we can trace derives from the word *breath*—*breath* of the body ("closer than breathing"), *breath* of life, then later *wind* of the cosmos. The root form in Hebrew is *ruach*, of feminine gender. However *spirit* appears to be far older than the Hebrew language. Breath (spirit) was seen as provided by the mother at birth. Broadened to cosmic dimension the image became that of the early Goddess—the source and nurturer of all living. Out of her very dust came the first creature and in the stirring dust breathed the living energy (spirit) of life. In this creation the body is not separated from spirit, nor spirit separated from woman, nor history separated from nature. Of the same movement derives *transcending*—rising up out of what already is. The ancient and proud history of spirit may be seen as a clear thread—a deep subliminal stratum of the feminine—running through patriarchal literature, suppressed and distorted but never entirely snuffed out.

I am not alone in holding the view that the patriarchal literature that has most affected Western thinking, culture, and political systems may be found in the Judeo-Christian tradition. In this tradition it is not too difficult to trace the suppression of women and the domestication of the spirit as one and the same movement. The Hebrew-Christian Bible, as well as many of the myths out of Greek and Roman history, may serve as paradigms of the way patriarchy reforged the terms of civilization to give women a subordinate status.[4]

Literary historian Katharine Rogers[5] considers the myth of
Adam and Eve to be the result of such a questionable misogyn-
ism, "...for it shows that woman was created almost reluc-
tantly, when no creature could satisfy man's needs."

Joseph Campbell points out in his *Masks of God: Occidental Mythology* that

> ...[in Genesis 3, the fall] Yahweh cursed the woman
> to bring forth in pain and be subject to her spouse—
> which set the seal of the patriarchy on the new
> age.... No one familiar with the mythologies of the
> goddess of the primitive, ancient, and Oriental worlds
> can turn to the Bible without recognizing counter-
> parts on every page, transformed, however, to render
> an argument contrary to the older faiths.[6]

In the same manner that these earlier images were
reforged in patriarchal terms, spirit was wrenched from its
organic origins, separated from the body—the mother
(woman) and the goddess—the mother Earth or Earth Goddess. The new manifestation of spirit, projected in hierarchical terms, emanated from the father in whom the "spirit of life"
as sperm was ejected as minuscule baby into the womb
(viewed as nutrient value only). The father as reflected in
early patriarchal mythology and later patriarchal science was
believed the sole parent. The cosmic dimension of the same
movement ripped spirit from its earth people origin and
placed it above the people, in the sky as originating in an
all-powerful Father—or male God. In patriarchal religious
ritual spirit came to be owned and controlled as property in
the one and same manner as women were owned. Patriarchs
usurped the exclusive right to define, interpret, and evoke the
spirit out of their experience and project it onto women and
children, as they deemed that women and children "should"
experience it. The moving verb *transcending* (synonymous
with breath and spirit) changed to a static noun, *transcen-*

dence, separated from the body and woman. The hierarchical direction assumed ultimacy—"down from up above" instead of the former direction of "up from down under." In hierarchical terms the dove (spirit) descends (transcendence). But in the organic, the dove rises—transcending—thus maintaining the powerful metaphoric movement as not separated from people themselves. Dove (spirit) descending suggests power over; dove (spirit) ascending—as the phoenix—suggests life out of the heart of a struggling people. The subliminal stratum of the spirit and the feminine may be identified throughout the Bible in spite of its patriarchal language.

Note how the imagery of an early Earth goddess ("out of her dust was made the first creature") comes through subliminally for the writer of the Adam and Eve story by having man, in the absence of a womb, reproduce out of his rib, then name his offspring "the mother of all living (the mother of all who breathe)." Yet, he made of himself and his god exceptions. The man already having been created "out of the dust of the earth" reflects clearly the early goddess imagery and the organic nature of spirit. In this sense the image becomes awkward and out of place (jars) when cast in patriarchal thought structures. The inversion continues in the male attempt to usurp the functions of the woman in himself and his male god, with whom he and not woman can identify.

The ground was thus laid for the separation of spirit from the organic, which is reflected to this day in the dualistic split of mind from body, reason from emotion, nature from history and the personal from the political and social. In partial contrast the hierarchical separation of spirit from body is evident in Genesis 1:1-2 which renders the earliest image of the creative process of all living as *spirit.* Note how the second verse reads:

> The earth was without form and void, with darkness over the face of the abyss, and a mighty wind that swept over the surface of the waters. (The New English Bible)

> The earth was without form and void, and darkness
> was upon the face of the deep; and the Spirit of God
> was moving over the face of the waters. (The Revised
> Standard Version)

Both wind (in NEB) and Spirit (RSV) derive from the same root word—breath, attributing the dawn of the creative process to spirit. Not the uttered word but the rhythms and patterns out of the universe itself, image-wise, become the source of creation. T. S. Eliot once described the birth of the spirit as that continuous interflowing of thought and feeling, of the perceiving self and the perceived world experienced by some people as reality.

> I know that a poem or a section of a poem tends to
> appear first in the shape of a rhythm before develop-
> ing into words and that this rhythm is capable of
> giving birth to the idea and the image.[7]

The image of creation in Genesis 1:2 comes through as breathing, brooding spirit. The image of chaos here, of which spirit is a part, stirring into form, is not, as ordinarily interpreted by the patriarchs, a great mass of disorder that God reduced to order, but a kind of order different from the hierarchically controlled. In *The Great Mother*,[8] Erich Neumann interprets it as the abode of the psychic processes from which energy proceeds and originates. He points out how many mythologies use the egg as the symbol of this world creation. The image of chaos appears as a powerful patterned rhythm— or to echo many early mythologies, a great cosmic egg laid by the brooding mother spirit. The creator-spirit is not a pantheistic deity, or a ruler from above, but a creative force (movement, breath, energy) in and through and a part of the total creative process. Cuthbert Simpson,[9] a Biblical scholar, indicates that the images, or ideas as he called them, were foreign to the rest of the first chapter of Genesis and to the creation story as a whole.

A number of theologians are seeking to restore the Holy Spirit in its present patriarchal context to a feminine image. But they inadvertently confront several problems. Perhaps the most obvious is that of a feminine Holy Spirit impregnating the Virgin Mary. The Eastern Orthodox Christian community has sought to preserve the feminine dimension of the divine in various ways through the Virgin Mother, the Mother of God, and Spirit iconography. Publicity has been given to a fresco in a small Bavarian church that portrays the Holy Spirit as a woman.[10] Dated to the late fourteenth century, it was traced to Eastern Christianity, in which Holy Spirit is referred to as Hagia Sophia and is still worshipped in many parts of Christendom. The woman in the fresco, shown clearly with breasts, is depicted between two men with long hair and beards. One has white hair, the other brown, while she, between them, appears to be held down by the men's hands—one on either shoulder.

Along with other patriarchal religious symbols Holy Spirit came to allow for such an increasing distance between the word and the experience for which the word stands that the patriarchs tended to structure a world of their own. A symbol, in itself, may witness to a mystery it cannot fully embrace. But patriarchal religious symbolization rests on the analogy that another world has a similar structure to this world. The tendency for a devotee is to bypass this world in favor of the other. At the same time the patriarchal symbols tend to dissolve this world—the flesh; the concrete; tangible realities of the human condition; what women now seek to recover in the organic, dynamic, inseparability of the spiritual and the political. The patriarchal symbols maintain the dualism that encourages life to be lived without presence and without genuine spiritual experience. The free transcending energy became lost between what was domesticated and that which was vague and vaporous.

Spirit, domesticated and made abstract, deprived the patriarchs and consequently modern "men" of whatever brought them into powerful presence of themselves and others and made them unable to relate except paternalistically to the hungry, the poor, and the dispossessed. Richard L. Vittitow from the Center for Designed Change, wrote of manhood (patriarchy) as such a symbol. It represents a task for men from which they can seldom gain a genuine sense of fulfillment despite all their efforts. He said that the myth comes about in the way men create their "ideal" (i.e., their god). For men to change and move toward any kind of genuine intimacy, he said,

> involves *acknowledging* the Myth of Manhood and the investment one has in it...*awareness* of how living and acting on this Myth and its commandments affects and influences one's life ... *experiencing* ... and intimacy with self, *encountering* who one really is. As this intimacy with self increases, so does the individual's capacity to genuinely and intimately experience others.
>
> I believe that the main reason men cannot be intimate with themselves or with others is their fear of coming to know their own aloneness. Rather than experience their own living and dying, they elect to buy into the Myth of Manhood which precludes them, except in their dream life, from having to deal with their own mortality.
>
> Staying with the Myth of Manhood and its commandments is an illusion. It means staying where one is, which means suffocation...The fear that we must live with and experience our aloneness and our death. Yet, ironically, it is in living with our aloneness and our death that we experience life.[11]

Political Nature of Spirit

In the male-defined assignments of aspects of the spiritual, not only the powerful mystical presence but also what may be called radical social change—a political dimension—was lost.

However, the social and political dimension of the spirit were still quite evident in some of the writings of the early Hebrew prophets.[12] Isaiah described the spirit as coming out of the hot winds of the desert to effect social change (Isaiah 40:1-5), but breath (spirit) he identified as belonging to the male Lord. The spirit judges those who make unjust laws...deprive the poor of justice...rob the weak of their rights (10:1)...The spirit brings justice and peace (2:4)...is an advocate for the wretched and the poor who look for water and find none (41:17)...is as a rushing stream which the wind driveth (59:14-19). Micah denounces the rich men as being steeped in violence (6:12)...and the spirit coming as a cry to the city... and as wisdom (6:8-9). See Isaiah 2:4; 7:7; 32:15-18.

Jeremiah cries out that there is in his heart the spirit as it were a burning fire shut up in his bones which he cannot hold in (20:7-18). Nor does the cry for justice, righteousness, peace, and deliverance end with the early prophets. It was the spirit that created the solidarity of Jesus with the poor, the captive, the oppressed (Luke 4:14-19) to such an extent that he was driven out of the city when he confessed it. His bias toward the poor, the hungry, and the dispossessed became explicit in one of his sermons (Luke 6:20b-23), and lest the point be missed, he struck out at the rich on innumerable occasions. The religious establishment of the day, unable to deal with the political and economic implications of such a stance, quieted his voice; and the patriarchal fathers of the early church finished the job by creating a theological superstructure that snatched him out of his humble estate and put him in the sky to shore up the ontological maleness of the old god.

The spirit, as women, appears to be denigrated throughout the early and patristic ecclesia except for voices that rose at intervals as the mighty wind and the fire in Acts 2 when everybody heard and understood the others' speech. Scholars now say women were prominently vocal in that gathering and quote Bernard of Clairvaux in the twelfth century calling Mary Magdalene (who the patriarchs and modern clergy have branded a prostitute) "apostle of the apostles."[13]

The Spirit as Sensual

Secular lexicon usage[14] supports the claim of the patriarchs that *spirit* is an ecclesiastical possession:

> Something that in ecclesiastical law belongs to the church or to an ecclesiastic.
>
> Distinguished from a worldly character. Incorporeal—having no material body.
>
> Related to religious or sacred matters; ecclesiastical rather than lay or temporal.
>
> Active essence of deity.
>
> One person of the Trinity: Holy Spirit . . . Came down from heaven as cloven tongues of fire.[15]

A lexicon further states that *spirituality* is opposed to *sensuality* and worldliness; and that *sensuality* equates with "the state or quality of being sensual; fondness or indulgence in sensual pleasures ... lasciviousness ..." Then, as if that were not enough, "lasciviousness or secular, opposed to heavenly, spiritual, ecclesiastical—devoted to pleasures of this world." Reflected here is the subtle dualism that claims for the male control of ecclesiastical organizations and whatever was called spirit or spiritual, but which women see as a distortion of the free-flowing spirit that was rooted in the universe itself and in the root sources of breath and movement. Reflected also is that aspect of spirit assigned to women as body—sensuous, lascivious, pleasure-loving—and placed in the private sphere. Women are made invisible in the public sphere and if one happens there she is made to feel out of place. She is usually described by her posture, her voice, her dress, or some other bodily feature rather than by her mind or the content of her commitment. Such a biased perception makes it difficult for men to be objective at the very moment they think they are being most objective.

Women are finding, from a kind of male scholarship, that men do not go back far enough to call the basic patriarchal presuppositions into question. Indeed, they may not be able

to, since patriarchy cannot admit it had a beginning. Therefore, men, conditioned as they are, cannot conceive of spirituality as women experience it. They perceive it in terms of
inversion—the opposite of a male hierarchical perception is a
female hierarchical perception. But that is not what women
perceive. Women refuse any longer to be bound by male
perceptions even if we have to fantasize about the paradises
before men took control. Fantasies have a way of shattering
narrow mind-sets and raising questions: "Just suppose...just
suppose there was a spirit who was in the beginning, as close
to women as men...even closer...and came as Presence in
the form of sister...just suppose!" But that is the way myths
are born.

It was Jean Piaget who, for me, first pointed to the significance of the sensory-motor in the small child. In the senses, he
claimed, after meticulous observation and study of many
children over a long period of time, lie the origins of intelligence (which men claim as their province, yet deny the body
in the process). Professor Piaget distinguishes the senses per
se—that is sight, touch, taste, smell, and hearing—from the
senses at their moment of sensing. As fire is known in the burning, not in the ashes, sight is known in the seeing, not in the eye.
As transcending is known in its acting, not in its noun, sound is
in the hearing, not in the ear. In the child, he observed, fresh
from the rhythms of the universe (the cosmic flow of energy)
the spirit, body, and mind may be seen as one. The material,
corporeal body equates with a sensory movement of spirit and
mind not unrelated to the vibratory rhythms of the cosmos
itself. One recalls sadly how it was once written that "the
Word became flesh," yet image-wise it was placed in the sky
again through one who was made both idol and a male god.

Spirit—Both Organic and Transcending

In that which was defined as sensuous, undesirable, and obscene appears now to be the origin of the mind, without which

the intellect would have no roots and no nourishment. The intellect without roots is tantamount to the body cut off from the spirit and the mind. Women are seeking to harmonize, to bring into a wholeness again, something that has been torn apart and has deprived men and women of humanness.

Antonin Artaud, a French playwright and founder of the Theater of Cruelty, approached Piaget's understanding of organic when grappling with the deeper meanings and power of speech...Artaud saw organic speech as the true and authentic expression of the mind dipping into the senses, interacting with all the senses at their moment of sensing. He saw as abstract, static, and supportive of the status quo thoughts and emotions that emanated from the intellect only. But thought and emotions came up out of the gut—the deepest innerness of the human spirit—he saw inclusive of both mind and body. Organic speech may be described as coming up out of the spirit in its most concrete and dynamic movement and not in its static or clichéd state; in metaphoric image and not patriarchal symbol.

A prominent male theological professor in an unpublished essay declared that women cannot have it both ways—"organic and transcendent." Obviously he was thinking out of the old dualism. *Organic* does not mean for us staying in the gut, nor is it limited to the senses as nouns. *Transcendent,* in itself, evokes a static immobility out of the sky rather than *transcending,* which stirs out of the organic as ever in process of reshaping self and society. Thus *spiritual* is experienced profoundly as sisterhood in its loftiest and most universal sense and, we may add redundantly, political action of the most radical sort on behalf of and ultimately including all humanity—women, children, and men.

The women's spiritual revolution calls into question direction, shape, and the source of the patriarchal. In reclaiming the organic and recovering the source of our energy flow, we are withdrawing our energy from the systems that siphon it off then name it their dove-spirit coming down from heaven. Little were the patriarchs aware of earlier images hidden in their own confession—images which in time could topple the superstructure of might and power. Up out of the Ark's dark womb the bird (spirit) flew to pluck an olive branch of peace. Jonah (the name means dove and is feminine) ejected from the belly of the whale—the womb of birth. The womb-tomb ejected its own dove-spirit.

Recovering Our Lost Humanity

Women of this century, to probe the root sources of our oppression, have tried on the stereotyped images in order not to evade or deny the way we have internalized them. We touched our bodies and tasted what had been denigrated and labeled sentimental. We owned our bodily functions as good. We have felt the pain of the images, followed them down to their source into the subterranean caverns of our own chaos. Through almost unbearable pain, we were sustained by one another. We know solidarity with other women and all women simultaneously as most exquisitely personal and powerfully political. Often our first utterance was a cry or agonizing gesture, but in that movement and sound we knew that we had been heard and understood even before the cry was uttered. Our tongues were loosened and we experienced ourselves speaking a new speech—boldly, perhaps, or haltingly, but authentically for the first time in our lives. We experienced a speech that follows hearing, as opposed to the going logic that demands precise speech for more accurate hearing to take place. Hearing, for us, became a personally transitive verb that evoked speech. We heard the person before the word was spoken. In that sense we can say we were heard to our own speech—to new creation. There is powerful spiritual movement in hearing one another to speech. The word in process of becoming visible flesh. It was not the word from the sky or from the patriarchal interpreter. The word was our word—our most human word. The word was ourselves. We heard one another to our own word—to our own self-birth.

For anyone to experience solidarity in world sisterhood is to break out of the patriarchal mind-set that cannot think in global terms outside of dualism. One of the most obvious expressions of a patriarchal mind-set is a parochial mentality that considers the other as stranger or enemy; a territory-bound mentality that cannot perceive the earth as a common home for us all. A patriarchal mind-set even at best is unable to see the point of view, except in a paternalistic manner, of those beneath. Constant reminders of what good things the fathers have bestowed upon us invite a demeaning and paternalistic response. That leaves all who are not patriarchs, and those who have not internalized the patriarchal perceptions of themselves, outside the decision-making and the production processes and denies them access to life-sustaining resources of the earth (except through the grace of the rulers). This exclusion has apparently been assumed by those in control. Note again the dictionary definition of *spiritual* quoted earlier: The spiritual is "related to...the ecclesiastical rather than lay or temporal," i.e., the masses of people. Within the ecclesiastical structure it is the clergy in control—not the lay membership. Outside the ecclesia, it is the rulers of the world—not the people. Those who claim to be the spirit's true interpreters are set against the masses of people both within and outside the ecclesia. And it is these masses who are kept powerless so that control may be maintained. By clear definition those laity (masses of people) outside organized religion and those nonclergy within are lumped together in relationship with one another in a way by which neither is related to the clergy or to the rulers. The freedom of the spirit inevitably becomes politically linked to the freedom of the laity (masses) in such a way that the political and the spiritual may be seen as one. But since in its present usage *spirit* is defined, domesticated, and controlled out of patriarchal perspective, women are compelled to search for a new word that brings to expression the new political/spiritual reality. The new word necessary to carry the full load of what is happening to women today must be powerful enough to transcend out of our organic body politic.

Liberation of the spirit and liberation of women are one and the same part of the struggle for a free society and world. I believe that the liberation of the human spirit from her captivity, the liberation of women, and the liberation of the oppressed of the earth will come at one and the same time and be the same radical movement that will make a universal, visible reality and unify the spiritual and the political.

1976:

Educating for Wholeness

This essay was a plenary address at the World Federation of Methodist Women, in Dublin, Ireland, on August 21, 1976. After much deliberation the quinquennium of the World Federation of Methodists was set for Ireland. Two reasons were given for the choice of location. The Irish civil conflict, going on for years, appeared to have reached its most violent form. It was hoped that the presence of the large Protestant World Body might give witness to a unity and peace that would transcend political, ecclesiastical, and national divisions. At the same time the economy of Ireland, at its lowest, enabled the National Tourist Association to make airway and combination tickets available so the beauty of Ireland could be widely shared by attending delegates.

The title of my address was chosen by the planning committee. I felt comfortable that I could interpret education in such a way that would make peace imperative as a woman's responsibility, and a just peace without presuming to offer the terms for settlement of the Irish conflict. I must say that the preparation carried some anxiety-producing anticipation that was eased partially by a party set up for me on my arrival by Bernadette Cahill of the Irish Press. I had come to know Bernadette at the World Council of Churches Conference on Sexism in the 1970s held in Berlin in 1974. I was far too tired to be my best at the party but it established for me a more personal relationship with ten members of the press including Bernadette. In all the conferences I have ever attended, I felt the Irish reporters the most understanding with the fairest and most in-depth interpretation. I attributed it to the fact that so many of them had been priests before they became journalists and were familiar with theological thinking.

Four days before the conference opened, Saturday the fourteenth to be exact, two women in Belfast had planned a memorial march for three children—victims of the Irish conflict. The shock had struck terror and rage into the hearts of the mothers and the memorial service drew ten thousand participants, many of them men and children. The conference women got the message of the Belfast women that they were fed up with the killing and they wanted peace. They had demonstrated a transcending hope for a peace with love and justice and urged a cease-fire until structures of justice could be worked out. Whatever the outcome, the message of liberation the women were so eloquently demonstrating appeared to offer the only possible hope. The women in Belfast were our sisters— church sisters, world sisters. In light of such overwhelming response a second march was scheduled for the following Saturday when the Protestant women could reciprocate by marching into the Catholic territory, in spite of the possible ridicule and physical danger. I was scheduled to speak just prior to this second march.

After my address and the affirmative vote of the conference women, they gathered on the lawn in gaily colorful dress from sixty countries, and marched down the street to a city park several blocks away. Many were in tears. Along the way others joined, women especially: single, in groups leading little children, and rolling babies in carriages. Men joined the march and others, many coming to the doors of their shops and moving out to the curb, crossing themselves, with tears steaming down their faces. By the time we reached the park local citizens had doubled the crowd. Most of the time we stood in silence. Off and on during the silence came the chanting of "Sisters, we hear your pain." Jean Skuse, a conference leader from Australia, explained: "We deeply admire the wonderful and courageous campaign being conducted in the north, and this is our way of demonstrating our heartfelt support."

On the way back from the demonstration one woman from Samoa said, "To think I had to come all this distance to know that commitment and action are the same." Another, "Marching itself can be a feminist act." Another, "There was no separation between personal and political."

The women in Belfast, who had not planned other marches beyond the twenty-first, were so moved by the Dublin conference support that they established marches throughout Ireland. Many of us traveling over the country afterward were often confronted with a march set up in the tiniest village. The larger World General Methodist conference in Dublin decided to march on August 28, when thirty thousand participated, with the lord mayor joining.

The aftermath of the witness of the women appears confused. Perhaps the world press gave too much publicity without being able to spell out the real witness the women were trying to make. Soon the IRA resumed the bombing. The English set up marches in London and other places which made it seem that they were trying to coopt the peace witness of the women. The People's Peace Prize in Denmark was awarded to the two women who had organized the march. Perhaps the publicity was too much. The women, along with many others, have moved out of Ireland.

And the fighting continues.

★

My sisters!

Sisters of one another!

World Sisters! Women of the world!

I do not say church women to begin with—though most of us are of the church.

I do not say United Methodist Women, though we have the United Methodist Women's Federation to thank for bringing us together.

I do not address you as from your specific country—though consciousness of our homes will be in our conversations and ever in our hearts these days.

To experience ourselves as world sisters is to break out of the patriarchal mind-set that cannot think in global terms outside of dualism. In patriarchy someone has to get "power-over" by putting others down; or have another globe to compare with our globe. See how we race to the moon and Mars before we can attend to world hunger, world poverty, world war, racism, sexism, classism, ageism, and colonialism at home.

The result of patriarchal mind-set for us educationally is parochial mentalities that consider others as strangers or enemy; territory-bound mentalities that cannot perceive the earth as the common home for us all.

Because of a patriarchal mind-set around the world we have never stood in greater danger of global destruction. The danger is heightened by increasing knowledge that we are using up the energy and irreplaceable resources of the world. Political analysts and social and economic scientists are at a loss for a solution or turn to the same authoritarian sources that have gotten us into our present dilemma.

The Urgency for a New Education

There is no question but that there is available knowledge and technical skills enough to feed, clothe, and shelter the entire people of the world with present available resources, but somewhere along the line our education has been such that we are unable to use them for this purpose. Denis Goulet, a prominent writer on ethical and value questions in relation to development and social change, points out that "modern communications render isolation among human societies impossible," then goes on to quote Lewis Mumford that if we forget our joint stock of knowledge and skills we not only enthrone superstition but undermine the essential basis of technology itself. Then he turned to the French economist François Perroux who said that "technical conditions for the establishment of a planetary economy now exist."[1]

We may not be isolated from one another physically, but we are hooked by a patriarchal mentality—a kind of dualism—which prevents hearing and the meeting of minds. The dualism is heightened by increasing knowledge that the earth's resources are becoming limited. One of the classic examples is the brilliant analysis[2] of the world economy by Professor Robert Heilbroner, who enumerates external threats that raise anxiety and introduce the doubt of human survival on this earth. He focuses on the increase of population beyond the world's ability to provide food, the potential and irreparable danger of a nuclear war, environmental disruption, limits of energy sources, tolerance of the ecosphere for absorption of heat, and the unbridled increase of industrialization, and their combined socioeconomic and political consequences for all the people of the earth.[3] After examining the capacity of two main economic systems to cope with the danger of global destruction, he appeals to authoritarianism, even though he confesses it is against his own inclination. He dismisses the male Greek god Prometheus, whom he evokes first, in favor of the mighty Atlas, with this closing doubt:

> We do not know with certainty that humanity will survive, but it is a comfort to know that there exist within us the elements of fortitude and will from which the image of Atlas springs.[4]

Here Heilbroner appeals to more of the same patriarchy that brought us to our present dilemma.

An even more disturbing note was struck by Dr. William Mensendiek of Japan when speaking from and interpreting the findings of a little volume entitled *The Limits to Growth*.[5] He said that with the aid of computers the complex interrelationship among five categories of data (which coincided with the external threats of Professor Heilbroner) had been analyzed. Then he said:

> Unless new forms of energy and synthetics are developed, modern civilization as we know it will suddenly fizzle out. Hope that the Science God will save us is not held by many scientists...for reasons too complicated to describe here...many scientists now fear that the length of the biosphere as an inhabitable regime for organisms is to be measured in decades rather than in hundreds of millions of years.

I believe it is too late for authoritarian patriarchy to turn the tide. It is too late for the rulers—those in control—to remedy the world's ills, even if they wanted to do so. They are too close to the causes of world disorder to have any kind of global perspective beyond saving their own skins and "inheriting the earth," which image the Bible keeps alive for them. A patriarchal mind-set even in the best can never see the point of view, except in a paternalistic manner, of those beneath it. That leaves more than half the world's people outside the decision-making and production process, denied the essential resources of the world with a deaf ear turned toward them.

If what I am saying has any semblance of truth then it appears that women and the disinherited have one of two choices. And these choices just may not be as oversimplified as they at first seem. First, we can go down with the earth ship, and prefer doing so, rather than live in a situation in which our energy is syphoned off for the continued race to benefit a few; or, second, we can take a bold stand to effect a global survival of humankind. But that would involve a massive educational venture and a coalition of all who are victims of the patriarchal habit of ruling and the mind-set that Germaine Greer called "sexism of the mind."[6] This mind-set spawns dualisms that split the self, alienate one people from another people, and prevent a worldwide common access to knowledge and the reverent uses of the resources of the earth now available.

Such an educational venture, many feel, would prove the reversal of much that we now have. It would focus at a different center from "power-over," getting ahead of another, racing to success. It would claim openly to have both a *political* and a *spiritual* dimension. Education as most of us know it now has a hidden political dimension while claiming to be objective and nonpolitical. In most countries it has a despiritualizing effect, while claiming to keep religion from indoctrinating education.

Before I go further with this line, I would like to repeat: If the world, this earth, and all of its people are to be diverted from global destruction, it is the exploited, the dispossessed, and the so-called powerless who will do it.[7] What I am saying should not sound new to you. Surely it was in the minds of your planning committee in arriving at your theme. It was what Jesus was really about. His teaching was both his spiritual and political vocation. It was his political activity, as an act of his faith, that put him to death. It was his spiritual sensitivity, as enabling power, that created the gospel. Was he not trying to reclaim the Spirit that had been suppressed and domesticated by the going religion of his day? The Spirit that enabled him to hear the poor, the prisoners, the women, the exploited, the hungry, and the powerless? Not once did he put the spiritual and the political in separate categories that would open them to labels of social issues so they could be dismissed. He listened to and heard the poor as his ministers. He heard them define their own agonies. Thus he experienced such solidarity with them that he could say: I am the disinherited, I am the prisoner, I am the poor.[8] He accepted his own powerlessness in order to have access to a power that did not domesticate the Spirit but respected its free movement as breath of life, enabling and available to all—even the least. And this, Jesus went about teaching. This kind of belief structure countered the mind-set and shattered the prevailing images of his day just as it shatters the mind-set of those who would control the nations and the churches of the world today.

The Power of Images and New Education

In order to break out of the dualistic mind-set we are compelled to deal with the way images shape our lives. We have been taught in various ways that education is to be rewarded; when we learn well, we receive stars, grades, labels, credentials, degrees, and titles in such a way that the essential learning becomes secondary. We have been taught mainly by images that an educated person is guaranteed power over the uneducated and can draw more money to enjoy more of this world's good life. In this process, there has been a breaking down of our natural person through the subtle images that mold us to fit into a competitive system and value human beings according to their sex, color, power, affluence, age, class, and nation. I see this as a subtle kind of politics of the most obscene sort. Images work subliminally in such a way that people can deny their intent and their existence. Images are created in words, repetitive events, ritualistic ceremonies of etiquette, hidden visual representation, structures that delude because of their invisibility so that all of us tend to be manipulated by them and their power in spite of our knowledge of their existence.

I can remember the history of Tennessee, which I studied as a little girl. It was filled with pictures of Indians scalping white settlers, Indian attacks on innocent whites, and stories that never allowed us to consider that anything worthwhile went on in the Appalachians before the kind English, Scottish, and Irish settled there and began to cultivate the land, build their cabins, and establish "civilized" living. I was almost grown before I realized that the image of "savage" was attached to the wrong group—that it was my own people who had driven out the Native Americans from the soil they had roamed and tended longer than history can document. The shattering reversal in finding the truth about my early white education recurred in examining textbooks that showed blacks as servants, docile, or sinister.

Images bring little children to attitudes of superiority and inferiority long before they are able to conceptualize. And after they can conceptualize all sorts of right concepts cannot change an image or correct the irreparable damage done. Images are woven into the languages of the world and our religious language so that we educate children and ourselves to speak to our own destruction. *Now* I am finding it the same with images of workers, older people, and especially women. I am shattered all over again to learn the subtle ways, in succeeding generations, we have created images of women who are sweet, clinging, dependent, with shallow minds and no political ambition, and limited to the private sphere.

Women have been assigned the task of carrying the moral values of the world but were not allowed power in the public sphere to do anything about them. You can see why in America we have sentimentalized the image of "mother," and established Mother's Day, which even the church supports. Mother's Day deludes us into thinking that the moral values are still intact and strong enough to support the fabric of public life. But mothers have no power, no access to the channels of social change, and no identity of their own outside their homes.

We have been taught that education is a matter of intellectual pursuit and have given little attention to the images that are projected in our educational materials, our methods of teaching, and the teachers as models. The church has supported such a system to the extent that it continues to express its faith in ancient patriarchal symbols that project images of "power-over," might, and rulership. See how we still address the deity as King of Heaven, Lord, Prince, Master, Father—all terms of early rulership, control, and dominance. Consider the beautiful metaphoric phrase of Psalm 90: "Thou hast been our dwelling place in all generations."

How delightful, energizing, nondiscriminatory! The expression appears passive but comes alive in "all generations" as it cuts through past and present to carry us into a future with all peoples. "Dwelling place" resists literalization. The direct address is profoundly religious. But it is negated by the jarring image of "Lord" at its beginning. "Lord" sets the "thou" within patriarchal limits and endows it with a certain gender. It evokes an image of maleness and rulership. Thus, women are excluded from the "dwelling place" as are children, blacks, the poor, the hungry, the prisoners, the colonized, and all who are the "other"—the woman. In the process of literalization of these images great political structures have risen to keep the control in the hands of the rulers and to keep us apart—as if forever. We cannot escape the fact that Lord, Master, King, and other such terms for deity were uniquely of a patriarchal culture. Use of overwhelmingly male language for God, educating and theologizing out of male experience only, as if it were the whole human experience, simply excludes far more than half of the earth's peoples. Remember, it is the image that shapes life-styles—not the concept. It is the image that perpetuates the hierarchical structures that would keep us all in bondage.

Images, as I have treated them here, are the powerful instruments of patriarchy and are kept alive by those of us who have not yet broken out of a patriarchal mind-set.

I have heard some of you say that patriarchy (or sexism) is not your problem—at the very time your whole nation is being victimized by patriarchy in the way your power is being usurped in colonialization, or the way you are deliberately kept powerless—cut off from earth's essential resources. Women and the disinherited who have begun to become aware of the real causes of their oppression have learned much through the bitter pain of being related to as an image; and have learned to perceive and hear the whole people from the bottom of the hierarchical ladder. We have one advantage over those at the top who cannot hear or know or see those beneath except through a relationship of paternalism. But paternalism works two ways. One cannot be paternalized without handing the privilege of power to the paternalizer. To direct one's energy from a paternalistic relationship is a matter of education involving wholeness of persons, a whole people, and a perspective of global wholeness.

Education for the Transformation of Self and Society

An astounding lesson that women learn when they come to new consciousness is that the self cannot be separated from the social structure of which it is a part. This moment of awareness is not something that happens in the head and must be transferred to a social and political situation. That dichotomizing of theory and practice, or knowledge and the application of knowledge, is part of an old method of education designed to keep the boat from being rocked. Even its more modern version of action and reflection is the same old dichotomy that misses the dynamic energy that is generated when the two mesh. That moment of meshing is action of the most transforming sort. The person is no longer an isolated being but a responsible social self...and has brought about the process of transforming self and society at one and the same time. As the ills or the causes are lodged in the social order, as well as the self, so also are its changes and healings. The gut knowledge that personal problems are public issues is not an individualistic but a community process. Women have claimed for years and with dead seriousness that the political is personal and the personal is political. If the two issues are separated again there can only be apathy or shallowness in the political sphere and a kind of individualistic, pious egotism in the personal.

The dualism of patriarchy has split the human experience into personal/political, theory/practice and has also split the human experience into male over female experience. Some attributes have been assigned exclusively to women and some to men. These attributes existing separately have become stereotyped images leading both men and women to live out of roles rather than out of their full humanness. The knowledge that this split was a political intention in order to gain and maintain control in the public arena is just now dawning on the world consciousness of women. Until the stereotypes that make up what we have come to call femininity and masculinity are shattered or transcended there can be no objective studies of the innate differences between men and women. When the time comes for such studies, they may reveal far greater differences than we can now enivsion. But even more serious, until the stereotypes are shattered it will be impossible to know or to experience what is fully human. Think of it! We have not yet come into the full human experience nor have yet experienced a genuine human community. For to shatter the stereotypes would at the same time crumble the patriarchal structure that cannot stay alive without the support of these stereotyped images. All we can know now is how the images shape the structures and program for poverty, war, economic exploitation, and colonialization.

No woman can be whole if she denies in herself part of her humanness—her initiative and her strength. No man can be whole if he denies that in himself which is tender and gentle. Carl Jung once made the statement that when one sex is denied essential human qualities such as those mentioned above that sex has the tendency to use the other, to possess the other in order to gain the qualities missing in oneself. Once we become aware that the assignment of certain human attributes to separate specific sexes opens the way for the economic system to use women and some men to perpetuate itself, we can readily see how our silence keeps us limited to the private sphere. We fall for the stereotypes to the degree we are not aware of our own self-worth and resourcefulness. Or to put it as Laurens van der Post put it, racism (sexism, ageism, classism) is a form of rejecting our own humanness.[9]

John Kenneth Galbraith wrote in *Ms.* magazine that women could change the entire economic system could we but come to the awareness of the way the economy hangs on our apron strings.[10]

I heard Thelma Stevens say practically the same about women of the church. What potential but unused power they have! They could change the patriarchal structures of the church if they would educate themselves to make their own decisions about their money, claim their own energy and their own time for genuine social change and spiritual renewal rather than frustrate themselves in projects that keep the present structures intact.

Few of us experience the limitlessness of the flow of energy in and about us. Dorothy Phillips, an editor of *The Choice is Always Ours*,[11] recently described an overwhelming experience at the sudden realization that the energy was *there—there already* working itself out in our lives. It is in such times Dorothy describes the Spirit as indeed healing. Often, however, it goes wandering. We lose its many splendored rhythms when we inadvertently try to manipulate it and bring it under our control (the egotistic, nonsocial, nonaware act) rather than reverence its own flow. "The Spirit bloweth where it listeth." It surprises us with good things far more than we now envision...and works in unexpected ways both within us and about us and in the community of mutuality.

The way sexual dualism is one and the same coin in shortchanging women personally and in the entire world has not been missed by Margaret Mead. At a 1976 meeting of the American Association for the Advancement of Science she denounced in no uncertain terms the American system of teaching scientific agriculture to men only and nutrition to women only. She indicated the disastrous effect it has had on the rest of the world, resulting in devaluing nutrition and related subjects because of their association with women in a society that views men's roles outside the home as being more important than women's. Mead called for a radical change in the educational systems in America and all over the world so that men and women alike would study both aspects. She called for a new name such as "human ecology" for, she added, women will get into agriculture but men will not go into home economics. A distortion of human experience, subordinating it to personal egos and the need to control, has hurt women all over the world and contributed no little share to the hunger of the world.[12]

"There can be no radical change without radical consciousness," say the authors of a paperback called *Moving Toward a New Society*.[13]

Long before the woman movement, some creative white teachers sought to develop independent children. One of their earliest experiences in the United States was when, after the Emancipation Proclamation, they organized schools among black children in the south. Politicians and official school administrators paid little attention to what was going on and supported them—at first. Then suddenly they moved in and assumed control. They perceived that the teachers had started a good thing as the response of the children had been phenomenal. But more serious, the pupils were becoming independent, resourceful, and self-reliant. That was dangerous to the system and had to be curbed.[14] To this day the black schools have never been fully equalized in the United States. And one cannot possibly understand the busing situation without knowing something of the history of these early days. The same problem is reflected in Britain's schools, according to Mariarosa Dalla Costa. There, black children are often confined to subnormal schools and in Europe the working-class child often sees the teacher as "somebody who is teaching him or her something against her mother and father, not as a defense of the child but as an attack on the class."[15]

Creative teachers see that the overloading of a teacher's schedule, the overcrowded classroom and the rigid programming run counter to their efforts. Many of the finest teachers dropped out of education when they became aware of the way the system (often through support of the parents) resists efforts in the classroom to break the heavy pressures which preserve the power and structures of an established order.

Nor are the universities and theological schools exempt from this kind of bias in their educational efforts. Perhaps they, more than any other schools, claim an objectivity that women find greatly missing. The choice of content, women students are now saying, is too often selective, partial, and even slanted to support a point of view of those in control. Much of the so-called scholarship is seen by many women, blacks, and the poor as emerging from a patriarchal perspective and training to fit into and support eliteness.

Far too many of these institutions operate on the model of the expert, the star, and the powerful teacher. History was so written. Structures are so ordered. Seminary women particularly have experienced bias under male professors who resist changing to an inclusive language or including woman history and woman contribution. One such professor who received a student paper on woman history rose to white heat, accused the student of being biased and unscholarly in her approach. It is assumed by many that seminaries and theological schools and even the churches are reluctant to take on a more whole approach because to do so they would have to re-examine their theology, which carries a kind of vested interest too costly to change.

Many women have been encouraged by the voices of Ivan Illich and Paolo Freire only to be disappointed later by their slowness to deal with dualistic patriarchy in both their content and their method. They have raised questions about the way these men operate as stars (gurus) rather than as participants in a mutuality of learning. Illich has earned the title of "deschooler" of education. Freire, from his office in the World Council of Churches Educational Department, made a brave effort to eliminate the dichotomy and recover the dynamism where action and theory become one and the same. However, in an article in *Quest*,[16] Lorraine Masterson gives more than usual credit to Freire's contribution as a tool for women to gain their lost identity.

Reliance on the "star" model or elitism in any teaching process tends to create apathy on the part of the majority and in its final expression can never transcend the status quo. An apocalyptic model means first, the discontinuity of the old hierarchical ordering; second, a reliance on faithfulness in the humanizing and the politicizing of every member of the body politic. It cannot afford to listen only to the expert and the star. Its ear is tuned to the heart of the community, thus allowing for a totally new break-in that cannot be predetermined, manipulated, or controlled by any one mind or by might. Since the apocalypse envisions the new society, the dynamic of its daily learning process actualizes it. Of course this implies a new kind of role for the teacher who may listen as much as speak; who may learn from the student—even the least—and is always refreshed as one after the other comes to a new sense of identity and self-worth while moving toward the new society. Anything less maintains an inequality that is a violation of basic human nature. Personal liberation and liberation of society become one and the same, and true education becomes the inherent right of a whole people in bringing both about.

Let Us Begin: NOW!

Since the ultimate issues in the new education are both political and spiritual, moral values assigned to women who are assigned to the private sphere must now become part of public life—that is, if we are to survive. The double standard, another form of dualism in present educational systems would no longer be viable. Teaching would involve public morality as women move more rapidly into the public sphere. No longer can women be dismissed by "you don't understand politics." We must make it our business to learn, become aggressive, and have initiative in public life. Not in the manner of men, but moving into the public arena with the moral values that too often have had a stillbirth at home due to society's hierarchical structuring of family life. We must bring our own way of working and our own understandings of life and interrelationships and our own vision of global peace and harmony as a viable possibility—indeed, the only viable possibility—for survival. The world is poorer and far from whole without all that women have to bring to it and that has too often been programmed out of the lives of men, especially as they operate in the public sphere.

What are some of these values that women have preserved? Would they not include: caring, mutuality, passion, intuitive depth of understanding, listening, and the ability to hear, capacity to cut through the claptrap and touch the core of an issue long before the going logic has started its committee research, patience to hear the least and in their own way, the recognition of a cry before it is uttered, and the sensitivity to smell a skunk before news of the graft reaches the press.

We must educate ourselves to public issues not just to keep informed or communicate with men, but in order to effect social change. We have been deluded long enough with that old false cliché: the hand that rocks the cradle rules the world.

This would lay a peculiar responsibility at the door of church women who might begin by examining critically the multiplicity of so-called good activities about which Thelma Stevens once spoke, including those volunteer projects which confine women to the private sphere.

Many women are setting themselves to the task of recovering woman history both in the secular and the religious fields. During the entire history of patriarchy its written records have been partial. Actually, women have been written out of history and in the process we have become invisible and a nonentity. The full story of human development has been neither whole nor honest since its authors have been men writing about the feats of men. Anne McGrew Bennett once commented that the control of historical records is another way the dominant group holds its power.[17] Such control not only tends to pressure women students to adopt the private sphere as "their place" but throughout the educational process has provided them with research materials in which they have no past and no contribution. Professor Sidney Ahlstrom once said: "A person who has no past is not a human being." And Mary Daly, commenting on the partial nature of history because the naming has not been mutual—that is, by both women and men—said: "To exist humanly is to name the self, the world, and God...The liberation of language is rooted in the liberation of ourselves."

We are faced with the need of finding a new language since the old patriarchal language can no longer express the spiritual longings, experiences, and visions that women are having today. We, too, must tell our stories and find new words and images out of the heart of our struggle that would help to usher in and liberate the spirit as well as women. We might begin with reclaiming the history of spirit which was a feminine word in Hebrew. The earliest word for spirit is breath, wind, *ruach*—all of feminine gender. It is also the earliest word for transcendence. Other aspects of spirit from our tradition also have feminine gender: *Chokmah*, or "wisdom," in Proverbs 8. She was before anything that was. *She-kinah*, Hebrew for "presence"—we might say abiding presence. *Torah* is the enabling guide. Dove, too, was a visible symbol of spirit—up out of the ark's womb she flew to pluck an olive branch of peace. The word *Jonah* means dove—ejected out of the belly of the whale—the womb of his salvation. Nor need we remind ourselves that the tomb itself, another symbol of womb, ejected its own dove spirit. Spirit is always movement, ferment, metanoia.

What was the Spirit's function?

What happened to her?

I am indebted to Richard Tholin[18] for some of the following images of the Spirit in Biblical witness: She filled inanimate matter and created human life (Genesis 2:7). She came out of the hot winds of the desert to effect social change (Isaiah 40:1-5, 59:17-19). The Spirit brings justice and peace (Isaiah 2:4, 9:7, 32:15-18). She is the source of power and justice (Micah 3:8-10). She is a burning fire in the bones that cannot be held in (Jeremiah 20:7-13).

It was the spirit that created the solidarity of Jesus with the poor, the captive, the oppressed (Luke 4:4–19). Jesus' bias on behalf of the poor and the hungry and the dispossessed became explicit in the Sermon on the Mount (Luke 6:20b–23) and lest the point be missed, he struck out at the rich with "Woe to you..." and "it is easier for a camel to go through the eye of a needle than for a rich man to get into heaven."

But the established religion in its dualistic manner somewhere along the line domesticated the spirit, brought the spirit under control of the patriarchal church fathers and secured her to the altar. They defined a part of it as vaporous and sentimental and assigned that part to women.

It is up to women to recover the lost history of spirit, rescue it from vaporousness and wraithlike sentimentality on one hand and domestication on the other, and restore it to its true heritage and true vocation.[19]

Liberation of the spirit is a part of the new venture in education for the new society. I warrant that the liberation of the spirit from her captivity and the liberation of women and the oppressed of the earth will come at the same time and will be a part of the same radical movement for global wholeness.

But that will not come, I predict, until women rise up boldly around the world, embrace the spirit energy, tell our real story, establish structures of justice, and bring the new reality to fruition. Women will, indeed, then become the second coming.

Rise up, Sisters!

Women of the World!

Rise!

Claim your heritage! Help shape the new day! Work for peace with justice, courage, and love.

The day is already at hand.

Can you, regardless of nationality, age, color, class, turn to any other woman as you turn to the woman standing next to you and say, as I would like to be able now to say to each of you, "Sister, I hear your pain!"[20]

Conference in unison: "Sister, I hear your pain."

The women of Northern Ireland are now getting ready for their second march for peace to take place this afternoon. Those of you who feel you would like to turn toward them and say to them: "Sisters, we hear you pain," will you do so now.

The conference in unison: "Sisters, we hear your pain."

Mothers of Soweto in South Africa, some of whom are present today, are still supporting their student sons and daughters against an apartheid language made compulsory for school use. Will you turn toward South Africa and say with me: "Sisters, we hear your pain."

The conference in unison: "Sisters, we hear your pain."

1977:

Beloved Image

By the time I was asked to prepare a paper on women imaging for the American Academy of Religion, I was aware that I was well on a journey into feminism.[1] Increasingly, I had become aware that we lived out of images more than concepts and that most of the images available to women were patriarchal constructs that we had internalized. I had become convinced also that religion was often used to suppress the valid, natural images that were part of the essence of our humanness.

Not only did many of the patriarchal images that shape our culture and our individual lives as women condone the denigration of parts of our bodies but *we* had joined in the pornographic hoard that created jokes about and laughed at parts of our bodily functioning. If we could claim unashamedly and proudly what belongs to us, that which is ourselves, and if we love these aspects in ourselves and others, we would be free from the patriarchal chains that bind us into a distortion of womanhood—making us ashamed of our created selves. Judy Chicago first gave me the idea conceptually. When she chose the cunt to be the core of her art, it was not a sexual move. She was after the symbolization of the whole history of women in Western civilization.

When I read *Of Woman Born* by Adrienne Rich, I knew she was not trying to destroy the image of mother, as so many reviews accused her, but to recover for women something precious that had been lost. She was not about to give up her experience of motherhood. She wanted to restore the image in all its power; to strip it of the sentimentalities and false images created by patriarchy for political and economic advantage. She was aware that patriarchy (including right-wing women) has deliberately and falsely accused feminism of being against motherhood and against family.

By this time I knew the direction I wanted my essay to follow, but how to begin was still a puzzle. I had worked hard on researching the work of Judy Chicago and Adrienne Rich, but I knew I was still in the cerebral stage. Then I saw Emily Culpepper's short film *Period Piece*. I knew what to expect. I knew what the film contained. I knew that it had been shown the previous year in this same meeting—the American Academy of Religion— and that then half the viewers walked out.

When Emily's vulva was flashed on the living room screen all my Southern primness surfaced. She could have used a picture from a book on physiology! I guess that is what Emily thought too. She too is Southern. It wasn't a picture of some unknown woman she had to deal with. It was herself. By the time the first "pure red blood" dropped from her vagina I was in tears. In one brief moment she had shattered the deep internalized patriarchal image within me, and I *knew*, not from my head but from the pit of my stomach, what Judy Chicago, Adrienne Rich, and Emily Culpepper were saying to me. I also had the title of my essay—"Beloved Image"! I knew that if ever I laughed at a "dirty" joke or condoned pornography in any way I would be laughing at myself and making my sacred images more distorted. I am indebted to these women, and others who have made me see more clearly.

★

...a part of me
is missing

Where is "me"
a part of me is missing

aborted—still born—
    since that Garden time

    yet, without plan or warning
    ever and ever again moving
    deep within my body
       and soul
    a person "image of God"
      WOMAN
    comes gasping, grasping
    for the breath of life
    struggling to be born
    and live—free

pushed back, covered over by
myriad words—intoned word
    you are not man
    you are woman
    created for man's pleasure
      and comfort
    created to bear man-child
      to rule you
    created to bear woman-child
      to be subject to man-child

Man-child, oh man-child
my father, husband, brothers, sons
do you feel a deep stirring,
    rebellion
at the intoned word for you?
    You are man, be big
    be strong, be powerful
    never surrender: succeed
    let no tears break through
    be mind, not heart
      heart is for the weak
    be arrogant-aggressive

CRY, CRY BELOVED IMAGE
Who calls us both?

—Anne McGrew Bennett,[2] April 1972

Feminist imaging aims beyond the dualism of mind/body, nature/history, personal/political, and organic/transcendence. It calls us to perceive the universe from a uniquely feminist stance rather than the internalized masculine perceiving with which we are already familiar. It presupposes that none of us—men or women—have yet come into the full human experience, and cannot without the new emerging feminine imaging. But feminine imaging demands a new way of hearing that precedes speaking, indeed that awakens speech, a new way of seeing.[3] It demands reversals from the going logic to openness for a new reality coming from a different direction—up from down under rather than down from up above, out from within; a new shape—cyclical perhaps, round or rhythmical, at least away from linear, which encourages no basic social, personal, and political change.

Imaging Is Out of Experience

The first thing to be said about imaging is that it is something one experiences, consciously or out of the personal or collective unconscious. All our lives we have been warned not to trust experience and never begin with one's own self. But the private self, as Elizabeth Janeway reminds us,[4] is the only source of authentic experience and this experience can be stated and understood only by public image. Both men and women, by and large, have lived out of patriarchal experience and male-defined images. These images, both historical and contemporary, have been transmitted through various cultural forms and have shaped society's values and expectations, including those that women have of ourselves. Thus we have been deprived of living out of images consistent with our own selfhood. As Robert McAfee Brown[5] points out: "All theologies emerge out of a certain set of experiences or out of a patriarchal historical context; there is no way in which a historical faith could be expressed other than through cultural norms and patterns in which it is located; and it may take others to show us how conditioned, parochial, or ideologically captive our own theology is." He goes on to relate an encounter from a South American at the Detroit Conference on Theology in the Americas: "Why is it when you talk about *our* position it is always 'Latin American theology,' but when you talk about *your* position it is always 'theology'?" Some women have tried to deal with this problem of bias and partiality by use of labels, "white, male theology."

Because of the dominance of men in society, culture has confused the full human experience with male experience, making it difficult if not impossible for men to hear women and our experiences, self-defined, out of which we speak. Objectivity, so highly prized in academic circles, is rarely found. Only recently a woman professor, a black professor, and a New Testament scholar pondered a passage of scripture in preparation for a faculty session on "Theologizing Out of Experience." After the N.T. scholar had expounded exegetically, the woman began with: "Now, I, as a white woman, perceive..." When the black started, "I, as a black," the N.T. scholar interrupted with "Hey, wait a minute. You're trapping me. Nothing is left for me but, I, a white and a male." Both his colleagues smiled. Not until that moment had the white, male, N.T. scholar considered the possibility that his maleness and his whiteness might have biased his scholarship.

All women's experiences are valid data and must be respected. It was reported from a recent consultation that one professor described her woman experience and the images rising from it in relation to her giving birth. Her respondent, a woman also, and single, challenged her position, making a plea that she theologize out of humanness rather than out of her feminism. But the respondent may not have considered that we have yet to know what the full human experience is, and may not know until many more women can get in touch with and affirm our own experiences. We are not yet to the point of saying that to be women all women must have such and such experiences. How infinitely deeper it would have been had the respondent affirmed the birth experience as valid for the speaker, then validated her own experience as a single woman by lifting up things that she knows and experiences which married women and mothers do not and cannot know. *Deep in the experience itself is the source of the new imaging.*

Hearing to Speech

It was in a small group of women who had come together to tell our own stories that I first received a totally new understanding of hearing and speaking. I remember well how one woman started, hesitating and awkward, trying to put the pieces of her life together. Finally she said: "I hurt. . .I hurt all over." She touched herself in various places as if feeling for the hurt before she added, "but. . .I don't know where to begin to cry." She talked on and on. Her story took on fantastic coherence. When she reached a point of most excruciating pain no one moved. No one interrupted. Finally she finished. After a silence, she looked from one woman to another. "You heard me. You heard me all the way." Her eyes narrowed. She looked directly at each woman in turn and then said slowly: "I have a strange feeling you heard me before I started. You heard me to my own story." I filed this experience away as something unique. But it happened again and again in other such small groups of women. It happened to me. Then, I knew I had been experiencing something I had never experienced before. A complete reversal of the going logic in which someone speaks precisely so that more accurate hearing may take place. This woman was saying, and I had experienced, a depth hearing that takes place before the speaking—a hearing that is far more than acute listening. A hearing engaged in by the whole body that evokes speech—a new speech—a new creation. The woman *had* been heard to her own speech.

While I experienced this kind of hearing through women, I am convinced it is one of those essential dimensions of the full human experience long programmed out of our culture and our religious tradition. In time I came to understand the wider implication of this reversal as revolutionary and profoundly theological. Hearing of this sort is equivalent to empowerment.[6] We empower one another by hearing the other to speech. We empower the disinherited, the outsider, as we are able to hear them name in their own way their own oppression and suffering. In turn, we are empowered as we can put ourselves in a position to be heard by the disinherited (in this case other women) to speaking our own feeling of being caught and trapped. Hearing in this sense can break through political and social structures and image a new system. A great ear at the heart of the universe—at the heart of our common life—hearing human beings to speech—to our own speech.

Since this kind of hearing first came to me, I have tried to analyze the process, but it resists analysis and explanation. It traffics in another and different logic. It appears to belong in woman experience, and I have found it in some poetry and some Eastern religions. The Pentecost story reverses the going logic and puts hearing before speaking as the work of the spirit.

There is no doubt that when a group of women hear another woman to speech, a presence is experienced in the new speech. One woman described the "going down" as nonspeaking—or speaking that is a lie. Even though she used the common vernacular she said she used it in the clichéd manner of her conditioning. It was the language of the patriarchal culture—alien to her own nature. "Coming up," she explained, "I had no words. I paused. I stuttered. I could find no word in the English language that could express my emotion. But I had to speak.[7] Old words came out with a different meaning. I *felt*

words I could not express, but I was on the way to speaking—
or the speaking was speaking me. I know that sounds weird."

While all liberation movements may be expected to rise
with a new language on their lips, I have been particularly
conscious of the new woman speech. Perhaps because it por-
tends such vast changes of both a personal and political
nature. It is as if the patriarchal structures had been called
into question and the powerful old maleness in deity had been
superseded by the new reality coming audible in woman
speech.

The phenomenon of women speaking runs counter to
those theologians who claim that God is sometimes silent,
hidden, or withdrawn *(deus absconditus)*, and that we must
wait patiently until "He" deigns to speak again. A more realistic alternative to such despair, or "dark night of the soul,"
would see God as the hearing one—hearing us to our own
responsible word. That kind of hearing would be prior to the
theologians' own words. It might even negate and ruffle their
words[8] and render them unable to speak until new words
emerge. Women know hearing to speech as powerfully spiritual, and know spirit as movement and presence hearing us
until we know and own the words and the images as our own
words and our own images that have come out of the depth of
our struggle.

Isolating the Images

When we want to begin with the image out of which we live
most of the time, we are not aware of what that image is or
how to isolate it. We may find it at the end of a diffused pain,
difficult to follow to its source. It comes clearer in telling
one's story or in keeping a journal. This is not like the early
consciousness-raising sessions in which women took turns
telling their stories. A woman must be granted all the time she
needs when it appears that her story is being told for the first
time. Depth hearing dares not interrupt but deepens when the

telling halts or the pain becomes intense. Hearing walks alongside the teller all the way down to her most excruciating agony. At such a point one suburban woman cried out, "I'm a sex object. I have been one all my life. I *am* one, now! Oh-o!"

Once the image is isolated a woman may savor its fit; ponder its power, the grip it has on her life; trace it to its source. Stay with it until it breaks from the inside and she touches her real self—that part of the self that the image has bound. The stereotyped image keeps us imprisoned. It is a false image to be shattered from within—false because it was assigned. The woman who discovered she was a sex object discovered also that when she dealt with it the image shattered and another more positive image emerged to take its place. The new image enabled her to affirm her sexuality—far more pervasive than she had thought—as a spiritual gift.

Women have tried to get at the image through drawing the self, then dealing with what the drawing indicates about our self-image. Often in such an exercise a woman may draw a much younger self than she really is. When this happens it may mean that there are experiences and living that she inadvertently has evaded, perhaps that she is not willing to take responsibility for. After I had turned gray, I found myself continuing for a year or so to put "black" on questionnaires asking for color of hair.

When working with children in the Deep South Robert Coles[9] used the method of drawing the self. He discovered little black children often drawing themselves with some sort of physical handicap when, as a matter of fact, they were not physically handicapped at all. Societal structures and cultural images had functioned so powerfully that the children had developed handicapped self-images long before they had come to the age of conceptualization. One child drew himself as a small and insignificant figure until he went to visit his grandfather who owned a farm in another state and who cultivated his own fields. The boy he drew on his return covered the entire page and was colored very black. His only comment: "When I draw God, He'll be a *great big man*."

An image is not just a picture in the mind's eye but a dynamic through which one communicates publicly or which communicates oneself. An image *is* its functioning—whether it operates consciously or deep in the unconscious; whether it operates in an individual or in the body politic.

There is such an experience as hearing oneself to expression, that is, getting in touch with deeply hidden or dominant images that may be unique with women. The following stories of women suggest the process by which each pursued an image within herself and brought it to authentic expression.

Judy Chicago

In her book, *Through the Flower*,[10] Judy Chicago describes graphically her struggle as a serious woman artist and her search for authentic feminine images. Judy did not make clear, nor is it the point of this essay to distinguish between images which may arise in women because we have been subordinated and images which may be innate in women because of physical and psychological make-up. When stereotyped images are shattered and we can make objective studies, we may discover differences between men and women vaster than we now imagine, or just the opposite. At any rate, Judy's image searching led her deep into her own experiences. She anticipated images rising within her powerful enough and stimulating enough to supply the substance of her work. She, like many women, struggled with a form consistent with her content. In the art world largely controlled by male standards, women appeared to have little or no place.[11] Judy knew she was a good artist. She knew and wanted to be accepted. She took the great risk of setting aside her own experience to meet the established standards. When she achieved recognition, she turned again to her own experience and began her work anew. Her first task was to get in touch with the images surging within her. How could she isolate them—even one? She chose part of her own body—an exploited denigrated part—the cunt. Starting with all sorts of representational drawings, she moved into deeper rhythmical levels with fantastic designs radiating out, yet drawing as magic within the core center. Playing with color, light, and vibrations in these designs, at some point along the way she broke through the literalism, shattered the stereotyped image that had been imposed upon her, and moved into a cosmic level. What daring and courage to so expose herself, as Arlene Raven put it,

> ...outside of—and without the support of—a social, economic, and cultural base. She had not participated in the mainstream of culture, and the culture does not operate from her perspectives. Her contribution has neither spoken to nor been understood by that system, and the content of her art has been bypassed by interpretations which could not reveal it.[12]

In Ruth Iskin's interview[13] with her, Judy described her art as an effort

> ...to formulate, namely, the spiritual rejuvenation of life. I think my work is metaphysical. People did not understand that; they thought I was interested in the image of the cunt simply as a sexual image, but I was interested in it as a metaphysical image, as a way of dealing with the entire relationship of the feminine to Western Civilization.

As early as 1970, Judy Chicago and Miriam Schapiro developed out of their own experiences a theory they called "central imagery," in the formal organization of which a woman's body was often a metaphor. Such imaginative experimentation, they believed, could blossom only in a feminist context and feminist environment. Their efforts led to the establishment of Womanhouse which is no longer in operation, but the Women's Building on Spring Street in Los Angeles creates an environment where women control the structures and program.

Overt female imagery has set off a wave of interest and concern in the art world with iconography made by women. One view insists that the physiological structure of a woman gives rise to unique feminine images. The opposite view, insisting with Coleridge that all great art is androgynous, presses the doubt of visual vocabulary unique to women. Still others insist that the images rising in women and the process of getting in touch with them and working them into some art form, whether innate or conditioned, are there at this point in woman history and are unique. Philosopher and critic Lucy Lippard writes: "I am convinced that there are aspects of art by women which are inaccessible to men and that these aspects arise from the fact that women's political, biological and social experience in this society is different from that of a man."[14]

Judy adds another dimension:

In my work I introduce not only women but feminine values as sacred. I believe that much of the alienation of human life comes from being out of contact with those values. For me, feminism is not only a political movement, it is a spiritual quest and a philosophical alternative...I see the issue of central core imagery as affirming self by making an image that grows out of one's body structure. The natural outgrowth would be building civilization from that impulse...People don't see the universalizing of the image of female genitalia in my work, because their perceptions and projections come out of the same sexist indoctrination that causes them to perceive a woman as merely a cunt.[15]

Something profound is being said here by Judy that has a powerful spiritual dimension. The spirit domesticated by phallic power in a sexist culture tends to obscure for the majority the spiritual aspect of the woman experience. To close one's eyes and insist upon hopping into human liberation without first recovering the feminist imagery does not make the evil of the fractured perceiving go away. Women, like Judy, have been seeking in the last decade to recover those images that have been programmed out of the male culture in general and assigned to women as denigrated, and to uncover new images in the new experience of women that yet remain to be expressed—yet to be made visible. Radical and committed women are, therefore, no longer willing to look at their work and themselves in relation to men's work and men's standards. We are committed to examine our work and ourselves in relation to other women and in relation to the uniqueness that is ourselves. Once committed to this vocation we have discovered all sorts of new images flowing out of the first image.

Emily Culpepper

By a similar process, Emily Culpepper* concentrated on menstruation. It, too, as a common experience of women, was denigrated, perhaps because of fear of female power or because women possessed the mysterious capacity to bear a child, which became symbolic of other powers of creativity. In papers and published articles Emily followed her study through taboos, myths, laws, customs, rituals in many cultures and many religions until it culminated in a film, *Period Piece*. The color red, in flowers, the heart, sacrifice, etc., was projected on the screen with interpretive singing and conversation. Finally, red dropped from Emily's own vagina. A climax of the short film, for me, was the spontaneous remark of Robin, an ethics professor, caught on the tape when the blood first began to drop: "Deep, dark, red, rich blood drop." Later he added, "Oh, this isn't superficial blood." A Harvard professor viewing the film gasped: "Emily, it's a jewel." Another viewer declared it had no substance. But this viewer

---

*A newly appointed faculty member at Harvard Divinity School.

had failed to see *Period Piece* as the pure celebration Emily intended—that which comes and which can come only after one has shattered the stereotype, passed beyond and through the taboo to the affirmation that what *was* is now ourselves. *Period Piece* leads to the door of the mystery of the universe itself—a taboo transformed into a new image of woman power and woman sensitivity, woman generosity and creativity, through hard research but more through Emily's own courage and imagination.

Adrienne Rich

Perhaps no clearer story of a woman going to the core of her own self-image is available than Adrienne Rich's *Of Woman Born*.[16] The author takes us through her pain of separating her genuine experiences of motherhood, which she affirms as good, from the image of motherhood as institution, which has falsified the image of woman and made her a political thing, an instrument through which patriarchy has perpetuated itself and accumulated wealth. It is unbelievable that most of the negative reviews of her book were by women who did not see, perhaps could not see, what the author was saying.

Images are a form of language, in this case English, which Otto Jesperson, one of the greatest students of language, has declared "the most masculine of languages, positively and expressly masculine...It is the language of a grown-up man and has little childish or feminine about it."[17] Since language is our greatest conditioner in which, as Adrienne says, "lie powerful secrets of culture," she was forced to struggle throughout with the English language itself in order to savor her own experiences of motherhood and communicate the self-image to the public without the institutional chaff along with it. But she could not find in the English language words to express many of the powerful emotions she had experienced. Twenty years ago, before the second feminist wave crested, Helen Lynd[18] had already pointed out how many significant human emotions had been dismissed as meaning-less—resulting not only in an impoverishment of language but an impoverishment of "the very concept of man [sic]." Linear meaning for the intellectual elements is amply com-municable, she added, but the nonlinear has inadequate or no language for expression. Unawareness of this poverty of lan-guage, along with lack of understanding the extent to which language shapes our perceptions, limits our ability to be objective, as was shown in the reviews.

A review of the negative reviews of Adrienne Rich's book written by Julia Stanley* carries the title, "The Rhetoric of Denial: Delusion, Distortion, and Deception."[19] The article vibrates with insights into language as well as Adrienne's intent and method of writing. She explains the way Adrienne resorts to quotation marks as a counterpolitical move to emphasize the vision and the possibility of a kind of freedom we cannot yet articulate because of the limits of our language. But even more—the quotation marks expose the way forms and standards are implanted in the consciousness so that we will not presume freedom—she quotes Andrea Dworkin who puts it even more strongly—

> ...so that freedom will appear—in all its particu-lars—impossible and unworkable, so that we will not know what telling the truth is, so that we will spend our time, and our holy human energy telling the necessary lies.[20]

When Adrienne struggled to isolate a new image of mother-hood shorn of the false images surrounding it, the very people she wanted most to communicate with could not hear. Frozen in the patriarchal language, they could not grasp the deepest feminine experience. Once the image is isolated, affirmed and revered, words will come. Words may evoke images, but the image creates the words—not the other way around.

---

* Now Julia Penelope.

Mary Daly

As powerful and intent in her form of feminine imaging as Adrienne Rich and Judy Chicago is Mary Daly.[21] Her book on meta-ethics, *Gyn/Ecology*, serves to disturb the going logic as she twists words and phrases into new/old meanings—forcing them to yield what they had long ago forgotten or what they are just now taking on in the new nonpatriarchal, free space. At the Women's Building in Los Angeles, she stunned, delighted, and shocked her audience by the brilliant way she summoned words into the service of women seeking to become our own exorcists—exorcising the fathers from ourselves. She called us to overcome the "numbing, ghostly gases at work to paralyze us, to trap us, so that we will be unable to move further." Each time we succeed, she assures us, in overcoming their numbing effect, dormant senses come alive. Inner eyes open. Inner ears become unlocked with each gateway we move through. The movement itself inward/outward is Being. It is spinning cosmic tapestries. She urged us into the spinning process that requires seeking out the sources of the ghostly gases "that have seeped into the deep chambers of our minds." The deceptive perceptions that separate us from reality were/are implanted through language—the pervasive language of myth, conveyed overtly and subliminally through religion, "great art," literature, the dogmas of professionalism, the media, grammar. "Indeed, deception is embedded in the very texture of the words we use."

She then defined the word *spinster*, a commonly used synonym for the deprecating term, *old maid*. One simple definition given, she said, had receded into the Background to the extent that we have to spin deeply in order to retrieve it: "a woman whose occupation is to spin." She sees no reason to limit the meaning of this incredibly rich and cosmic verb. For a woman whose occupation is to spin participates in the whirling movement of creation.

> She who has chosen her Self, who defines her Self, by choice, neither in relation to children nor to men,

who Self-identified, is a Spinster, a whirling dervish, spinning in a new time/space.

Spinster is merely one of the many images Mary resurrected from its deadened, chaotic past, redeemed from a doomed present, and freed it to usher us into the new time/space. She described this kind of journeying of women breaking through the maze of deception and falling into free space, as both exorcism and ecstasy. Literally, before us she spun her way into the Background and beyond the father's Foreground with words that led to the images that created them and the images restored the words to the time they were not yet caught in the grammar trap of our current thinking and habit.

More on Imaging

Feminist book stores and feminist restaurants project new images in their titles; *New Words*, in Cambridge, Mass. reflects the new woman speech; *Page One*, in Pasadena, implies beginning again; *Joie de Vivre*, a restaurant in Madison, N.J., *Mother Courage*, in New York City; and *Amazon Sweet Shop*, in San Diego.

Women's journals and women's centers committed to creating a new women culture and a new woman consciousness spring up like mushrooms. A few of the many are: *Chrysalis*,[22] out of Los Angeles; *Quest*, of Washington, D.C., seeking to define feminist theory and political strategy; *Signs*, published by the University of Chicago Press, carries excellent research by women; *Sinister Wisdom*, a fine literary magazine, presupposes the lesbian in all women; and *Woman-Spirit*, of Wolf Creek, Oregon, on woman spirituality. Many feminist newsletters and journals have sprung up out of religious communities.

Other legitimate imagings come through taking dreams as well as fantasies seriously. Working on dreams (which Jung says are images in their totality), and pursuing the image in fantasies, will provide enough content for women to be able to go back into history, literature, and religion to recover images long bypassed, hidden in texts, myths, and legends—suppressed but never entirely snuffed out.

Once we isolate the images and consider them deeply, we shall be better able to recognize the difference between those ancient goddesses and archetypes which have risen out of the experiences of women and prepatriarchal culture and those constructs of goddesses and feminine stereotypes which have been male defined—reflecting women as men would like to see them and have them. Jung's archetype of the feminine actually pointed beyond the stereotype, but his patriarchal background and patriarchal language never made the distinction clear enough to save doctrinaire Jungians from falling into the trap of confusing the two. Through imaging women can better equip ourselves to reclaim from the writings of our foremothers those images and authentic models which fit our experiences as opposed to those which meet the going standards in the service of male culture.

Virginia Woolf closes the last chapter of her brief volume, *A Room of One's Own*, with a fantasy—a call to all women to bring to life those women of the past who have never been able to express themselves in their own culture.

> I told you...that Shakespeare had a sister...She died young—alas, she never wrote a word...Now my belief is that this poet who never wrote a word and was buried at the crossroads still lives. She lives in you and in me, and in many other women...she lives; for great poets do not die; they are continuing presences; they need only the opportunity to walk among us in the flesh. This opportunity, as I think, is now coming within your power to give her. For my belief is that if we live another century or so—I am talking of the common life which is the real life and not of the little separate lives which we live as individuals—and have five hundred a year each of us and rooms of our own; if

we have the habit of freedom and the courage to write
exactly what we think; if we escape a little from the
common sitting room and see human beings...in
relation to reality;...if we face the fact, for it is a fact,
that there is no arm to cling to, but that we go alone
and that our relation is to the world of reality and not
only to the world of men and women, then the opportunity will come and the dead poet who was Shakespeare's sister will put on the body which she has so
often laid down. Drawing her life from the lives of the
unknown who were her forerunners, as her brother
did before her, she will be born. As for her coming
without that preparation, without that effort on our
part, without that determination that when she is
born again she shall find it possible to live and write
her poetry, that we cannot expect, for that would be
impossible. But I maintain that she would come if we
worked for her, and that so to work, even in poverty
and obscurity, is worth while.[23]

Analysis of Given Symbols, Pursuit of Given Images[24]

Through her fantasy on Shakespeare's sister, Virginia Woolf
envisioned the imaging of women accelerating generation
after generation until patriarchy itself is threatened.

Patriarchy has been defined as a system whose political
structures and institutions are dominated by the Fathers.
Patriarchy—a culture whose language and religion have been
shaped by the dominant rulers—the Fathers. Patriarchy—a
nation or nations built by power of the Fathers until the ruling
deity has appropriated the image of this dominant sex.[25]

"When a system is on the verge of crumbling," wrote Brita
and Krister Stendahl[26] in the *Boston Globe* when reviewing
Mary Daly's *Beyond God the Father*, "it is always the images of
deity that first come tumbling down." Not since the death-of-
God movement some years ago has the white male God been

called to reckoning as today. But neither the death-of-God theology nor black theology reached the radical depth that has characterized the rising woman consciousness. For neither theology left the circles of male theologians.

Rebellion against the idolatry of whiteness and maleness gathers momentum among the most ordinary women and some men. The surging spiritual move among women who never were in organized religion, those who have made an exodus from it, and those struggling within its confines seeks to recover a dimension lost when spirit was domesticated and women were subordinated. Sweeping efforts to recover the Goddess have merged with calling into question the most fundamental traditional religious symbols—symbols that have filtered out of the patriarchal symbol system and mind-set.

The word *God* may be said to be the chief traditional symbol. The symbol carries its own "mystery of its power." It is kept alive by language, ritual, and political structures (all rising out of patriarchy). In turn the symbol supports the language, ritual, political structures, and institutions of the nation and world at large.

When the word *Father* is added to the word symbol *God* to make *God the Father*, *God* ceases to be a general symbol and becomes a symbolic image that functions more actively and more specifically and more directly than does the general symbol *God* when used alone. As image, it can no longer be analyzed. It can only be pursued and observed in its functioning. *God the Father* (read male) is a live symbolic image in the sense that the living of the people (read male-dominated) shapes the image and fills it with content. In turn, the image shapes the life-styles of people, coercing them to conform (consciously or unconsciously) to its own gender. At this point the image becomes irrevocably sexist, reflecting a sexist people or vice versa. Male dominance is thus strengthened both within and outside organized religion. Note how the nuclear family structures derive from the way the maleness of God functions to brook no other authority than that of the

Father. (See William Blake's illustrations of Job in which Job sits among his family in like manner and in like pose as God—an exact replica of God in his heaven above with his holy angels.) The symbolic image, *God as Father,* has served to legitimate male dominance as desired and innate to the human situation. In its partiality it can no longer function on behalf of justice except paternalistically. It has defined women out of male perspectives and created institutions in which we have no power. Its projected images of women conform to male desires and provide the model for keeping minorities powerless. It has created a kind of biased scholarship so that discriminating alternative institutions, and more political and economic equitability are in the final analysis tolerated only long enough to be co-opted. *God the Father* functions now, not for change, not for liberation, but to support that which already is. Its character has become synonymous with the character of the culture that provides the rhetoric for its audible expression.

How would *God the Father* function when evoked in times of crisis? "He's got the whole world in his hands." Trust no other. Lean on Him, He will take care of you. Surrender and you will be saved. One thing He asks, be totally obedient to Him. Give thanks daily for the gifts He bestows upon you. *God the Father* has lost its power because it has become synonymous with a patriarchal culture, in which men demand like response from women.

It is not my purpose to argue that God has a maternal side or that the nature of God is both male and female. That is beside my point. To argue such, I am convinced, serves to keep women shortsighted and the Goddess suppressed. My primary concern here is to deal with the image—not as theologians interpret its alleged intent but by following the image and observing the way it functions in public. Images have shaped the consciousness of people so that their response is literalism on one hand, or dualistic thinking on the other. Dualism demanded by patriarchy separates the image evoked from the theologizing and intellectual interpretation of it. In either case, the power of the image is ignored. Images have the power to shape styles of life, values, self-images, ecclesiastical and political structures, in the same manner that subliminal images have caused black children to feel inferior and white children superior long before they reached the age of conceptualization. Conceptual thinking and imaging are of a different genre due to the kind of dualism we have inherited. Concepts can be corrected and changed, not so images. They must be shattered or exorcised. They have a life of their own and often function subliminally in the individual or the body politic.

Since the feminine image as perceived by women is contrary to the character of society, it appears powerful enough to elicit strong response—demanding specific choice—to remain with the old logic or risk the new. In that sense *God the Mother* or *Goddess* cannot be so easily analyzed or characterized as symbol but functions as metaphoric image. Each tends to produce shock, for neither is harmonious with the culture. On the other hand, *God the Father* remains a symbolic image in that it is taken for granted and assumed—no change or movement required, as is consistent with the going culture.

Now, call on *God the Mother* or the *Goddess.* What happens? For women she appears. She says your life is the sacred gift. Pick it up. Receive it. Create it. Be responsible for it. I ask nothing in return. It is enough that you stand on your own feet and speak your own word. Celebrate the new Creation that is you. Move in the new space—free. The response from women who have become aware is an overwhelming sense of acceptance and belonging and identity. At least the society at large and the religious community appear awkward and uncomfortable. At most, women respond with resistance, ridicule, anger, tolerance, or indifference. *God the Mother* requires from women no transfer from the male experience to the female experience, as when evoking *God the Father.* No paternalizing. No demand for payment. Women sense a "forever dependence" asked from *God the Father.* But only independence and resourcefulness from the *Goddess.*

God the Mother or the *Goddess* tends to be transparent, to make herself dispensable in such a way that in time we will be compelled to seek a totally different way of speaking of reality.

There may have been a time when *God the Father* functioned as a metaphoric image. If so, that had to be when there were goddesses and women had more freedom to define ourselves and society was not male dominated. But over the years the image has done its work so well that there is now little or no tension remaining between *God the Father* and the prevailing male culture. Those women who seek authentic images for ourselves are putting ourselves outside of patriarchal space and making ourselves no longer subjects for the old conditioning.

Having drawn a comparison between *God the Father* as a symbolic image[27] and *God the Mother* as a metaphoric image on the basis of their respective functioning let us return to analyze the word symbol *God*. The word on its surface appears inclusive. Indeed, we are told by scholars that its earliest form had no sexual identification at all. Hear Old Testament scholar Gerhard von Rad:

> Although Jahweh himself was conceived as man, any thought of sexuality in him, or of his acting in creation by means of sex, was completely alien to Israel ...But for Israel the polarity of the sexes was something belonging to Creation, and not to the deity himself.[28]

But von Rad's language tells us otherwise. Unquestionably the word *God* is a symbol. Throughout patriarchal history the symbol appears weighted in favor of the Fathers. In the hands of the Fathers over the intervening centuries the symbol has been filled with male content and used interchangeably with King, Lord, Master, Shepherd, Prince, Son. Thus it assumed male character. Once the symbol was participated in and analyzed, the feminine imagery became hidden or suppressed in the same way women disappeared from history, politics, and public life in general.[29] As a result, the word *God* itself lost its inclusiveness and its power to change the culture or society. Women are not alone in calling the word *God* a patriarchal symbol, empty of its redemptive power. There has emerged an increasing effort in the theological world to find another way to speak of God.

I do not argue for the use of *God the Mother* or a return to the *Goddess*, except for iconoclastic purposes. It may be the only way to shatter the old male god image and return a patriarchal culture to the *Goddess* along with the restoration and public expression of worthy self-images of women. As I see it these are one and the same movement out of our present bondage. I believe the *Goddess* could ultimately become the same kind of idol the male god has become. But in a sexist culture and sexist religion the option for the *Goddess* may be the only, the only sane, redemptive move. Human liberation and androgyny at this point are illusions until the "coming of woman."

Patriarchy, which supports the continued use of patriarchal symbols, could well be the system predicted by the Stendahls as on the verge of crumbling. It may now be thought of as global. The welfare of the world in the hands of the Fathers may indeed be in jeopardy. Witness the plutonium controversy: "Once into plutonium there is no turning back." Robert Heilbroner presents a gloomy analysis[30] of the human situation and appears to know no other solution—or even be able to consider one—but to call on the old patriarchal god, evoking Prometheus first, then Atlas. His explanation that Atlas is ourselves became an intellectual exercise. These symbols from a long-ago culture hold no power or even hope for today's survival. Many male theologians, far more astute than Heilbroner, appear to be more honest and allow themselves to be vulnerable. We remember how when Bonhoeffer was in prison he predicted that we could never do theology in the same way, if we could do it at all, after the war. Theological professors Thomas Altizer and John Cobb, and many others, are struggling with ways we can speak of God with integrity. What kind of language is usable? How can we get beyond the symbols—the ancient images—back to the reality before the word was named; ahead where the reality moves before the new word comes visible? Some women iconoclastically hammer away at the male imagery in culture and organized religion, or make an effort to put the female image along with the male image in the word *God* to fix up *God* in what appears to be a ludicrous hermaphrodite or a male constructed androgyne. Others are evoking the *Goddess* or *God the Mother*, along with emerging images of women, believing that the only way to shatter the male god (idol) is to regain lost images of ourselves incorporating the new imaging, which women are about today. Once we, out of our own imaging, establish our selfhood and affirm the spiritual, which has been experienced but has not yet been named, men will be forced to deal with the patriarchal. Beyond that point we cannot now see.

1978:

The Goddess as Metaphoric Image

Over a period of ten years—the decade of the 1970s, to be exact—I have been trying in one way or another to exorcise male images from the patriarchal religion I had internalized far more deeply than I had dreamed. During this period I have had many experiences with the Goddess. In this essay, I relate the story of five of these experiences. Some of them were intimate and exposed me at vulnerable points I was not prepared for. I have told the stories to friends, and their reactions still puzzle me. In each case, they seemed not to understand what I meant when I said these were experiences of the Goddess as metaphoric image.

The first reaction came from a self-labeled radical feminist who is deep into the psychic. The story to which she referred was the third—the levitation. "It really happened, didn't it?" she asked. I was completely taken aback and stuttered, "Of course it happened." I could have added that the experience was more real than if it had been literal. If literal it would have been something out there coming in to me, a supernatural event taking place. I could say no more, for her question was entirely beside the point.

The second question pertained to the last experience: "It was a dream, wasn't it? You *had* gone to sleep!" A dream might not be reality and could be easily dismissed; the implication was that if it had not been a dream I might be losing my sanity. Again the question had missed the point.

The third question came from another radical feminist: "Did you have these visions when you worshiped the male God?" This question puzzled me perhaps more than the first two, for it seemed to imply that she saw something "out there" coming in to enlighten me.

The most frequent question comes from my more traditional friends: "The Goddess!!!! Do you believe in the Goddess!!!!" To that there is no answer, of course.

Note: Although this essay was written in 1978, I updated the references when I presented it to a group of graduate women in religion at Claremont in 1983.

★

THE GREAT MOTHER, the Great Goddess, early Greek and Roman myths of gods and goddesses, fascinated me when I was a little girl. I read as many myths and fairy tales as I could find, and often on a bright day my sisters and I searched the moving clouds for pictures of gods and goddesses and for the horses pulling Apollo's chariot across the sky. It is possible such early interest prodded me to take so many Latin courses —every year in high school and four years of college. I had one of the leads in our college play, Euripides' *Alkestes*, played on the Greek-columned portals of Flora Macdonald College in North Carolina. By the time it was presented I had memorized most of the lines of the entire play. I was an avid reader and collector of early Greek plays. My interest persisted well into my adult professional life and led me to Greece and the Greek isles, especially to Crete, to enjoy the "real" land of the gods' activities and expose myself to the setting of the ancient Minoan culture. Not once did I perceive that this part of my history had to do with religion or spirituality even in its broadest sense except to deepen my understanding of culture, archeology, history, and art. It stimulated my appreciation of the earth and the relationship of a people with the soil.

Not until my seminary days did I discover that many of the earliest words for the Judeo-Christian deity derived from Goddess history and that the Goddess had been suppressed or dismembered to make way for the monotheistic God. I became aware of the many references in scripture to God as mother but I was not interested in an androgynous God any more than I am an androgynous person.[2] Nor have I made wishful efforts to depatriarchalize the Old Testament or the New Testament. It is a thoroughly patriarchal document and must be allowed to be what it was in the time it was written, not studied out of context. However, I am still interested in recovering the early history of the goddesses—the prepatriarchal history of a civilization and even a religion. I probed the earlier Goddess stories prior to the Greek and Roman myths.[3]

Now that I am in the woman movement I support efforts to recover women history as far back as we can trace through tablets, documents, and artifacts and to provide an interpretation from a feminist perspective. Many of the artifacts of these periods have been dismissed as fertility figures and pagan idols by male archeologists and historians when from woman perspective they are something else again.

Since there has been much resistance in patriarchal religion to reexamination of ancient symbols, I have moved into women's support groups with their indigenous rituals for the source of my energy. And many of these groups are Goddess groups, though I have attended only one that actually addressed the Goddess as deity. And, of course, I have read the Goddess literature—both the earlier classic works and the ones that have come out of the feminist/Goddess movement.

I have been interested in Jung's interpretation of symbols and myths and deeply impressed with the later works of James Hillman and Naomi Goldenberg, and especially with Edward Whitmont's book, *The Return of the Goddess*,[4] all of which have moved in the direction Jung was pointing. (Jung assumed his archetypes had to do with psychology and did not claim them as religion; however, doctrinaire Jungians give archetypes such religious overtones that they have difficulty distinguishing between the feminine archetype and the feminine stereotype.) My analysis under Dr. Esther Harding directed me into the woman movement in the first place and her books have been helpful.

While I consider myself a Goddess woman, I am not interested in a Goddess as an object of worship. But she is part of my history and I want to claim my history. She is also a part of my present and I am nurtured by her. We are moving toward a time of wholeness and global community, or annihilation. But a global community is not possible until women can come into our own and use what we have for the health and freedom of all human beings. For the first time in world history we recognize that we cannot depend on a great leader. Any one of us is too prone to error to be trusted with the present instruments of destruction. For the first time in history it appears possible for structures of justice to emerge from the common people—the masses; but this cannot happen until patriarchy is called into question by the common people and it begins to topple. That is why I speak of *feminism* exclusively; of *woman* liberation; of a *feminist* perspective of the world and its people. To speak of or to work overtly and exclusively toward human liberation at this crucial point in history is to take us all off the hook and continue in the old boys' club. (Examine the theology of those crying for human liberation.) Nor am I interested in working toward getting more women in the inflexible patriarchal structures without allowing the structures to be reshaped to deal with what women have to contribute.

And here is where the Goddess comes in. The resistance to changing the male God language would indicate (even in the face of violent denial) that *the male God is meant.* Patriarchal religions are not about to give up the symbols carrying this maleness, because these symbols are related to nostalgically rather than redemptively. "Redemption" means radical change. Nostalgia keeps things as they are.

Behold what has happened in black theology. The word *God* has been filled with white imagery, controlled by whites, to the extent that the laws, the educational systems, the cultural advantages, the social arrangements, have balanced in favor of whites of the land, and so long as the adjective *white* was silent, though inviolate, the blacks cooperated unconsciously with the system. Indeed, many of the old spirituals reflect a white supremacy understood as ultimate: only another world or existence could yield anything different.

Note with what prophetic insight the black theologians came out with black theology, black God. Action began to take place once this was broadcast. Blacks challenged the unspoken whiteness in the old God and exposed it as idolatry.

What if the blacks had proposed a black/white God, or a black/white theology! The metaphor would have been removed, and the phrase would have restored to the word *God* its former conceptual "reasonableness" and become weak and insipid. In the same way I see male/female God language as an attempt to appease both sides while leaving untouched the image of the male God.

To introduce Goddess/God, God/ess, mother/father God, or even Mother alone, reckons the holy in sexist terms, and removes the possibility or even the inclination for change. It gives the false impression of having arrived when it merely supports the status quo because it has not touched the image out of which daily living takes place.

But to substitute Goddess, an exclusively female image, and one classed as pagan, in the place of God immediately confronts the maleness in God, which produces a shock, a shattering, and opens the way for exorcising the old image. Those who respond (as some of my most sexist friends respond) with "But I don't think of God as male!" are immediately putting the issue in the wrong place—on the level of reason rather than on the level of alive imagery.

I should remind us that at this point I am not speaking theologically. I am merely exposing the power of images. Therefore the question: What is evoked in you by goddess? Is it dismissal? Fear? Anger? Discomfort? Then we do have some unfinished business to take care of.

In the following section I will examine metaphor itself and how it functions. I will then relate five experiences I have had of the Goddess. She appeared to serve me as a metaphoric image to change my life.

I shall close with more about metaphor.

Metaphor

When one speaks of metaphor one actually refers to a metaphoric process that may appear immediately as a drop of a penny, a sudden kindling of the imagination to a new horizon, a new insight. Metaphor begins with the concrete and demands total presence to it.

Metaphor is not a static word or a frozen image. An image cannot become metaphoric until it is on its way—like a meteor. Where it explodes, or how soon, when it burns out, how long or how far it journeys, are unknowns. That is why metaphor can never be subsumed under analogy. In an analogy there are two knowns; in metaphor, only one—the concreteness of its beginning, with the degree you can be present to this literal, factual beginning. Where the metaphor ends, how long it takes to get there, whether you stay by to its finished action, whether your imagination is such it can follow the process and participate in the surprise, the new reality, is another matter. The final metaphoric action is always a surprise, for the new reality it ushers in is like a revelation. James Joyce once called it epiphany because a metaphor reveals itself as in a burst, a celebration, and draws the participant in as celebrant.

The journey of a metaphor includes two activities. The first may be called the shattering (of an inadequate or phony image out of which one lives) or the exorcism (of what one knows one has outgrown) or the blotting out (of the image with which one comports oneself). The second is the ushering in of the new reality: the transcending to a totally new horizon or perspective that the old horizon kept hidden so long.

Within a brief span of time I was confronted by three graduate students with the same question: How long in time is the journey of a metaphor? I had always thought the two actions or prongs of a metaphor were the same and came at the same time. "Could loneliness," asked Linda, "be an awful abyss that occurs after the shattering and before the new reality appears?" The little work I have done on loneliness has convinced me that it is a patriarchal construct—with quick remedies to keep us in shape. It may be that some of these remedies are more of the same syndrome that made us lonely in the first place. "What about an awful bereftness?" asked Sue when we spoke of the metaphoric process; "can so much shattering take place that the very ground is pulled from under one?" Michelle asked, "Could Susanne Langer's formative function of language be a drawn-out metaphor?" These three questions made me realize that metaphor is a rich, unexplored field for women seeking liberation.

Current writers on metaphor have not disproved or corrected Goethe's comparison of symbolic image with metaphoric image. Symbolic image is a figure of speech that can be analyzed, that is, to the degree that it is a known or experienced aspect of reality. Thus it can be participated in. Tillich added that to participate in symbol is to participate in reality itself. But symbol can never *fully* reveal or *disclose* reality. Esther Harding once pointed out how symbol rises in a community to enable it to function as one body and not as a group of individuals. But, she added, when the community is dispersed and passed into history, the symbol becomes a historical, not a living, entity. As a community changes, the symbolic image, to remain alive and function actively, must ever be re-examined and allowed to reshape itself.

Not so with metaphoric image, said Goethe; it can be pursued and observed only in its functinng. James Dickey would have us remember that "for it to live, something from within you must come to it and meet it and complete it." Modern language philosophers and philologists agree by adding that metaphor cannot be defined. It can only be actively followed on its journey and perceived in its functioning. Therefore, I repeat, metaphor is not metaphor unless it is *on the way*; metaphor is not metaphor until it is perceived as metaphor, until the metaphoric movement draws on the creative imagination of the perceiver. Metaphoric action may become ecstatic and enlightening, disclosing wholly new dimensions of human powers and energies. But it should not be termed *psychic*, a revelation from "out there" as from another world. James Joyce sought to describe a community metaphoric action as an epiphany arising from within the community itself. As the energies and vibrations become unleashed in ritualistic movement, he said it is almost as if the participating individuals are swept off their feet.

Once metaphor is understood as process, one can readily see how its action is never repeated in exactly the same way for all participating, nor indeed for the same person twice. The external context from which all enter the metaphoric process may be the same. For example, a child peeps through a door into a room where her mother is serving tea to a guest; the child, wide-eyed, announces that "a big bear is coming through the door to eat you up." The two women see the same child physically and hear the child's voice and words. They agree perhaps exactly on the concrete visual and audible action. But the perceiving of what is there or what is going on may be totally different depending on the degree each woman allows her imagination to be tapped and allows herself to be drawn into a new logic. The mother, embarrassed at the interruption, closes off the child, intent on serving her guest tea. The guest, however, sets down her teacup and hides behind a chair.

The guest has allowed the mundane tea world to be shattered by a whole new reality that has made its appearance. She is able to enter the new logic—the new world of the child, which now has become her world also. She is renewed and her horizons have been pushed beyond where they were when the child entered. She has become totally present to the concreteness of the child and thus has been able to follow the movement into the new world the child offers her. In gratitude the child rushes in and throws her arms around the visitor.

This brief story suggests the process of the metaphor, if not its timing or spacing. It suggests a two-part journey—first, an iconoclastic movement that shatters the tea world; second, a revelatory one that discloses the glorious imaginative world of the child. Both are possibilities depending on the particitative imagination of the perceiver and the degree to which she is able to be fully present to the concreteness of the situation before her. The child (without her intent or knowledge) becomes the carrier of the metaphoric process—but the real metaphoric action takes place in a woman drawn into a new world and a new logic and allowing her presence to the concreteness of the situation to lead her on.

When I speak of the Goddess as metaphoric image I am in no way referring to an entity "out there" who appears miraculously as a fairy godmother and turns the pumpkin into a carriage. I am not even referring to a Goddess "back there" as if I participate in resurrecting an ancient religion. In the sense that I am woman I see the Goddess in myself, but I need something tangible, a concrete image or a concrete event, to capture my full attention to the present and draw me into the metaphoric process. In the same way that the world of the tea-party was shattered by the appearance of the bear (child), the Goddess injects herself into my experience.

The context in which I experienced the Goddess the first time grew out of a kind of unconscious awareness that, even though conceptually I no longer accepted a God "out there" nor defined a "God within" as male, on the level of imagery the maleness was still alive and functioning in me on most unexpected occasions.

The Goddess Appears

In 1972 at Grailville[5] the second national conference on women exploring theology was held. One morning its sixty-five or so women delegates gathered for worship sitting informally in semicircular fashion on the floor of the oratory. The atmosphere of conditioned meditation—soft lighting, high altar up front, much space—was bypassed by the women perhaps intuitively, perhaps by overt intent of the leaders. A space indicated by cushions on the floor set aside was marked off as sacred. A screen hid the phallic symbol up front. A bouquet of wildflowers on the low table in front of the screen added to the informality. The women faced one another.

Most of us did not understand at the beginning what was taking place. I was aware early, however, that something new and different was happening to me—something far more than the caring I experienced in the presence of an all-woman community. The climax came near the end when the leader said: "Now, SHE is a new creation." It was not something I heard with my ears, or something I reasoned, or something I was being told. Everything seemed to coalesce and I felt hit in the pit of my stomach. It was as if the leader had said, "You are now coming into your full humanity. That which has been programmed out is authentically yours—essentially you." It was as if intimate, infinite, and transcending power had enfolded me, as if great wings[6] had spread themselves around the seated women and gathered us into a oneness. There were no ifs or buts. I was not hearing a masculine word from a male priest, a male rabbi, or a male minister. I was sensing something direct and powerful—not filtered by the necessity to transfer or translate from male experience and mentality into a female experience and then apply to myself. The words used in the service were exclusively female words.

Suddenly I came to, my hand on my stomach, my mouth open. I was almost sure I had said aloud, "Oh!" I wondered if I had made a fool of myself! When I looked about me, it seemed many other women were responding as I had. The leader paused. Then one of the women lifted her fist into the air and shouted "Yeah! Yeah!" All the women followed as the oratory rang with "Yeah! YEAH! YEAH!"

That is the first time I *experienced* a female deity. I had conceptualized one before, but I had not experienced one directly. It was also the first time I realized how deeply I had internalized the maleness of the patriarchal god and that in so doing I had evoked cosmic support of male rulership of the earth and had reneged on my own woman identity. Not until that moment did I realize that women had no cosmic advocate in any of the five major patriarchal religions of the world. I knew that I had much unfinished business, which I have been working on now for ten years.

My second experience of the Goddess occurred in 1976. I had already moved to a retirement community in California.[7] In August, en route to Dublin to address the World Federation of Methodist Women, I had stopped at Grailville as resource leader to the Seminary Quarter for Women.[8] Soon after my flight to New York had left the Cincinnati airport, the sky turned dark and we were caught in extremely turbulent weather. All my life I had been frightened of heights. I couldn't remember a time when I was at ease in the air—even in smooth skies. I must have had some traumatic experience with heights when a child, since each time I boarded a plane I reverted to a most irrational state, far from the mature faith I considered I now had. Usually I clasped my hands together and called on the powerful male deity in the sky for protection. I must have reverted to the faith I had when the phobia first latched itself in my unconscious; the phobia and the child faith images surfaced simultaneously. I usually asked the God Father to keep the plane safe. I even made promises and confessed my wrongdoing. I always asked safety for others in the plane and for all the planes flying as "He had the whole world in His hands." Once seized by such fear I had to keep up the pleas for safety throughout the journey. Then at the end of the journey, there was always much thanking to do.

In this particular storm en route to New York I decided it was past time to let my mature intelligent self take over. The thought came—what would happen if I invoked the Goddess! How does one call on the Goddess anyway? And which Goddess? I no sooner had such a thought than I leaned back in my seat and closed my eyes. Suddenly, it was as if someone had eased into the vacant seat next to me and placed her hand on my arm. "Relax," she said. "Let go of all your tightness. Feel your weight heavy against the seat and your feet heavy on the floor. The air has waves as does the ocean. You can't see them, but if you let yourself be carried by them you can feel their rhythm—even in turbulence. The pilot has been here before. He knows what he is doing. Even in the worst weather. Ever so faintly...now...can you feel the currents, the ordinary currents of the air? Now breathe, breathe deeply. Ride the waves. Let yourself become a part of the rhythm."

I did as she directed. Fear left my muscles. I did indeed feel the rhythm. Soon, I was enjoying the ride. Then came the question, How does one thank the Goddess? I opened my eyes. The seat was vacant. She had gone. I began to feel such power within, as if she had given me myself. She had called up my own energy. I was unafraid. Nor have I been afraid in a plane since that day. A new thing I recognized immediately: the Goddess works herself out of business. She doesn't hang around to receive thanks. It appears to be thanks enough for her that another woman has come into her own. I did not feel guilty.

I next experienced a bona fide Goddess celebration. I had met Z Budapest at the 1977 Annual Meeting of the American Academy of Religion and had seen her several times since then. I, with three other women from Claremont, visited one of her coven meetings.[9] She called herself a Dianic High Priestess and as such was presiding over the Susan B. Anthony Coven in Santa Monica. Her tiny shop was filled with all sorts of Goddess books, artifacts, statues, and altar equipment. The scent of burning incense welcomed us as did the flickering candles. We spent much time browsing and buying.

When time for the celebration arrived, Z pulled the shades and seated us with her coven members—on the floor in a semicircle. More candles were lighted and she waved incense over us all. As she began to talk I became intrigued with the names of goddesses printed in large square letters around the tip of the four walls. Many I recognized and was curiously stirred by those I did not know. I found myself unable to follow what Z was saying, so I turned to creating my own world. In the service Z invited us to join in the "OM." Having my voice coarsened by medication, I did not sing but closed my eyes and soon was in the rhythm—mesmerized by the sound. Something, however, caught me unexpectedly and was singing me without my knowing when the sound began to vibrate my throat. All at once I felt lifted in the air above the heads of the seated women—on up to the ceiling until my eyes were on a level with the goddesses' names. How close I felt to each in turn as I floated around the room! Suddenly the goddesses began to take form, clothed in garb appropriate to the country and the century to which they belonged. And I...floated in and out among them, at home with them as if I were a goddess myself. Finally, the "OM" softened. The goddesses became their names again. I felt myself lowered gradually to the floor and seated between the two sisters I came with. I squeezed their hands, which I had never let go. They squeezed back as if they had had the same experience. When I opened my eyes and looked into the beautiful faces of the seated women, I cried out to myself, "Why! These women are goddesses and maybe I am also!"

Z began to talk again. I wondered whether she expected any of us to participate and, if so, whether I would or even could share the experience I had just had. Z talked on and on. We thought Z was great. As we left, I pondered the difference between a High Priestess and a male priest. I still had much unfinished business to work through!

I returned to my usual source of energy, spiritual nurture, and support: three small groups of women in my own community and a powerful network of women on the West Coast, the East Coast, scattered over the United States, and extended throughout other countries of the world. We spoke together over long distances (never have our telephone bills been so high!); travel brought many of us together regardless of the cost of fares. My most intimate and powerful group locally, Sister Circle, enabled us to share our joys, pains, angers, and plans and celebrate together with new forms of rituals, songs, and meditations.

It was part of the wider network of woman support that drew me to San Diego to celebrate the opening of the Amazon Sweet Shop in Campus Square on El Cajon Boulevard. It was there I sensed most deeply the spiritual dimension of our network —that woman commitment is related to all facets of life and has metaphysical implications and that the Goddess is indeed ourselves. We had come to love her and to love one another, as Ntozake Shange said, "fiercely."[10]

The story of the Amazon Sweet Shop centers on two women from Boston who left graduate theological school on a wild leap of faith, crossing the entire United States to a city neither had lived in before nor had any ties to. They took jobs. They learned how to make ice cream on a commercial scale, how to operate the equipment for doing so, what the costs for the layout and maintenance are. They started slowly, surveying the community, estimating operating costs for one year, and borrowing money to begin.

When they announced their grand opening for July 1978, balloons and banners waved throughout the square; pure ice cream was served—no artificial flavoring or sweetening, no alcohol. Feminist music set the tone of the day with T-shirts and health, nutritional, lesbian, and feminist information available. Women came from Boston, San Francisco, Berkeley, Oakland, Claremont, and many communities around San Diego. Flowers and Mailgrams came during the day. Temporary booths had been set up in Campus Square, where friends and wellwishers demonstrated the making of art crafts (for sale)—ceramics, metal work, carvings, silk screening, jewelry, leather tooling.

When the doors of the sweet shop opened, in came people of all nationalities, sexes, ages, races—men carrying babies and caring for children, professors, students. Many were casually dressed, many dramatically so, many poorly dressed, and a few elegantly attired. We mixed as if we had something very important in common, which many of us believed we did. We ate ice cream together next to strangers who became unstrange, sat together and talked of a new humanity envisioned by what was taking place between us and within us. I became convinced, all over again: Yes, the Goddess is ourselves and we love her fiercely.

If needing some visible legitimation for what was taking place, we had but to lift our eyes to the parade of goddesses' names printed in large square letters around the top of the four walls. We were struck by names we had not heard before—then came familiar ones, many names of those present and others we knew who could not be present, the mothers and the grandmothers of the proprietors, along with numerous names of foresisters. The only bona fide ancient Goddess listed was Kali, on whom I did much research on my return to Claremont. Often called the dark Kali from India, she created all and all returned to her. Her need for the blood of animals and sometimes of humans was for new creation. It was a comedown later to learn that Kali referred not to the goddess but to the black cat of Emily from Boston—yet it seemed entirely appropriate in light of the chosen list printed.

An hour before midnight the doors were finally closed to the outside world, which in a strange way had come inside and changed the atmosphere of the shop. The close friends who remained, with no hint and no direction, began cleaning, scouring, disinfecting, mopping, washing dishes, and dusting. The usual cleanup at the end of each day's work was done in record time to Meg Christian's singing along with Holly Near and Willie Tyson. Then, toasting the two ambitious Amazons who had reached another milestone on behalf of us all, we concluded that the entire day had been a broad and loud statement of a new global vision for women of the world.

Toasts were made to that future as we entered it together in this extraordinary celebration, standing under the parade of our foresisters, blood mothers, and the network of women living and dead represented by the names on the walls above.

Each year as we return for the annual founding celebration, we become increasingly aware that this purely secular event has taken on profound spiritual overtones.

It was midafternoon some years later. I sat in my living room in a large armchair with my feet on a hassock, facing windows that opened onto the street. I could not throw off a blueness that had nagged me off and on all day. As I relaxed, I decided to give myself to it wholly, go to the root of it, release its energy and learn at least why it had not let go of me. As I began following it down, ready to face most anything to be rid of it, I thought of the Goddess and how she had come to my rescue on the plane, and nurtured me in other situations. As I let go and opened myself to her, in she swept suddenly through the left side of the windows in front of me. As she reached my chair she stepped aside, bowed my mother into the room, then disappeared. My mother floated in on a river of blood. It seemed all the blood in front of her was blood she had shed in her lifetime, and behind her, all the blood I had shed. She came directly to my chair, bent over me, and began speaking: "Nelle, I have made a great mistake with you children. I have allowed you to think—no, I have *taught* you—that menstruation is an illness. You were the oldest and I did learn something from you, but you suffered more than your two sisters. Never did I let you go swimming, play tennis, or hike during your periods. I didn't even let you do dishes, or take your turn with the chores about the house. It seemed the more I cared for you, the more pain your period brought. Huge clots of blood could not be absorbed by any napkin. Often the first day you had to miss school. Many times we had to have a doctor give you a shot, the pain was so intense. He kept promising that having a baby would be your only cure. Not only did you learn from me that menstruation was an illness but also that it was something to be ashamed of.

"I began sensing my mistake when you reached menopause and your doctor suggested that your dread of menopausal distress might be due to internalized negative attitudes toward blood and the body. He then proposed you purchase bath oils, bubble bath soap, bath powders, and luxuriate in your body, revel in its sensuousness. You did and have never to this day had a hot flash. Now I have learned that many of these conditions derived from patriarchal attitudes toward women and the mysterious power women possess. While I had these negative attitudes and passed them on to you girls, you, Nelle, internalized them—so deeply that they are now in your very bone marrow and too deep to be exorcised.

"Remember years ago your doctor prescribed sperm to start a baby. Now another doctor has fed you male hormones for six years. Both referred you to a male for a cure of patriarchal attitudes. Ha! Forget it! And forget all this visualizing of whole red blood cells which you will never have. Remember the hematologist who described your cells as shown under a microscope—'wild and bizarre.' Be thankful for your 'wild and bizarre' blood cells. They are keeping you alive. They are now normal for you."

My depression lifted immediately as I received this beautiful gift from my mother. I jumped from my chair and kissed her on the mouth, which she had never allowed us to do because of a lung disease she feared she might transmit to us. But in that kiss I had all the loving hugs she had ever given me. Then she disappeared.

Immediately on the right side of the window appeared an enormous spider with a gray body and large orange legs. She lifted one leg high above the other as she walked toward me on the darkness. I was not afraid, somehow. As the spider reached me she held out her two front legs on which hung some woven material. All she said was, "Your mother spun this for you." As I took the material the spider dissolved into me, as did the Goddess and then my mother. I opened my eyes. It was dark outside. My entire attitude toward my illness[11] had changed. But I remained puzzled by the spun cloth, which was neither practical nor by my standards particularly beautiful.

The Goddess as Metaphor

In not one of the above incidents was the Goddess actually summoned or invoked. Therefore, her coming, and the way she came in each case, was a surprise. The nearest to contrivance was the visit to Z Budapest's Dianic coven—in a sense we went to the Goddess' abode to meet her. But she greeted us with so many manifestations of herself, many of whom I had read about at length, some strange to me, that I became unexpectedly aware how improper it is to refer only to "the Goddess." By speaking of "the Goddess," I appear to be merely transferring my image of a patriarchal male God "out there" to a matriarchal female Goddess "out there." And that is not what women mean at all when we refer to the Goddess or to a specific goddess. Naming a specific goddess, as Isis, identifies her own history, tradition, and attributes. Naming the gender only, as Goddess, confronts the gender of the patriarchal God, calls into question its partial nature, and affirms the woman experience and our woman-selves as visible, with our own power. It is not surprising that the Goddess in my experiences would appear as a wholly different reality or order of being from the old male God.

My greatest surprise and shock came perhaps in the last experience—the surprise of relating my internalized male attitudes toward women's blood to my present very serious blood difficulty—"too deep to exorcise." I am able now to receive the "bizarre and wild cells" as a special gift. In that sense the Goddess gave me back my life and called me to live fully with what I have, adjusting my activities to what energy I can summon and use creatively. Since then I have resumed my writing. I participate in social and political issues as I am able. It is as if the Goddess restored that part of myself that was wasted with fear from false images in my unconscious.

I began to see more clearly how we act out of images rather than concepts, especially in crisis situations; how the fear of heights automatically summoned up the God-image I had as a child when the phobia first planted itself as image deep in my unconscious. The Goddess caused the old image to surface and shatter so I could experience the flight from a more mature perspective which in many ways was mine already, but unused. I began to see more clearly how the God of patriarchal religions could have been a living metaphor at one time. But over the centuries the word has been filled with such male, power-over, and status quo images it has become a dead metaphor.

The Goddess ushered in a reality that respects the sacredness of my existence, that gives me self-esteem so I can perceive the universe and its people through my woman-self and not depend on the perception conditioned by patriarchal culture and patriarchal religion. I do not have to receive my identity or renew it through another gender, be the representative of that gender a minister, father, boss, professor, colleague, husband, or male lover. As I see the gift of myself aborted by social and political structures I renew my responsibility to the world—to help break the patriarchy that creates discriminations, oppressions, poverty, and wars. These for me have become woman issues and never again "causes." I perceive the world and its people from the perspective of where women have been put as women in the hierarchy.

The Goddess introduced me to a profound sense of community I had never before experienced. The bonding of women—from that small group at Grailville in 1972 to the small ritual, working, and action groups to which I now belong and the celebrating groups and the networks of women across the country and even around the world—continuously energizes and supports me. Beyond these groups, or because of them, rises the vision of what women can be and will become as we receive our full humanity and achieve political power. The vision enlarges to include those women still blinded by the patriarchal fog,[12] and imprisoned in a seemingly unbreakable vise. There is something of the past the vision resurrects (as Virginia Woolf urges us to resurrect Shakespeare's sister). Our research in history, literature, theology, and other fields is beginning to break open the tombs of our foresisters and enable them to walk the earth again, to claim the earth as sacred and for the good, health, and justice of all people.

The Goddess has cleared away much of the theological mystification to which I had subjected myself—which kept me from seeing and enjoying the sheer humanness of another as we came into physical proximity. Human beings did not come from another world nor are we headed for one. Nor did we descend from the sky but out of the womb of our mother, our mother's mother, and our mother's mother's mother. Recognizing our origin, we experience *presence*, as in the Amazon Sweet Shop celebration. The pure secularity of the celebration in the sweet shop was an experience of woman's spirituality. This kind of physical experience that is nourishing and loving and in touch with cosmic energy rises out of our common bonding and vision and our rootedness in the earth. Julia Kristeva[13] pointed out that such an experience is answerable to a logic other than scientific," that it is experience dedicated to the search for "a little more truth" and for power shared and power from within rather than power-over.

Since the Goddess works herself out of the picture, we are better able to come into our full and whole inheritance that would make us one in our bodies, minds, and spirits. We can claim our sexuality as pervasive and as ourselves. We can claim our bodies as ours and as ourselves and our minds as our own and ourselves. This sense of oneness within and with one another has brought us into more erotic relationship with one another as women. For once a woman comes to see beauty in another woman's mind and in her own mind and to love with the mind, she discovers another dimension of power that is self-fulfilling.

The Goddess shattered the image of myself as a dependent person and cleared my brain so I could come into the power that was mine, that was me all along, but that could never have been appropriated until the old limiting image was exorcised or shattered.

The last experience with the Goddess ushering in my mother has proved most profound of all—the gift of my mother herself. Since blood is a powerful symbol of life, I see her blood as saying she has rebirthed me, and my blood as saying I have given birth to my mother. The kiss, still vivid, remains the seal of that blood covenant.

The spider! Surprise again! Who could have imagined a spider in this sequence! Especially one so large (about my size), orange and gray with elegant long legs stepping so lightly on the dark, and one which did not evoke fear!

I have not been able to identify the spider scientifically. The spider that comes closest to her color and shape is a tiny American House Spider—the *Sisyphoides*—a cobweb weaver. But since the Goddess does not allow herself to be limited to patriarchal time or space, the myth of the spider should be much more fruitful than the scientific identification or study of it.

Several tribes of the early American Indians, especially the Hopi, reverenced the Spider Woman as Creator of the earth and all underneath the earth. Making her home underneath the earth, she was known as the Earth Mother, "as old as time...as young as eternity." She was said to croon, "I receive Light and nourish Life. I am the Mother of all that shall ever come." Yet the Spider Woman resided in the Underground.[14]

The Mexicans saw the spider in a great hole in the west where the sun went down and perceived her as an archetypal womb sucking into death all who have ever been born. The Aztecs called her the "place of the Women" from which all humankind once crawled. The spider as this womb represented life and "time before time...before the birth of the sun."[15]

As Goddess of life and death the spider was also the Great Mother, a spinner of destiny. The new child is the fabric of her body or, to turn that about, the fabric of her body is the new child.[16]

Finally, the Spider Goddess appears as a "journey or a way, always as walked or danced archetype," as labyrinth or spiral.

Relating myth to my experience, I see that the spider's prominent legs "walking on the darkness" affirm my journey; the spun cloth—fabric of my mother's body—affirms my own new birth. Yet the cloth being not usable in patriarchal time and space, and the Goddess not limited to time or space, the cloth could have a double meaning—death as well as birth. Since I possess no tangible evidence of the cloth, it must have disappeared in me along with the Goddess, my mother, and the spider. So *I am the new child.*

The afternoon's journey brought the relationship with my mother into sharp consciousness. "The true mystery," declared Erich Neumann, "through which the primordial situation is restored on a new plane is this: the daughter becomes identical with the mother [and she is] transformed in every respect. This unity...is the central content of the Eleusinian mysteries."[17]

The triple appearance of the Goddess—as herself, as my mother, as the spider—and ME! Blessed thrice!

> Anger and tenderness: my selves.
> And now I can believe they breathe in me
> as angels, not polarities.
> Anger and tenderness: the spider's genius
> to spin and weave in the same action
> from her own body, anywhere—
> even from a broken web.
>
> —Adrienne Rich[18]

The appearance of the Goddess in the present wave of the woman movement looms as an important phenomenon and promises to become more so as the people of the world turn to our own inner power and integrity. Its importance will increase with more serious archeological and historical research and interpretation by women. As responsible women take the Goddess seriously there will be less dismissing by male archeologists of Goddess artifacts as mere "fertility figures" or temple prostitutes, and more relating of them to the whole of creation in both a spiritual and physical sense.

The Goddess has been the means of recovering a history of ancient peoples in which many women-centered cultures revealed ability, leadership, and inventive skills. The women in these cultures are being rediscovered as healers with ceremonial connectedness to the earth and cosmos.

The Goddess has begun to expose the artificiality in the elaborate hierarchical system of a male-oriented deity.

But perhaps the most important function of the Goddess is the transformation of women ourselves. Adrienne Rich hints of it in *Of Woman Born* as she describes the possible power of early Goddess images:

> These images...express an attitude toward the female charged with awareness of her intrinsic importance, her depth of meaning, her existence at the very center of what is necessary and sacred. She is beautiful in ways we have almost forgotten, or which have been defined as ugliness. Her body possesses mass, interior depth, rest, and balance...She is...without age. She is for herself even when suckling an infant, even when, like the image of the Ephesian Diana, she appears as a cone of many breasts. Sometimes she is fanged wielding a club, sometimes she is girded by serpents, but even in her most benign aspect the ancient Goddess is not beckoning to her worshippers. She exists, not to cajole or reassure man, but to assert herself...imagine what sense of herself it gave a woman to be in the presence of such images...If they did nothing else for her, they must have validated her spiritually (as our contemporary images do not), giving her back aspects of herself neither insipid nor

trivial, investing her with a sense of participation in essential mysteries. No Pieta could do this, not even the elegant queen of the Amarnan divine family of Egypt....The images of the prepatriarchal goddess did one thing. They told women that power, awesomeness and centrality were theirs by nature, not by privilege.[19]

The reappearance of the Goddess at this time in history takes on profound metaphorical significance and global proportions. Women are no longer minus a cosmic advocate, rooted in creation itself, to provide legitimation for and to affirm our experiences.

Unfinished Business

Philologists and language philosophers tell us that the meaning of metaphor cannot be determined nor its content fixed, since it has no content. In this sense metaphor is unique. It must be set apart from simile, analogy, allegory, and other figures of speech which have two knowns,[20] one to be compared with the other. In metaphor there is only one known— the concreteness from which the movement takes off. The context out of which the movement emerges depends first on our being present to it. The movement that is the metaphoric process, including its end surprise, can only be followed and observed, and that depends on intuition, imagination, and open flexibility in which there is involvement and participation on the part of the "pursuer or observer."

The action of metaphor, then, cuts two ways: 1. iconoclastic and 2. revelatory. Metaphor begins its movement by exposing the nerve of daily existence (the false gods, the narrow horizons, the mundaneness), causing it to surface, then shattering it in order to create space for the new. Metaphoric movement ends by introducing a new logic—by ushering in a new reality and greater vision.[21]

This process may be observed in the stories related in which the Goddess serves as the metaphoric word. In each case the exclusive maleness and authoritarianism of the old God of patriarchal religion was confronted, called into question as inadequate and even destructive for women. The new reality that appeared to me in each case pushed back my horizons to unanticipated visions and new sources of energy and new ways of comporting myself.

While metaphor rarely functions in the same way for two people and just as rarely functions the same way twice for the same person it appears to me that metaphoric language is a natural for women...

...since metaphor begins with ordinary everydayness and women have been assigned menial tangible work.

...since women have been assigned the flesh often denigrated. New efforts have been made in the feminist movement to reclaim the body as ourselves and as good.[22]

...since mind and spirit have been assigned to men, women are now in process of reclaiming our minds as ourselves and redefining and re-experiencing spirit on another level. In so doing we have reclaimed imagination and creativity as inseparable from intuition and inseparable from reason.

...since most women have intimate and frequent contact with children, and children's speech is spontaneously metaphorical and playful.

...since for sheer survival women have been forced into another direction from the hierarchical scale of values. We have gone inside and down into the deepest labyrinth of ourselves and social and political issues. We have begun to find ourselves emerging with a new speech on our lips.

In *Anatomy of Feminism* Robin Morgan wrote of "feminism [as] that vision which enlarges the incipience of all other visions.[23] And well it might be, since sex is the deepest cleavage in the human experience, excluding no one in all the world and offering unexplored metaphoric avenues for corrections, connectedness, enrichment to women and men, children and aged, of all races, classes, and nations, the earth and cosmos.

It is mainly through metaphor that language expands and is enriched; that new words emerge; that social, personal, and political changes are forged. However, as new words come into common usage many of them become filled with status quo images and their meanings often become fixed and static, in the same way that myths lose their power when they become literal. Owen Barfield calls such words dead metaphors.[24] As a word loses its power to evoke change, no longer can it evoke imagination; thus it becomes fit only to communicate from one mind to another without changing either.

The word *God* may at one time have been metaphor, but in common usage over centuries, along with many other religious symbols, it has lost its redemptive power. Since it has been identified with power-over, male rulership, and male control, it has been separated from the reality it first ushered in. The entire culture and political structures are extensions of this dead metaphor. Barfield points out that "progress involving change comes about only when we question (and because we question) our fundamental assumptions."[25] The idolatry arises in the worship and devotion of the word symbol rather than the reality behind it—the reality for which it once stood. In time the Goddess may become a dead metaphor if she is set "out there" and literalized. Indeed when the Black God ceases to become iconoclastic in confronting the White maleness in the patriarchal god, becomes literalized and exclusive, it, too, will lose its power and become a dead metaphor.

While Barfield himself dismisses as nonsense the theory that all language originated as metaphor, Antonin Artaud, considered by Julia Kristeva as one of the two greatest authorities on language, did believe that the earliest speech of "primitive" peoples was metaphorical and that the further back their origin is traced the more metaphorical the words become. Artaud even said the earliest sounds of humans coming to consciousness (like the first cry of a baby) were not for communicative purposes but to cry out to the cosmos a state of change, aliveness, and affirmation. The sound marked a new state (or perhaps the beginning) of consciousness.[26] Several generations later Rubem Alves[27] made a similar statement regarding all liberation movements—they rise with a new language on their lips. This is consistent with a statement made by Helen Lynd[28] long before the current cresting of the woman movement: that we are having emotional and imaginative experiences today the patriarchal language has no words to describe.

Women are experiencing today in the area of spirituality that which the patriarchal language has no words to describe. This might be called the metaphorical interlude, referring to that time after experience has shattered the old logic and before the word can name that which is beginning to take place. The interlude itself may be a frustrating and even lonely time until the fuller reality makes its appearance. But the right naming of the metaphor calls into being far more than what the women experience. Women become aware that the word in embryonic state has been there shaping them.

If the origin of language in metaphor has any validity historically, it may offer insight into the methodology of Mary Daly in *Gyn/Ecology*[29] as she seeks to follow words to their sources. True, she uses patriarchal tools, but she traces them through the smog of patriarchy nearer to their source, and the further back she goes, the more powerful the words appear. Note what she has done with *hag, spinster,* and *crone.* The closer they approach their metaphoric origin, the more powerful they become and the more their journey from there until now reflects the history of language itself as well as the history of culture. Daly used a similar method in *Beyond God the Father* as she made the patriarchal word symbols turn back on themselves, on their own history, to expose the way they have been used to control and dominate.

It is possible that the history of language offers even greater hope for women and other liberation movements. For this we turn to Owen Barfield again and his little-considered theory of the origin and history of language.

In a series of lectures at Brandeis University in 1965[30] Barfield created no little stir when he called into question the way findings from one discipline have been allowed authority in another. Perhaps the most common conflict between disciplines may be seen in science and religion when the findings of one are applied to the other without first going down through their separate symbol systems to discover their commonalities and their differences. He points out how this sloppy methodology shows up in the way we have applied findings that supported the Darwinian theory of the evolution of species to an entirely different field—the origin and history of language.[31] There is no reason to doubt, he asserts, that plant life, animal life, and human life developed in that order. The evolutionary theory applied to matter has become undeniable. To assume, however, as has been the case, that the world therefore began with nonconsciousness and to apply that assumption to language (another discipline) leads to the conclusion that language emerged from a primitive state into today's highly sophisticated symbolization system.

But suppose, as Barfield proposes, that language has been subjected to reduction rather than expansion; that first sounds and all new sounds emerged with great surprise and boundless possibilities; that new words arose out of presence, connectedness, new realities, riding in on community sensibility, intuition, imagination; that at the heart of nature moves a great pervasive wisdom. Barfield proposes that the history of language and the history of thought corroborate this theory, and he claims it to be in the grand tradition of Goethe, Coleridge, Woolf, Steiner, Artaud, and others.

With use and control of words reductionism set in until words evoked certain images and tended to signify only one thing or only one content. Thus filled with status quo images the content of many words became exact, completely understandable and usable, so that they tended to move away from metaphorical action and to become what may now be called dead metaphor—good only for communication. But since language is expressive as well as communicative and is constantly in ferment, we look to radical social change, questioning basic assumptions and frozen symbols, new forms of technology, poetry and other creative arts, to push horizons out, usher in new realities, and create new metaphors. We begin to understand how new naming for the new experiences women are having is necessary for our further liberation.

Barfield asserts that history as we know it was preceded by prehistory and that prehistory was the period of developing language. But, as he says, we cannot stop with prehistory but must continue back to a primeval period or to nature herself. Then, he adds "we find ourselves with a nature very different from the nature assumed by the evolutionists...once one has got over the shock, this nature turns out to be *more*, not less, like the nature we actually see, hear, smell, and generally experience around us."[32]

It appears obvious that women have much unfinished business. Wisdom is feminist and suggests an existence earlier than Word.[33] The writings of women today, based on new perceptions of solid research as well as on fanciful projections, suggest that we have reached the periphery of our known knowledge but are already on the journey of knowing by another route; and it is on that route we are compelled to be in touch with that pervasive wisdom hearing us to new metaphors.

1979 and into the 1980s:

Unfinished Business

Originally this essay was one of three plenary addresses
on "Doing Theology in the World in Which We Live,"
delivered at a national conference in Montreat,
North Carolina, Summer 1979. My address was from a
feminist perspective. The other two were given by a
black theologian and a Third World theologian,
each from his own perspective. Later I adapted mine
for a group of feminist graduate students in Claremont,
California. By that time I saw that Montreat had
become a paradigm of my life journey as well as a
paradigm of each job I have held since then. By that
time, also, I was nearly overwhelmed by the vast
unfinished business opening for women—a business
demanding a new way of thinking and a way of knowing
that have been programmed out of a patriarchal, hierarchical culture.

The second essay in this volume indicates how
woman's story became central in the rising woman consciousness. It became inseparably connected and clearly one with historical, social, political, and religious
structures. Our stories began to make clear the origin of
our oppression. They broke through a dualistic perceiving
so that our very personal story did not have a political
side and then a personal side. In its deep dynamic it *was*
political, thus was born the phrase, "The personal is
political. The political is personal." Structures of injustice
could no longer be conceived solely as "out there" in

institutions. They were seen at the same time within the very structures of our psyches and senses.

Recovering the authentic image out of which women live meant exorcism of the false images. False images could now be seen as one with as well as created by the structures of institutions. Kept alive by the very language we speak. A vicious circle!

Our major institutions place the responsibility of the country on the most powerful, the wealthy, the one with most credentials, the star, the leader. But in a nuclear world no one person can be trusted to save us all. The button is there to be punched. Where is the one who could be trusted to punch it at the right time—assuming there might be a right time? Any human being on earth would be corrupted by the acceptance of so much power. Therefore, the new perception must conceive a structure that is not based on power-over but power shared. It appears to me that there are sprouts of a new order trying to emerge from the common people of the earth. Witness the nuclear freeze and "Green Politics"—up from down under—in which the most ordinary person is politicized.

As I write this introduction the 1984 Olympics are in full swing in Los Angeles. In spite of its politics and manipulation from above, what comes through is the powerful emotion, energy, discipline, and commitment of the most common people of all nations participating. They appear to be saying what the nations are not yet perceiving—that the time for global community is past due.

And so in 1979, the invitation to speak in Montreat, the summer conference center of the Presbyterian Church, U.S., became crucial to the collection of and the publication of these essays and to seeing my life as a journey with much unfinished business, but a journey in which the "traveling" itself is home.

I have never loved work more than I did in the Presbyterian Church, U.S.—for it pulled up out of me, in the formative years of my theology, some of the deepest passions I have ever experienced for justice, and peace, and freedom for all people. And yet, not more than any other work, and not as much as some, it aborted through its unexamined structures, images and language, the very meaning of freedom and liberation.

I am convinced that to see violence and injustice clearly demands a passionate, forgiving, and committed love. It demands a new way of perceiving and a new way of hearing, which women are already beginning to experiment with boldly. It demands a new way and a new reason for researching woman history to release the full power of a suppressed past and to open up and bring to expression the vision of a good and sane human existence for the future.

★

MY LONG PAST and shorter future appear to me to be a personal/political/spiritual pilgrimage. I can see now how in my most unaware moments I was being shaped for realities that made their appearance often many years later. Oppressive aspects in time have proved unexpected sources of insight and energy.

I make no apology for a certain kind of theological flavor to my language. After spending more than four decades in professional religious work I could hardly emerge with a totally new speech on my lips. Yet during my nine years of retirement I believe I have been heard to a new speech.[1] Even though I may use many of the old symbols, they have taken on new and often radically divergent meaning. I am now in search of new positive images faithful to woman experience; a new way of writing that transcends the old dualism. In this process I can be grateful for a kind of theological thinking in the past that led me to rebel into a new woman space—not separated from the concreteness of our daily living, yet transcending[2] into global/cosmic dimensions. Doing feminist theology, as experienced by myself and other women, is both a process and a communal enterprise.

My chief concern has been to deal ruthlessly with ways I myself have internalized patriarchal images and to recognize the degree to which all of us are living in a patriarchal culture that makes women invisible and legitimates the status quo by the image of a male God. While pondering how religion has shored up patriarchy, I happened on Anne Wilson Schaef's small volume *Women's Reality*.[3] She confirms my contention of the necessity of all feminists (whether they are religious or not) to be theologically aware, lest we miss the more radical aspects of feminist theory and action.

Patriarchal religious symbols have shaped and pervaded our political, educational, economic, social, and international systems with such violence toward women as to call for iconoclastic action before the woman vision can become a reality.[4] How do we respond to the overtly authoritarian and autocratic theology out of which President Reagan now speaks, out of which the new political climate is being shaped, which the secretary of the interior used to legitimate the exploitation of the sacred earth for private gain? Theological mystification has blinded us to the fact that the world constructed by patriarchy is *not* the real world. In arguing for women's history Gerda Lerner points out: "Everything that explains the world has in fact explained a world that does not exist, a world in which men are at the center of the human enterprise and women are at the margin helping them. Such a world does not exist—never has."[5]

I invite you to engage with me in a process that seeks to view the world and its people from a woman perspective—I will share enough of my life story so that the forces within and without that have determined the path of my life may be glimpsed. I hope, to some degree at least, my story will evoke your story. When you find that happening, you will engage yourself consciously in your own story.

In order to enter the process, three common illusions need to be cleared away: first, only the religious expert can do theology; second, theological images are handed down from above or from the past and do not grow out of human experience; and third, the personal can be separated from the political.

Three Illusions

> The mind hath its own snares. What sins of the mind
> Trouble thee now?"
>
> —Dorothy Sayers

Everyone, even the least of us, lives and speaks out of some kind of theological context that either supports the patriarchal symbols and structures in our society or seeks to expose them and exorcise them so that we can go about our business of creating and naming a new world of justice, freedom, and peace. In my first association with families of severly mentally retarded children, prior to and during my few years of teaching their children, I was amazed at the theological implication of their questions: "What have we done that this should happen to us?" "Do you do everything you can to help Jerry get well, or will a child with Down's syndrome never have a chance? How unfair!" They did not have to be addressed to a deity to give them a theological dimension. As Anne Wilson Schaef[6] points out, whether we commit ourselves consciously to the theologizing process or whether we lambast and walk away from the institutions that perpetuate patriarchy, we live in this false world pervaded by a closed system. Even a small child on the street who couldn't care less about a transcendent being will say any time, "Of course God is a man. He has a beard, hasn't he?" And the male child, as the man, and the male-identified woman unconsciously identify with the male rulership of the world. Unless exorcised, these images latch themselves deep in the individual and community psyches, form a life of their own, and at most unexpected moments rise to action, regardless of our correct thinking. Concepts can be expanded, corrected, or revised. Not images.

They can only be rid of in some cataclysmic action like shock, shattering, or exorcism.[7] Of course, there are good images as well as destructive images, but any image that becomes fixed, that is, not lifted into the consciousness and owned, is idolatrous. It rules us and denies our humanness.

All ultimate values whether male, female, black, Third World, white, or whatever, grow out of human experience. When we do not recognize the part experience plays, we develop a tendency to see our view as the only one. Often whole traditions are like this. Some men can hear this from other men when they have difficulty hearing it from women. Robert McAfee Brown has admitted: "All theologies emerge out of a certain set of experiences or out of a particularized historical context; there is no way in which a historical faith could be expressed other than through cultural norms and patterns in which it is located; and it may take others to show us how conditioned, parochial, or ideologically captive our own theology is."[8]

Thus it is customary to label women's theological work as "feminist theology" while maintaining the mainstream theological work as "theology," instead of the more accurate "male theology"; or to dismiss the rising new spirituality among women as vaporous, shallow nature worship, while maintaining the traditional nomenclature as the true spiritual in spite of its domestication and control.[9] It is not wrong to be partial. The wrongness comes when the partial parades as the whole. Theological awareness requires an overt effort to be conscious of a pluralistic universe and the specific context in which we work.

The third illusion has been partially explained by the second. The personal cannot be separated from the political nor the political from the personal. We have had a running controversy for years on which is more important, the personal or the social, or which comes first, theory or practice. Then along comes feminist theology to tell us that they cannot be separated—that the political is not *out there;* that all theologizing, philosophizing, and politicizing take place within the context of a social and political situation that both conditions the way we act and think and in turn, is affected by our thinking and acting. No longer can we separate theory and practice or their corollaries action and reflection. In a feminist perspective both are fused into a new kind of dynamic. It will be surprising to many to learn that the phrase "the personal is political and the political is personal" became currently popular from a lesbian-produced document on the woman-identified woman. Perhaps its use was an effort to strike down the erroneous concept that the lesbian life-style was deterministic, when as a matter of fact countless women have chosen it as a powerful political protest against a pervasive homophobia as well as a way of entering into a loving relationship.

Those who claim to be apolitical are merely withdrawing their energy from effecting change, while at the same time giving silent support to the status quo. Justo Gonzales, at a Hispanic Ecumenical Theological Conference[10] accused U.S. Americans of doing theology without being aware "that since the fourth century there has been an alliance between the church and political power." In Hispanic countries, he claimed, a sociological and economic bind constantly reminded them where they came from. "It's a theology," he said, "being done from below. And every single Christian doctrine looks different when viewed from that perspective."[11] In the United States, he insisted, the theologians buy into the dominant system to avoid conflict. Their appearance of choosing not to be political he sees as overt action and partially responsible for the way injustice and poverty are built into our system. Today, Gonzales would only have to point to the Moral Majority to illustrate the degree to which unexamined religious symbols give impetus to widespread capitalism unmindful of the poor, the needy, and those without legal recourse. Feminists would call Gonzales himself on dualism. While most feminists are supportive of the economic analysis of the Latin American liberationists, we are appalled at the way they then invoke the old patriarchal religious symbols and images, which confuse and separate the political from the personal, and resort to a hierarchical form of direction.

Symbols and images out of our past tradition and history must be seriously examined so that we may let go that which is crippling us and reaffirm and reinterpret what has been liberating. I quote Audre Lorde when she warns against using the tools of patriarchy to examine the fruits of that same patriarchy: "It means the most narrow perimeters of change are possible and allowable."[12]

A Personal/Political/Spiritual Pilgrimage

> Flow backward to your sources, sacred rivers
> and let the world's great order be reversed...
> Story shall now turn my condition into a fair one.
> —Euripides, *Medea*

> For we know when a nation goes down and never
>   comes back,
> when society or civilization perishes, one condition
> may always be found. They forgot where they came
>   from.
> They lost sight of what brought them along.
> —Carl Sandburg, *Remembrance Rock*

Since the stirring of early memories was stimulated by the invitation to lecture in Montreat, North Carolina, the official conference center of the Presbyterian Church, U.S., and since I had been a member of the administrative staff of the Board of Education of that denomination from 1937 to 1944, I include some details of that generative event.

The moment the invitation arrived deep memories began to stir within me—some almost primordial memories—that long ago I thought I had put to rest. But there they were and try as I might I could not fight them off to begin working on my address. Finally, I was forced to give in and hear the voices.

They spoke in a most unexpected manner. I dreamed I was already in Montreat beginning to lead a seminar. Women began filling the room, standing and sitting on the floor. Somehow in the background, unseen but a powerful presence as if in a large grandstand, were men observing. Many of the women, I felt, has been resistant to me at one time. Today, they were anything but hostile. I could not use material I had prepared. So I suggested that we share with one another what had happened to us in the years of our absence from one another. It became a dynamic session, difficult to end. When I started to say goodbye all of them rose to go with me. "But you can't," I insisted, "I am going far away." "Oh, but we can," they replied in unison, "for we are a part of you. Today you have owned us. Together we will go where none of us has ever been before."

What could I do after such a dream? I began at the beginning —with my family. And this is what came to me.

I am from a profoundly religious family—not pious but religious in the best sense of the word. I am sure this had much to do with my early experience of the church and why I chose the church as the institution through which to express my vocation. I have always been a Presbyterian. I am also a Southerner. I am sure I had and still have many of the prejudices that white Southerners are supposed to have and which I have found also in other parts of the country. However, both my mother and father were able to entertain hard questions about our culture, politics, and religion. We were active in community and political life, and church. While I have lived in the North most of my working years, I have never lost my parochial loyalty for the South. I am an Appalachian. That means I am a mountaineer in a literal sense of the word. My father was a bookkeeper and manager of a commissary in a logging camp on top of Holston Mountain, East Tennessee, where I was born in one of the company cabins. I spent my early years in Sullivan County on a farm which had been in our family, we thought then, since the beginning of time. Now we quote from *Historical Sites in Sullivan County* that our place, "one of the earliest, was . . . homesteaded from the Indians."[13] The implication of that in today's world gives those of us who are left great pause.

We were an independent and frugal people. Because of my Biblical rootage and my Appalachian speech I learned early to think metaphorically and to recognize the power of images. This is affecting much of what I am doing today on women, language, and theology. "The mountain's a-roaring," a farmer might have stopped any day to say. It forebode not only bad weather but a disastrous happening in the community. "Wind in the valleys" told us of an approaching death. "Rock," "pilgrim," "tree planted by the waters," "sowing seed," "winding river," "milk and honey" were of course Biblical but became part of our everyday speech. The mountains, the winding river, the fields of corn and wheat, the people I knew as a child, will never be out of my memory. The games I and my two sisters played, from creating moving pictures in the clouds to creating whole villages out of morning glories turned upside-down, stimulated our imaginations in ways nothing in today's culture could. We knew the joy of taking off winter union suits every spring and going barefooted. We were fortunate enough to have a grandfather live with us and at intervals several cousins, as well as an occasional stranger so that we experienced something of generations and extended family life instead of the narrow nuclear family. We lived near a cemetery. The whole countryside stopped working when a tolling bell sent out news that a neighbor had died. Many times we sat up all night at wakes and in our earliest years we were lifted up at funeral services to view the "remains," so that we were never shielded from the reality or the finality of death.

My high school years and later were spent in the newly developing city of industry, Kingsport, also in Sullivan County. Kingsport was designated as a model city, having been planned from the beginning to bring industries that would develop the raw resources in the area. One of the raw resources I soon found was drawn from the surrounding hills—the people of the mountains. Managers and owners of new industries were brought to our school and introduced as helping to save the mountaineers by giving them a good place to live and good wages for the first time in their lives. They came to our Sunday school and we began to wonder if economic development was an aspect of religion, and labor organizing unnecessary or a work of the devil. I might always have believed them had I not taught for three years in Kingsport schools and had occasion to visit many of the homes of these mountaineers who had moved because of "good pay and decent housing." It wasn't a pretty picture. Even then, I was aware how my own mother had to work impossible hours in order to keep boarders that we might make ends meet, and scrub windows week after week to keep the cement plant dust from etching the glass permanently. She contracted a chronic bronchial disease that took her life. A piece of research prepared for a citizen's forum on occupational and environmental health placed Kingsport's death rate from cancer, heart diseases, and stroke far above the state and the national averages.[14] My brother-in-law, who died from a brain tumor a few years ago, and a dear first cousin, who died by heart attack, were both employed for years in a prominent Kingsport industry reported in the research document. Images of poverty, unhealthy workspace, and unequal pay stored themselves away in my unconscious—images that did not surface until years later. And it was many years after that before I was able to comprehend and articulate what I had seen and heard and experienced.

As I have already hinted, accepting the Montreat invitation was near trauma. At first I wasn't even sure I wanted to visit there again. Yet, I wanted to go back desperately. I loved Montreat and my work with the Presbyterians. Montreat represented the heart of my early church work. Those had been the days when the consciousness of the South was beginning to stir and expose the vast chasm that existed between white and black people. Many questions had to do with including black young people in Montreat conferences. Until then it was all white except for speakers. No schools were integrated. Train and bus travel was segregated. Even integrated travel in private cars often was dangerous. Finally black young people were allowed in Montreat if they secured jobs of menial labor that provided housing space in shacks on the side of the hill. (This was in the 1930s and early '40s.) They could attend workshop sessions if work permitted. Many questions were raised about the living conditions of the black council members. In the light of what was said in our materials about faith, it was hard for the young people and youth leaders to understand the restrictions.

It was also hard for the church administrators and those who controlled Montreat to hear and understand the questions that were being raised by white and black students and young people—and even harder to deal with them. I remember the first time the black young people were to attend a customary banquet held during a youth assembly. The right was suddenly taken away, and if I remember correctly, all young people then refused to attend. I remember when one of the black young women drowned herself in Lake Susan, prominently located in the middle of the conference center. Her good friend and former president of the black youth council told me she became confused by the overt discrimination she had experienced in Montreat and could take it no longer. The tragedy of her death was compounded by the fact that the incident was never dealt with, but hushed up and attributed to other causes. Some of us tried to get action with no result. Two of us later went back to Montreat. We walked around the lake, then went into the water. We vowed together that, so far as we were concerned, this young woman's death would not have been in vain. We would probe its meaning all our days and would seek to express it in our lives and our work as long as we lived. I never went into Lake Susan again.[15]

I also remember stories that were told repeatedly of the poor working conditions and low pay of the mountaineers who had constructed the buildings in Montreat, yet could not afford the admission required in the early days to enter the grounds.

I am convinced now as I look back forty years that the student and youth questions were often labeled as a "cause" or "riding an issue" in order not to take seriously what was going on in the world and thus dismiss them with a guiltless conscience. From what I know now such issues pinpoint the place where the young people stood on the edge of the times, where a new reality was trembling to break into the human experience—making visible the transcending nature of faith.

For many years I had been a member of the Women's International League for Peace and Freedom and of the Fellowship of Reconciliation. However, peace activities during the years immediately preceding World War II became very unpopular. Pressure was placed on the administrative staff of the Presbyterian Church, U.S., to purchase war bonds, for instance. Since my commitment made it impossible for me to cooperate, I contributed an equal percentage of my salary directly to peace organizations. When draft registration became compulsory, the church did not stand by the young people who sought alternative service. Finally, there remained only three Southern Presbyterians of draft age who persisted as conscientious objectors and chose alternative service. I stayed in constant touch with these three men and continue to be close to one of them.

From the educational branch of the Presbyterian Church my work took me as executive secretary of the Fellowship of Southern Churchmen—a band of committed leaders across the South pioneering in racial and economic justice. Often at physical and social risk its members sought to interpret and act out the social and political dimensions of faith. One of my most vivid and frightening memories was at a work camp we had set up in eastern North Carolina to help build a credit union building with citizens who were losing their small farms to loan sharks. Everything went well until a day or so before the camp was to close. The members of a camp we had helped set up in Virginia decided to visit us. They came in an open truck entering the small town singing and waving banners. Like us, they too were interracial. News went out over the countryside like wildfire, "They're bringing reinforcements!" By dusk the camp heard the rumor that a mob of four hundred local citizens, including police and sheriff, had gathered. Lights were turned out and the entire camp membership spent the night in deep grasses in nearby fields. White members of the camp experienced for the first time in their lives being in a position in which there was no recourse, no protection, no means of getting in touch with help. They were afraid to go to a single white home to call the Fellowship office, the state patrol, or even the state department of agriculture, which was cooperating with us. They dared not go to a black home lest the family be endangered or their home burned. Yet that experience was formative for the campers— all living members of whom have continued as agents for social and political change.

Failures as well as successes during the days of the Fellowship helped to create a climate for the Civil Rights Movement, as well as to provide the movement with many of its early leaders. Several times I have heard Dr. Benjamin Mays answer a question that was directed to me, "How is it that a nice, white Southerner like you could get so deeply involved in race and economic issues?" "Because she is a woman," came Mays's reply.* I did not know what he meant during those days. Now, I suspect I understand his answer far better than he did.

The "first" sit-in in Greensboro, the one that received such wide publicity, could have happened, I am sure, only because we had an intercollegiate, interracial, ecumenical council in Greensboro, Raleigh, and other university centers—thirteen in all—quietly challenging segregation in churches, public meetings, and eating places, letting people know that desegre-

---

* Dr. Mays died in March 1984.

gation could happen and without fanfare. Part of the genius of the Fellowship was involving local people in such a way that the Fellowship as a movement never sought or claimed credit.

The first Freedom Ride in 1947 to challenge segregation in interstate travel in the South was initially planned by the Fellowship of Reconciliation and the Fellowship of Southern Churchmen. The Fellowship insisted the first ride must take place in the border states; that half the riders be Southern; and that some training be given in nonviolent behavior. The Fellowship of Reconciliation conceded only to our first condition, but even in the border states reaction of taxi drivers at a bus depot was threatening enough to end the ride in North Carolina.

While Charles Jones, a white member of the FSC Executive Board, went to bail out the riders, I found anti-segregationist homes in and around Chapel Hill for the riders to spend the night. Conrad Lynn, a black lawyer from New York, stayed with me on Airport Road. All night long taxis buzzed around my house frightening a white student couple then living with me who took to the woods back of my home. No further harassment followed, but a rock was thrown into Jones's house, because of riders there, necessitating removal of his family for safety.

The riders were apprehended and served time on the road gang and in prison in Raleigh, North Carolina. Bayard Rustin, one of the riders, kept careful and minute notes of the conditions inside the jail and when released appeared at a meeting with us and Dr. Howard Odum, then head of the sociology department at the University of North Carolina, to present a report and make recommendations for prison reform in North Carolina. Dr. Odum himself took the recommendations to the governor. Several years after I had left the Fellowship for other work, I was informed that the state had finally fulfilled all three of the recommendations. Two that I remember included removing prisoners from the road gang, and initiating a rehabilitation program for prisoners.[16] It is a little discouraging at times to read the number of books written in the '60s by people who spent a few months or a year working in the South, describing their work as if there were no history. Three important indigenous pioneer rights movements in the South began in the '30s: The Fellowship of Southern Churchmen, the Southern Conference of Human Welfare (later the Southern Educational Fund), and Highlander Folk School.

I thought during my work in the South that I saw clearly which people were oppressed and which were the oppressors. At that time I thought I was unprejudiced, identifying myself with the blacks, with workers, and with those whites who were in deep pain because of a discriminating system. Not until years later was I able to recognize my own prejudices and myself as an oppressor. And I never saw that until I knew myself as oppressed.

I was well into my second decade of teaching in the Theological School of Drew University when the woman movement crested and its profound theological implication dawned on me. The very foundation of my earth shook. Then the pieces of my life began to come together and make more sense than they had ever made. Feminism was not a new cause to me any more than the race issue and the peace issue had been causes for me and the young people in the South. It merely set me at a new cutting edge to view myself, the universe, and other human beings on this globe in a more radical way, and to raise theological questions I had never dreamed of before. It was out of the radical feminist perspective that I began to see racism, war, poverty, anti-Semitism, class, economics, compulsory heterosexuality, and politics as connected and interconnected for all these are women's issues. I began to see clearly why women had been kept out of decision-making positions—that is, women who refused to be identified by male definitions. The moment we reached a high position and raised the economic, the political, or the war question from a woman perspective—OUT!

It came clear to me that discriminations I had experienced all my life were not because I was incompetent but because I was a woman; that the humiliating putdowns women experienced in seminaries as students, in church as leaders, and in the world at large were conditioned by a patriarchal culture, a patriarchal political system, and a patriarchal religion. I experienced disillusionment in the theological school as I began to realize how many of the male theologians had become comfortable with the present culture and political and economic system. I saw women who were now beginning to enter theological schools in greater numbers as doubly bound. I began to realize the degree to which patriarchal religion, espoused by male theology, was violent to women and destructive of the humanness in us all. Perhaps my greatest disillusionment was when I discovered that I, too, had internalized the same brand of theology and realized that all my life I had been worshipping a male god. Even I, like the men, declared at that time that I was not thinking sexist and that language did not make that much difference.

The internalization of such male imagery prevented me from fighting for myself during my years at Drew University. Without hesitance, I could fight for and support women students but the promises made to me when I joined the faculty were lost in the internecine conflict that developed among the faculty a few years before I retired. At that time I was the only woman faculty member in theological school, which did not ease my situation. I understand that affirmative action has since been introduced in Drew University in order to address across-the-board discrimination against women.

The rising anger among women first coming to this new consciousness was healthy. So much of our early anger was directed toward ourselves because we had bought so long into a political/religious system in which human beings were valued by sex, race, class, and nationality. We blamed ourselves for reneging on our own identity—thus denying the sacred gift of ourselves. In coming to new consciousness women began to experience great personal liberation that enabled us to transcend our feeling of victimization and creatively work through our anger, and begin shaping a new vision for the future. We came to see this process in itself as a new way of shattering the maleness in the old sytsem—a first step toward allowing a new reality to break into the human experience. Early we began to repudiate the image of the white, male god as idolatry. We saw how patriarchy projected a male god to support and maintain a male position of rulership on the earth. Thus, through the woman sensibility we came to see how the exploitation and enforced powerlessness of blacks, workers, the hungry, the poor, the exploited, and the pollution of the holy earth derive from the same root source.

For six years now I have lived in a retirement community in Southern California. I am freed from the pressures of remunerative work. I experience freedom in living in a beautiful and comfortable house and in association with highly intelligent people whom I care for deeply and increasingly. Freedom from an activist life because of ill health allows time for reading, meditation, research, and writing, and—when I am able—lecturing. I am in touch with radical feminists in the immediate area and on both coasts. I participate in a network of women across this country and in several other countries. I do not feel isolated from involvement in the political, religious, and cultural pressures of the world. Indeed, I am convinced there is no place where patriarchy has not left its mark. In that sense, my immediate community could be considered a paradigm of the paternalism (patriarchy) in the nation at large, even to an appeal to a male deity for cosmic legitimation, thus blurring insight into many urgent social and political issues of our time.

I am near the end of my story and my essay and am just now beginning to be grateful for all that has happened to me—not because everything has been good or right or easy, but because everything from my past is now becoming a means of grace. At one time I sought to recover and reaffirm only that which had been healing and redemptive; and slough off that which had been crippling and destructive. Now I gather the whole of me in these pages and discover some of my deepest learnings have emerged out of the pains, the discriminations, and the angers. It is in the whole I see more clearly the feminist vision emerging. Because many of us have lived through these groundbreaking times, we nurture the hope daily that other women, younger women coming along, will not have to retrace our steps but go on and on from here.

The Feminist Vision

> Images of God dictate who will feel worthy in society and who will feel inferior, who will be respected and who will be despised, who will get easy access to the literal material goods of culture and who will have to fight for those same goods.
>
> —Naomi R. Goldenberg
> *Changing of the Gods*

Considerable headway has been made in an effort to eliminate sexist language. I have served on area and national committees to make changes toward this end. But in spite of widespread efforts, it is obvious that something more is needed—something far more drastic than inclusive wording, much of which is still sexist. To reckon deity with Father/Mother God, or with God/ess not only removes the metaphor but becomes purely androgynous. No really basic changes have taken place. The same masculine imagery remains. Sexist words can be seen as but the tip of an enormous iceberg. Sexist wording over a long period in our history has evoked such sexist imagery that in spite of recent publications on inclusiveness these images have established themselves with a life of their own deep in our culture and in our psyches. Here is where Amos Wilder offers hope. In a charming little volume, *Theopoetic*,[17] he points out how many of the symbols and images in our language are no longer creative and healing but actually work to our destruction. We do not readily give them up, he says, because they have a nostalgic hold over us. Unlike concepts, images cannot be corrected or changed at will. They can be changed only by shattering, exorcism, or shock, he says.

Only after I had done an in-depth study of images and their functioning did I come to see the radical meaning of "God is black" and "God is woman" and the inevitability of evoking the Goddess. The very word *God* has been so filled over the centuries with male imagery and, as blacks have pointed out, with white imagery that the word no longer functions metaphorically or redemptively. The whole culture has come to respond automatically and comfortably to the image of a supreme deity as white and male. But deity as black, woman, and Goddess goes against the cultural and religious grain and produces the discomfort, anger, or shock Wilder calls for. Thus these images function metaphorically. It may be that evoking a Goddess of color is important for all of us, especially when we consider that although our society is multiracial and pluralistic, its laws, theology, customs, and social arrangements operate as if under a supreme mandator, who is white, male, autocratic, and all-American.

When I realized that metaphor has a double function—the clearing away of the old logic and ushering in of the new—I experimented with "Mother God" and exclusively female language in liturgy. But soon the Mother got confused with the Virgin Mary, who was always *Theotokos,* the God-bearer, the Mother of God, and never God the Mother. Finally I resorted to Goddess and Goddess energy. I and other women experienced a whole new reality. The male interpretation of the Goddess as pagan did not keep us from evoking the Goddess in whom we did not have to make a transfer from a male experience to a female experience. Indeed, for the first time in our lives it was as if boundless energy and inexhaustible loving had come directly and immediately to us and we were wholly and fully accepted. Our experience was validated and affirmed and we sensed a healing never before dreamed of. In the same way that the Goddess, who of course is female, shatters the maleness in the word/image of God, it would be extremely important for white worshippers to be confronted by a black God in order to shatter the unspoken, exclusive whiteness in the God of the Judeo-Christian tradition.

In time, the Goddess may cease to be metaphorical: that is, when sexism is eliminated from our religion and society, or when (if) religion and society become exclusively feminine. Then evoking her would become sexist and idolatrous; just as when racism is eliminated the black God that now functions powerfully may become racist and idolatrous. It is then we will be forced again to seek a new language and new images to express the new reality—the new humanity. It may take several types of experimentation to show how idolatrous and authoritarian we have unconsciously become, and how far from human.

Resistance on the part of the church, the synagogue, and the public at large to dealing with the full human experience has made it clear that theology as we have known it grew out of white male experience and is bound to the tradition of British and continental scholarship which has been patriarchal to the core. Gayraud Wilmore from Rochester (New York) Divinity School* pointed out:

> In order to...be human—black people invested their blackness with positive theological and psychological values...those values...have served to frustrate every tendency of the white world by confirming and strengthening the black humanity.[18]

When I worked with the Fellowship of Southern Churchmen, I learned how in every small Southern community the blacks knew two languages—the language of the black community and the language of the white community. For survival, blacks had to know the white community and every white person in it who could be counted on. Since becoming deeply involved in the woman movement I see how in the same way women have come to know two languages—the language of the woman world, used for nurturing, and the language of the male world, for survival.[19] Men know only the language of the male world. Logic would tell us then that women of color

---

*Now from New York (City) Theological School.

know four languages—and because of that knowledge may be the key to the final liberation of us all. The white males knowing only one language (their own) are perhaps the loneliest of the four groups of people.

Some profound understandings of human existence have come out of the black community and the woman community. Our existence indeed has to do with Be-ing itself.[20] It is possible to eliminate poverty, colonialism, class, wars, and other overt human injustices. These are obvious human errors within a patriarchal system that judges the value of human beings through manmade standards. The origin of race and sex, on the other hand, is not so easily identified. They have to do more with the order of human existence in such a way that it is infinitely more difficult to determine whether they could be the results of patriarchal requirements or whether they are biologically distinct. For all practical purposes, with our present knowledge, they are givens. But in order to mystify this fact and make them unquestionably distinct, a cosmic legitimation is projected in patriarchal religion, which has named the creator one sex only and that male; and one race only, and that white. Hence race and sex become the most profound political, social, and theological questions of the century.[21] Women do more than raise the question. *We are the question.* Our invisibility shows that the stake is not reform or improvement. The stake is far more revolutionary—the recovery of the spiritual and the survival of humankind.

Let me state this more strongly. As long as men (supported by male-defined women) internalize the cultural images and stay in control of the schools, the religious institutions, the political and economic systems, they are forced to project a male ruler—a ruler in the image of themselves. For they must have cosmic legitimation and enough followers in order to keep power. The same kind of creator who legitimates male rule legitimates a government's interfering in another country such as Chile, killing its ruler and overthrowing its government. Furthermore, it legitimates the way poverty is built into the system. The human rights question in the Reagan administration has been pushed to the back burner or eliminated entirely, and the effect of the U.S. corporations' policies on the poor in this and other countries is glossed over. Perhaps the multinationals have learned only too well from patriarchal religion "your seed shall inherit the earth."

Black theologians from South Africa claim to see a direct connection between their oppression and the images invoked by the language religious leaders have brought them in describing Western religion. I quote from *Black Theology: The African Voice:* "Black theology cannot afford to have any truck with these images which lend religious support to a fascist type authoritarianism...sickening reflections of the white man's power...we need new images which are freeing...images of unity and wholeness, images of humanizing relationships of love and truth and justice and kindness and mercy....[22]

I hear what they are saying. I had my ears unstopped years ago by the baptismal waters of Lake Susan in Montreat.

There is a growing vision among feminists as we are getting in touch with new images, new symbols, new connectednesses, and new arrangements for human interaction. Already these images are emerging in networks of woman culture. They can and must function to heal, redeem, reshape, and bring peace and survival for all. The new vision is beginning to penetrate patriarchy, expose its idolatries and name a new order. Joan Martin says, "This vision is our future." "This vision," added Judy Mintier, "is our present."[23] Perhaps both are right. Our present is our future and our future is now. In the kind of movement and change we are committed to there is no dividing line. I remained silent. I could have added, "The past is present." In living out our vision in the present, we create a new reality for all the past and the future are there.

Now when along the way, I pause nostalgically before a large, closed-to-women door of patriarchal religion with its unexamined symbols, something deep within me rises to cry out: "Keep traveling, Sister! Keep traveling! The road is far from finished."

Appendix
Journal Jottings

Notes

Index

Journal Jottings

M𝚈 ꜰᴀɪᴛʜꜰᴜʟ journal, which has changed form and face many times since the '30s, has carried all sorts of miscellany—quotations, dreams, joys, angers, pains, failures, stories of experiences, happenings, reviews, poetry, and all of these interacting with one another. Isolated seeds of ideas in time sprouted and grew into questions and resources that have shaped my living. At first they have no name—twisting amorphously over the years until some happening, reading, a person, as the woman in Illinois, articulated "hearing to speech" (see p. 202). The germ of the idea had been there many years.

Long before I heard the Hebrew word *chutzpah*, meaning "the arrogance of challenging God," I was a child running through the house opening doors quickly, making no noise before turning on the light, demanding that God show himself if he really did exist. If God were everywhere, if he could see us at all times and we couldn't see him, there seemed to be something awry. Almost two decades later, sitting by a window in a college class on the prophets, some of my juvenile skepticism turned into pure excitement. I saw the Old Testament prophets not as foretellers and miraculous supernatural predictors of the future but as people who had minds who could read the signs of the political and social ferment and point to what they would inevitably bring forth. Many years later, indeed, when I was already teaching, I came to respect the language form of the parables in the New Testament and the parable of Jonah in the Old Testament as a new way of speaking—when the content and form of language were inseparable in spite of many translators and redactors. The parabolic form had remained so pristine that the functioning over the years still disclosed ever new paradigms of reality. These parables Professor Robert Funk described as extended metaphor.

Therefore, the sections of my journal I have selected to include in the appendix are not the result of current research so much as they are the maturation of journal entries: Hearing to Speech, More about Metaphor, and Questing the Quest.

Hearing to Speech

If one can be heard to one's own speech, then the speech would be a new speech and the new speech would be a new experience in the life of the speaker—that is, the one heard to speech. It was so with David, the young son of my colleague. I first met David when he was nine years old. He had been diagnosed as a retarded child when one doctor discovered his deafness. He had not learned to speak a word for he had never heard words. He could communicate only through facial expressions and touch and embrace. David was placed in a school for the deaf—one of those schools that taught children to speak words they had never heard spoken. I was in David's home when he returned for his first holiday. In a broken but understandable fashion he began to tell his parents things he had never been able to tell them before...could never communicate to anyone before. He was able to share his own history. He opened up the innermost part of his life to those hearing most deeply and most anxiously the new knowledge never spoken before. The family, perhaps far more than the teachers, brought David to speech. The silence that had stifled him now yielded his own story. Almost overnight David's entire personality changed from the quiet wistful boy to a shiny-eyed vibrant new kind of family member.

★

Patricia Moore in the *Los Angeles Times*, wrote of special schools for the deaf in which no finger spelling or sign language are taught at first in the hope that the deaf ones learn to recognize the sound of words coming alive out of their own vibrating vocal cords.

What an astounding experience that one can learn to speak words without ever hearing but only with having been heard! It is strange that we have never understood before that this is what often happened among women. It is tied up with telling our stories. When Helen Keller out of the darkness of her life reached out her hands under the water pump and struggled to speak a word she had never heard spoken by another living being it was far more than memorizing a new word. "Wah! Wah!" and again with great effort "Wah! Wah!" It was not just a word or a number attached to an object to designate or signify utilitarian purpose. This word was her own experience. This word opened to her the concept of words—the secret of language—of self-identification—of history—of literature—of connectedness to other human beings. Once the concept dawned it was the connectedness with the other—a special other—she immediately sought. Where was that loving ear, that persistent hearing, that had tried and tried again to break through Helen's silence and hear her to this new world of speaking? When she found her teacher, Helen threw herself into her arms, grateful for the profound gift of herself.

During the Seminary Quarter for Women, Grailville, 1976, a folded sheet of paper was placed in my hands by a blind woman student.* She called it a prose poem, "On Finding Our Stories." I became aware of the endlessness of this kind of hearing—hearing onself, one's own past, one's own heart beat. Kathi Wolfe's precious gift read in very large, square letters:

> We find our stories through the
> hallows of time;

---

*Now a minister in New Jersey.

through the corridors, halls, byways,
and sidewalks of history.

Our stories jump out at us;
taken by surprise
in
their locked up corners;
chained
to the walls of the past of men.
They leap to freedom—dancing—
hopping with joy—at being set free—
unchained—unlocked.
They leap into presence—
creating—
becoming—
the true (free) past and present
of women.

We reclaim—see our stories—
through the cleansing (freeing)
mirror of women's history.

It was in 1971 that I received a totally new understanding of
hearing. It came from the lips of a most ordinary woman in a
workshop I was conducting in Illinois. I repeat this story for
comparison with the one following. I remember well how this
woman seemed a loner at first—quiet and almost frightened.
Perhaps the idea of women needing to be free was new to her
and she did not know what to make of it. Perhaps she was
resisting and her silence reflected a subtle hostility or hesitance. As was my custom in such groups I was careful not to
push her but wait until her time came and only she could
judge that moment. I knew the easy talkers would in time run
down and a more realistic, deeper level would emerge. The
last day of the workshop, the woman, whose name I do not
know, wandered off alone. As we gathered sometime later in
small groups she started to talk in a hesitant, almost awkward

manner. "I hurt," she began. "I hurt all over." She touched herself in various places before she added, "but I don't know where to begin to cry. I don't know how to cry." Hesitatingly she began to talk. Then she talked more and more. Her story took on fantastic coherence. When she reached a point of the most excruciating pain, no one moved. No one interrupted her. No one rushed to comfort her. No one cut her experience short. We simply sat. We sat in a powerful silence. The women clustered about the weeping one went with her to the deepest part of her life as if something so sacred was taking place they did not withdraw their presence or mar its visibility. Finally the woman, whose name I do not know, finished speaking. Tears flowed from her eyes in all directions. She spoke again: "You heard me. You heard me all the way." Her eyes narrowed then moved around the group again slowly as she said: "I have a strange feeling you heard me before I started. You heard me to my own story. *You heard me to my own speech.*"

I filed this story away as a unique experience. But it happened again and again in other such small groups when we allowed the pain to reach its own depth, or as another woman told me later: "You went down all the way with me. Then you didn't smother me. You gave it space to shape itself. You gave it time to come full circle." It happened to me. Then I knew I had been experiencing something I have never experienced before. A complete reversal of the going logic. The woman was saying, and I had experienced, a depth hearing that takes place before speaking—a hearing that is more than acute listening. A hearing that is a direct transitive verb that evokes speech—new speech that has never been spoken before. The woman who gave me those words had indeed been heard to her own speech.

★

It was in the early '80s that I sat on the floor in a circle of women. Candles burned in the center. We sang a few ritual songs and then sang to each present. As we held hands, one woman began talking. Tears moved in all directions as her voice, already low, became lower. She told how her life was no longer her own. She loved her children. She wanted them but they were there with her during every waking hour. No moment was her own. She wasn't herself any longer. One tear waited not for the next as she moved steadily, surely near the abyss. The pain became almost more than any of us could bear. I felt the women cluster closer and move with her down into deeper pain. All women were motionless, their eyes fixed on her. Suddenly the woman next to her turned to the woman on the other side of her and with her hand on her knee interrupted as she asked: "P____, you have two children also. Do you ever feel that way? Tell us about it." P____, who was hearing the sobbing woman, nodded but kept her eyes on the woman. "Tell us about your experiences," insisted the woman who had now broken the journey of the first woman and left all of us stranded along the way. P____, embarrassed, mumbled something, then the talk was passed to the next woman, and the next around the circle. One told of her grandmother. Another of an aunt who died too late to hear her story. Finally a woman suggested that the candles and food be moved back and the one whose aunt had died move into the center. She directed that all hands be placed on her and that the group give her energy. All followed instructions.

What had happened to the interrupted hearing and the unfinished story and word that never came to sound? The broken connection and the interrupted story and the word that never came to speech were finally squelched by the comment of a woman in training to be a counselor: "That is one of the cleverest techniques I ever saw!" I could not bear the pain of having the grace a woman pleaded for intercepted by women who could not go through the pain of hearing another into the depths of her own abyss where sound is born. Clever techniques seen as positive agents for creation and change are not good for the kind of hearing that brings forth speech.

★

I go back again and again to a time when I was inadvertently drawn into teaching severely mentally retarded children. I was not prepared to teach them. They were severely retarded—most of them with Down's syndrome. Twelve children had been screened for the class. Community and state money had been secured. The parents and the board could not secure a teacher though they had possibilities for securing one within a month or so. "Would I please take them for this short time?!—a month or so?" It was a rather fortunate learning experience for me since the school was located on a state line and the two states were experimenting with setting up curricula for the severely retarded.

I have never listened to so much and so attentively as I did to these children. Finally I think I learned to hear them to their own expressions of themselves. I found myself talking little but hearing them more. I remember one dark rainy day Sidale pressed her nose against the windowpane. "Mor" she called me, the first syllable of my last name. I moved to her side looking in the direction she was looking and wondering what was going on in her mind. I did not speak. I waited. Then with her nose pressed against the window with the drops dripping down on the outside of the pane she said:

"Rain!
Rain wet,
Window wet
Mud wet!
Mud...Wet? No! Mud wet...wet? No
MUD!"

I nearly wept and she was so proud. I printed the poem on a large sheet of paper for all to see and respond to. For that little Down's syndrome girl to figure that the word *mud* by itself was wet and did not need a modifier not only produced a poem but a whole new insight for her. What if I had interrupted her?

★

Betty was older than the others but there was no other
class for her to go into. At six years of age she had stopped
speaking. Now she was twelve and still did not speak. Something of a profound traumatic nature had happened to her at
six, concluded the psychiatrist who was on our board and on
the committee to screen the children. She had not spoken for
the two months she had been in the class except occasionally
to repeat a word that had been said to her, but no more.
However, she seemed happy and was cooperative. Her drawings were as hesitant as her speech and she could not dance
with the others unless someone led her. Together the children
made a large puppet theater out of a refrigerator box; then
each one made a puppet. One by one, they went into the
stage/box/theater, put their fingers in the head and arms of
the puppet each had made and talked for the puppet. Sometimes more than one would carry on a conversation and
sometimes several would have their puppets sing together.
Betty finished her puppet with help, put three fingers in the
head, the thumb and little finger in the arms with help, then
the children urged her to go into the stage. She did. She waved
to the children with her free hand. They cried: "With the
puppet!" She waved with the puppet, then leaned down near
the puppet to hear the puppet speak. The puppet did not
speak. She turned it toward her and looked it squarely in the
face. Then she turned it back toward the children. "Speak!
Speak!" they cried together. Suddenly she made the puppet bow
toward Sidale and said, "Hi, Sidale!" Then she went around the
room calling each by name. The children were ecstatic. I wept.
All clapped their hands and rushed toward me. "Betty speak!
Betty speak!" And Betty, laughing with them, said toward me:
"I speak! I speak!" From then on Betty began very slowly to add
words to her vocabulary. When I moved from that community
her family said that she was still trying to talk. The psychiatrist on our board took her on as a most interesting client.

John Calvin referred to hearing as the miracle of Pentecost and saw the reversal of hearing/speaking as crucial to the event.

★

After he had received his degree in medicine, Carl Gustav Jung interned at the Burghölzli Hospital with women who had become withdrawn and mute. The doctors who treated the women assumed they had no language. Therefore, they tried to give them a language by speaking words that had alienated them from the world in the first place, words to which they had closed their lives and could no longer recognize. The doctors' vocal antics and their performances of meaningless jobs and routine activities led Dr. Jung to conclude that the doctors were in a greater state of alienation from the women and from themselves than were their patients. They were trying to speak the women to hearing. Dr. Jung directed his efforts toward finding a way to make contact with the women—not as they "should" be but as they were. He observed certain repetitive movements of their bodies and certain repetitive words disconnected from other words; certain characteristic gestures of their hands or their heads. These he tried to imitate both to himself when alone and then with each woman in turn. He repeated the first word the movement seemed to suggest to him. He concentrated on one woman after another for some recognition of familiarity with the sound or the gesture. He repeated and waited. Again and again. Finally one after the other woman recognized a connection with their gesture, and began to speak a word. Then ever so gradually another and another. He had touched the place where the connection had been broken. But he did this through their language and not the language of the doctors. He had heard them to speech...to their own speech.

In this way Jung was able to help many of them recover their own story...the story they had forgotten or had never known...or to create a new story for themselves. Through appropriating their own story they were restored to health. And to the amazement of the doctors many became well enough to be released from the hospital. (Retold from an out-of-print bulletin of the Analytical Psychology Club of New York.)

Not only a new speech but a new hearing. Not just cleaning out the ears, as Fred Paddock used to say, but having new ears. Hearing from a new center—the whole body.

Hearing to speech is political.

Hearing to speech is never one-sided. Once a person is heard to speech she becomes a hearing person.

Speaking first to be heard is power over. Hearing to bring forth speech is empowering.

More about Metaphor

If you could say it, you would not need metaphor. If you could conceptualize it, it would not be metaphor. If you could explain it, you would not use metaphor.

James Dickey once said that the poet is not trying to tell the truth, the poet is trying the make the truth. That is metaphorically close to what George Bernard Shaw once said, that in worship we do not adore God. We create God.

Allow the pictures to come. Remember! Imagine! Create! Alistair Cooke told of a schoolboy in England who preferred radio to T.V.—"because the pictures are better," he explained. (*TV Guide*, 1982)

★

Dickey reminds us that when things connect they are never the same as before in isolation. Yet the connecting itself is new with each venture.

★

God guard me from those thoughts men think
In the mind alone;
He that sings a lasting song
Thinks in the marrow bone.
—W. B. Yeats, "A Prayer for Old Age"

★

A literalist could be described as one who both takes metaphors too seriously and does not take metaphors seriously enough.
—Michael McCandles (*PMLA*, March 1976)

★

The literalist is unprepared to recognize when his own or other lexicons are used literally and when they are used metaphorically.
—Michael McCandles (*PMLA*, March 1976)

★

Donald Davidson was so right—"in metaphor there is no meaning available except the first concrete literal meaning." Barfield, I hear also: "The truth appears." The gap is bridged when the hearer is forced to make some response at the moment of first awareness. It is then not too late to return to the old logic or go courageously along with the new.

★

The following eight quotations on metaphor were taken from the book *On Metaphor,* edited by Sheldon Sacks (Chicago and London: University of Chicago Press, 1979):

> Metaphors speak of what remains absent. All metaphor that is more than an appreciation for more proper speech gestures toward what transcends language.
>
> —Karsten Harries

> ...for the truth of the past is not necessarily the truth of the present, and the work of art may succeed to the extent that it diverges from the past models rather than resembling them.
>
> —Richard Shiff

> We are forced to recognize the importance of sound pattern for metaphoric success.
>
> —Karsten Harries

> The metaphorical meaning compels us to explore the borderline between the verbal and the non-verbal.
>
> —Paul Ricoeur

> Poetic language, says Hester, is this language which not only merges sense and sound...but sense and senses, meaning by that the flow of bound images displayed by the sense. We are not very far from what Bachelard called *retentissement* ("reverberation"). In reading, Bachelard says, the verbal meaning generates

images which, so to speak, rejuvenate and reenact the traces of sensorial experience...These images bring to concrete completion the metaphoric process.
—Paul Ricoeur

No theory of metaphorical meaning or metaphorical truth can help explain how metaphor works—what distinguishes metaphor is not *meaning* but *use*.
—Donald Davidson

What metaphor adds to the ordinary is an achievement that uses no semantic resources beyond the resources on which the ordinary depends.
—Donald Davidson

It is no help in explaining how words work in metaphor to posit metaphorical or figurative meanings, or special kinds of poetic or "metaphorical truth." These ideas don't explain metaphor, metaphor explains them.
—Donald Davidson

★

Metaphor in its deep creative sense results in wisdom.

★

I saw no God, nor heard any, in a finite organical perception; but my senses discovered the infinite in everything...
—William Blake

★

The whole earth is charged.

★

Individuals and groups live by their images and dreams, and...it is harder to change the archetypes, symbols, and myths of men than it is to change their ideas and doctrines.

—Amos Wilder

★

It is always the pressing concern of religion to seek after and seize its own vital essence and spiritual center, but that is poor reason for supposing that spirituality came naked into the world, or could exist without the images which condition it.

—Austin Ferrar

★

We cannot short cut divine wisdom by manipulation, nor should we confuse psychic pyrotechnics with the fulfillments of a long period of gestation.

—Amos Wilder

★

It is as natural to fabulate, as to breathe, and as necessary.

—Amos Wilder

★

Language and mental habits change. Old maps of reality based on different apperceptions seem quaint if not grotesque. When retained they subvert the original vision.

—Amos Wilder

★

Children speak metaphorically out of ignorance—but always out of movement. They speak out of playfulness in putting words together when they were never intended to meet. Something exciting happens in the process.

Children are not used to standing alone mentally. They are forever seeking connections. They make connections, as when Henny Penny sat opposite me at the birthday dinner for him. Between us were tall narrow blue candles in small blue glass holders shaped like stars. He lighted them by himself then looked wide-eyed across the table at me: "Nelle! I see stars in your eyes!" In the same way foreign students in classes often open new insights with their broken English, and speak metaphorically without being aware of doing so.

The metaphor serves to draw the imagination into a new logic which now can be recognized as the imagination's own world. If entered and accepted the old logic is broken and a radically new relationship to reality in its everydayness is ushered in.

All good liturgy and ritual that has power to change is filled with metaphor.

As Stanley Hopper often reminded his classes, metaphor has no content. A metaphor is known only in its functioning.

To work magic, we begin by making new metaphors. Without negating the light we reclaim the dark, the fertile earth where the hidden seed lies unfolding, the unseen power that rises within us, the dark sacred human flesh, the depths of the ocean, the night— when our senses question, we reclaim all the lost parts of ourselves we have shoved down into the dark, instead of enlightenment we begin to speak of deepening.

—Starhawk, *Dreaming the Dark*

★

...As imagination bodies forth
The forms of things unknown, the poet's pen
Turns them to shapes, and gives to airy nothingness
A local habitation and a name.

—Shakespeare

★

...if metaphor, taken in this general sense, is not just a certain development of speech, but must be regarded as one of its essential conditions—then any effort to understand its function leads us back, once more, to the fundamental form of verbal conceiving.

—Ernst Cassirer

★

Transcendence is no longer the issue. But healing the web of life is.

★

Since metaphor opens up new space and ushers in a new reality, without metaphor we look in vain for open space that demands no shattering. We must claim our own space by shattering that which usurped it in the first place.

★

When metaphor becomes analogy it means metaphor has been literalized in order to make two knowns. In this case the process has been intercepted and the power of metaphor is lost. Thus metaphor has ceased to be metaphor.

Metaphor intends to increase the sensuous element—primarily because it is organic—derived out of the senses.

The first metaphor the human mind uses in the act of cognition is the translation of sensual perception in image.

—Bedia Allemann

Hope is the thing with feathers
That perches in the soul,
And sings the tune without the words,
And never stops at all,

And sweetest in the gale is heard;
And sore must be the storm
That could abash the little bird
That kept so many warm.

I've heard it in the chillest land,
And on the strangest sea;
Yet, never, in extremity,
It asked a crumb of me.

—Emily Dickinson

Too many women in the Goddess movement see the Goddess as "out there" or "up there"—all powerful and all loving. In other words they perceive with a patriarchal mentality which does nothing but make a matriarchy the opposite of a patriarchy structurally and functionally. The authoritarian ruler has only changed sex but the authoritarianism has yet to be exorcised from one's consciousness.

The maleness of the patriarchal God is reflected in many areas—but perhaps the most obvious is the prevailing political systems of the world including their militarized cultures and pervasive hedonistic mentalities.

★

The word *God* can no longer claim to be a metaphor, though quite likely it was at the beginning. Filled with male images through the centuries it has done its work well in spinning out political, social, and economic structures of control and dominance. The maleness is so well established in cultures and mentalities it is responded to almost universally as revelatory, whether one is religious or not. Indeed, whether one is in church, or synagogue or another institutional religious order matters little. That is why the challenging of and shattering of this male image is the task of every citizen...every human being—not just the overtly religious. All, even the most common masses of people, have been too well indoctrinated to leave room for change, the calling into question, breaking that which is in tight control. A metaphor opens up new space and ushers in a new reality—iconoclastic first and then epiphanous action.

★

If the Goddess can function as a metaphoric image, perhaps a dragon can—even a small clay dragon made by a mentally retarded boy only twelve years of age.

Larry was a Down's syndrome child and they have the reputation of being sweet and loving children most of the time. Usually the times they are not—the times they go into tantrums and have difficulty controlling themselves—are those times when the adult world is demanding from them a performance equal to a so-called normal twelve-year-old. It was not unusual for Larry to have two or more tantrums during the week. And when one began it had to run its course. All of us in Larry's class were aware of that.

One day while sitting at the table working with clay, Larry was trying to make a dragon. Time after time it fell apart. I sensed the first symptoms of a tantrum coming on. Since it was the adult world putting him into a squeeze (which of course he did not realize) and Velma, the assistant teacher, an adult, was standing by him, I suggested that he let his dragon eat Velma. He started smiling through his tears. He took the head in one hand, the tail in the other and gobbled Velma from head to toe. Then he turned on me. After he had demolished me, he started on the children. One by one he had the dragon eat all the children. By that time the children were laughing with Larry and when we were ready to put the clay away, Larry would not give up his dragon. He carried it to his locker and carefully placed it on the shelf above his coat.

The next time a tantrum began gathering I suggested that he get his dragon. It worked as effectively as the first time. In time the children began to sense when a tantrum was coming on and suggested the dragon. It seemed to work every time. One day, Jerry, who ordinarily used beating copper to handle his anger, was given the dragon by Larry. It worked for him. To my surprise, once when I was tense and speaking sharply I found the dragon in my hand and Larry was motioning for me to go ahead and use it. I found not only that it worked for me but that I was getting all kinds of support from that little community of children that enabled me to weather my tension.

At the end of the semester when I knew that I would not be returning to the children and was clearing all my things away and putting materials in order for the next teacher, there on Larry's shelf I found the dragon. It was dried and almost turning to dust as I lifted it in my hands and dropped it slowly into the wastepaper basket. It could mean nothing to a new teacher nor could the bit of clay now disintegrating out of shape mean anything to me and twelve children. But the dragon had functioned and functioned well and probably was still functioning in various ways for those of us who had come into the presence of one another through it.

★

Images, as clues to language, are not purely psychological, nor can they be limited to linguistics. They are theological in the profoundest sense of the word. But theology as feminists are coming to experience it now refers no more to a male God nor, for that matter to a female Goddess. Professor James Robinson worded it as, "a stance toward the ultimate." Perhaps it is giving one's all in the search for Self (meaning individual Self, the community Self, and the pervasive Self in the universe). It therefore becomes more universal and healing rather than transcendent; pervasive rather than wholly other; connected rather than separate; up from down under rather than down from up above.

★

Some controversy is arising over the relation of metaphor and analogy. In the early days of language philosophy, analogy was allowed by some to subsume metaphor as it did simile and allegory. With more attention to the power of metaphor as it operates in liturgy, poetry, drama, and now that feminists are beginning to see in it hope for social change, it is important to clarify the difference between the two.

After a metaphor has functioned in a certain context— that is taken off from a concreteness and observed to its end journey—it is proper to say that the concrete beginning is analogous to the final functioning. But together they cannot properly be referred to as analogy. Analogy would mean that each would be analogous to the other. As an example: "There are roses in your cheeks." The concrete beginning to which the observer of the functioning metaphor must be present is the red cheeks. In certain situations they may be called analogous to a rose but only to a particular kind of rose which is red and blooming, even though the particular color is not referred to in the metaphor. But to say a rose is analogous to a cheek becomes absurd. It is impossible to identify the end of the metaphoric journey before it takes off or before the creative migration is awakened to provide energy for the metaphor to function. That would be placing the concreteness of the beginning process in a rose—but what rose? What color? Where would the rose be concretized? It would be irrational to produce the end process to insure the concrete beginning, which direction makes no sense whatever. Not least of which the power to change would be decimated. Max Black points out that "in this form of words, the absurdity of postdating causes is flagrant."

Max Black reminds us that Aristotle ascribes the use of metaphor to delight in learning. Black also adds that metaphor may evince feelings or predispose others to act and feel in various ways—but a metaphor does not typically say anything.

We know a metaphor only by the way it functions, Stanley Hopper reminds us. To speak of a new reality which has not yet come, as if it had come—using the old language to do so—is a lie, or can kill the new word/image taking shape. To conceptualize metaphor, domesticate it, control it, destroys it. A metaphor creates its own words to bring to new light the old meanings.

Questing the Quest

Gertrude Stein opened her eyes and asked family and friends gathered about her bed, "What is the answer?" A deep breath followed her closing eyes. Then she lifted her head and asked, "But, what is the question?" In the stunned silence of her waiting family she died.

What is the question?

Rainer Maria Rilke is often quoted as admonishing us to stay by the question and then perhaps in some future the answer will come.

Always there are questions posed directly to Faith out of Faith. These become sharper and sharper until at the very end they become addressed to the bare core of Faith itself.

★

Judith Plaskow raised the great *what if?* question in
MENORAH, Sh'vat 5782 (February 1982), vol. III, no. 2:

> In an extraordinary article on the situation of Jewish
> women (*Lilith*, 1979), Cynthia Ozick offers fourteen
> "meditations" pointing to the sociological status of
> the woman question in Judaism. The subordination of
> women, she argues, is not deeply rooted in Torah but
> is the result of historical custom and practice which
> can be halachically repaired. Only in her last medita-
> tion does she raise the great "what if?": What if the
> Otherness of women is not simply a matter of Jewish
> incorporation of surrounding social attitudes but is in
> part created and sustained by Torah itself? What if the
> subordination of women in Judaism is rooted in theol-
> ogy, in the very foundations of the Jewish tradition? . . .
> If the Jewish women's movement addresses itself only
> to the fruits but not the bases of discrimination, it is
> apt to settle for too little in the way of change . . . Clear-
> ly the implications of Jewish feminism, while they
> include halachic restructuring, reach beyond halacha
> to transform the bases of Jewish life. Feminism
> demands a new understanding of Torah, God, and
> Israel: an understanding of Torah that begins with
> acknowledgment of the profound injustice of Torah
> itself. The assumption of the lesser humanity of
> women has poisoned the content and structure of the
> law, undergirding women's legal disabilities and our
> subordination in the broader tradition. This assump-
> tion is not amenable to piecemeal change. It must be
> utterly eradicated by the withdrawal of projection
> from women—the discovery that the negative traits
> attributed to women are also in the men who attri-
> bute them, while the positive qualities reserved for

men are also in women. Feminism demands a new understanding of God, acknowledged in the mystical tradition, but even here shaped and articulated by men, must be recovered and reexplored and reintegrated into the Godhead. Last, feminism assumes that these changes will be possible only when we come to a new understanding of the community of Israel, which includes the whole of Israel and which therefore allows women to speak and name our experience for ourselves.

What if, when you take sexism out of God language you have nothing left? What then?

If the images out of which you live should prove phony (false) would you be willing to have them shattered in order to let the shining reality of truth come through?

But there really is a prior question: Do you have a mind-set to search for a little more truth and then for a little more truth?

To what degree are we open to change? History offers many examples in which the work of the spirit and the surprises of grace have outrun the laggard frontiers of orthodoxy.

A twelve-year-old once asked his church schoolteacher: "What would you do if I said I don't believe a thing you and my parents are telling me?" The teacher to the twelve-year-old: "I would say you had begun to think for yourself."

"Are you making your faith a hitching post or a signpost?" is a question Scotty Cowan kept asking the Fellowship of Southern Churchmen in the '30s and '40s.

Is the problem a search for ways to speak of God properly or is the God of your present religion so totally male-conditioned a new reality is in order?

If language is such a primordial, elemental phenomenon arising only when no present known symbols serve reality is the world forced to wait until men know themselves oppressed to listen for the new word to be spoken?

The central point for both Artaud and Beckett was that the most powerful and authentic speaking does not arise from careful and precise syntax but only when these are recognized as rapier liars to keep human beings out of relationship one with the other.

The "OM" uttered in many theater games is a part of the search for new human words that as Artaud said would become more ritualistic than what we commonly know as speech and once it is experienced it will be close to worship.

The only route to the new words is down through our common life together, letting go our logic, our authority, our control, our pride, and our use of one another.

We tear away the ancient myth to get at the reality which originally gave the myth birth. But what we find back of it is the Source, the Energy, the Wisdom that created the myth in the first place. Once freed from literalism the myth is released to interact with the Source of energy and so a new myth is given birth which is passed for other generations to shatter and create anew. Once the myth becomes ultimate, creativity is stifled and one can only obey that myth or symbol which has become creativity's god.

—Paraphrased from Dorothy Sayers

★

I'm tired of a militarized culture, of mentalities which produce hunger, poverty, power over others. So I am willing to take the chance. That is why my last essay is the most important in this collection and toward it I have been slowly moving all my life. All I can say at this point is that what brought me into the world and has sustained me thus far can be trusted. That which has given me a glimpse of love and a vision of justice is now giving me new hope and energy at this time in my life and can be trusted—come what may.

★

viii   Margo
The one who can't say it
says it.

The one who can't figure how
pictures what.

The song no one can sing
sounds, quiet
air in air.

—Denise Levertov, *"Footprints"*

★

If we take our tradition (Jewish, Christian, Buddhist, Islamic, humanist, or what have you) with dead seriousness and remain faithful to it will it push us beyond itself or draw us inward, separating us further from one another?

★

If we go to the depths of our traditions, down through our separate symbol systems, do we come closer to one another and to a common truth?

★

For this is the thing the priests do not know, with their One God and One Truth: that there is no such thing as a true tale. Truth has many faces and the truth is like to an old road to Avalon; it depends on your own will, and your own thoughts, whither the road will take you.

—Marion Zimmer Bradley, prologue to
The Mists of Avalon

★

What has been lost is more than a childhood notion of some sort of superior being, it is the whole supporting fabric of our lives.

—Joseph Campbell

★

Let us measure defeat
in terms of bread and meat,

and continents
in relative extent of wheat

fields; let us not teach
what we have learned badly

and not profited by;
let us not concoct

healing potions for the dead,
        nor invent

new colors
for blind eyes.
        —H. D., *Trilogy* ("The Walls Do Not Fall")

★

I fear to know me
I who am mystery
mostly to myself.
What would I discover—
grace and peace,
anger and pain,
all knotted together
in some vulnerable
    passionate place
called the heart of a
    woman.
        —Catherine Leahy, the Grailville Community

★

You are destined to fly, but that cocoon has to go.

★

Maybe "journey" is not so much a journey ahead, or a journey into space, but a journey into presence. The farthest place on earth is the journey into the presence of the nearest person to you.

Notes

Prelude

1. Ruth Duck, "Lead on, O Cloud of Yahweh," in *Because We Are One People* (Chicago: Ecumenical Center, 1974).

2. The Seminary Quarter for Women on feminist theology, held at Grailville, Ohio, offered credit to students already enrolled in an accredited seminary or theological school.

3. See Emily Dickinson's poem, "This Is My Letter to the World," in *Emily Dickinson*, The Laurel Poetry Series (New York: Dell, 1960), p. 53.

4. See the Owen Barfield reference in "The Goddess as Metaphoric Image," 1978 essay (note 23, page 247). Also Owen Barfield, *Speaker's Meaning* (Middletown, Conn.: Wesleyan University Press, 1967), ch. 4.

5. See Susan Copenhaver Barrabee, "Education for Liberation: Women in the Seminary," in *Women's Liberation and the Church*, ed. Sara Bently Doely (New York: Association Press, 1970), pp. 47–59.

6. See Brita and Krister Stendahl's perceptive comment on language, note 25 in "Beloved Image," 1977 essay, page 244.

Also on the power of images: In 1974, prior to her ordination as a priest, Professor Carter Heyward, as deacon, was assisting with communion in an Episcopal service.

A male priest came forward and stood with others before her. She approached each communicant intoning, "The Blood of Christ shed for you." As she neared the male priest he reached for the cup, but instead scratched the back of her hand deep enough to draw blood. Then, he turned and was lost in the crowd.

What really happened? Many saw in his act a premeditated anger at a woman daring to fill the role of a male priest.

Something jars with so simple an interpretation. Could the priest have approached the Eucharist in all good faith? But as he heard a woman's voice intoning words shaped for a deep voice, a long-embedded image stirred in his unconscious. Suddenly, the image assumed a life of its own, in spite of the male priest's possible good intention, and struck at the usurper of "his divinely appointed office." (Interpreted with Carter Heyward's permission.)

Another version of this incident may be found in Malcolm Boyd, "Who's Afraid of Women Priests?... And Why They Won't Admit It," *Ms.*, December 1974, p. 49.

7. Hebrews 12:27.

8. Statistics now tell us that the majority of church and synagogue members are women. Before his death Saul Alinsky said that he was turning his labor organizing efforts toward the churches and synagogues for they held the majority of middle-class America. He believed that as the middle class goes, so goes America. When Alexander Miller was head of the Atlanta office of the Anti-Defamation League, before he became national director, he said in conversation with me that the rabbi, priest, and minister hold the key to the solution of social issues in every community. That influenced my going to theological school to teach. If we admit that there are more women than men in churches and synagogues, it would follow that women in local communions are in a peculiar position to effect social change.

1970: Women—on the March

1. *The Women's Bible* (reprint, Seattle, Wash.: Coalition Task Force on Women and Religion, 1974).

2. Matilda Joslyn Gage, *Women, Church and State* (1893; reprint, Watertown, Mass.: Persephone Press, 1980).

3. Eleanor Flexner, *A Century of Struggle* (Cambridge, Mass.: Harvard University Press, 1959); Aileen Kraditor, *Up from the Pedestal* (Chicago: Quadrangle Books, 1968); Alice Rossi, *The Feminist Papers* (New York: Columbia University Press, 1973); Gerda Lerner, *The Grimké Sisters from South Carolina* (New York: Schocken, 1971).

4. See Kathleen Barry, Charlotte Bunch, and Shirley Castley, eds., *International Feminism: Networking Against Female Sexual Slavery* (Report of the Global Feminist Workshop to Organize Against Traffic in Women, Rotterdam, 1983).

5. Simone de Beauvoir, *The Second Sex* (New York: Random House, 1953); and Betty Friedan, *The Feminine Mystique* (New York: Norton, 1963).

6. Valerie Saiving Goldstein, "The Human Situation," *Journal of Religion,* April 1960.

7. Judith Plaskow, *Sin, Sex and Grace* (Washington, D.C.: The University Press of America, 1980).

8. "Women-on the March" was published in *Tempo* (National Council of Churches, October 1970), and in *Drew Magazine* (Drew University, Winter 1970).

9. For a preliminary report of the results of the United Methodist study see Sarah Bentley Doely, ed., *Women's Liberation and the Church* (New York: Association Press, 1967), pp. 119f.

10. Mircea Eliade, *Gods, Goddesses, and Myths of Creation* (New York: Harper and Row, 1967). I would use the story quite differently today (1984).

11. In the reference to early Hebrews, I never intended to imply that patriarchy began with them. Dr. Phyllis Tribble, now Professor of Old Testament at Union Theological Seminary in New York, once, in a personal conversation, indicated there was far more sexism in the New Testament than in the Old Testament.

12. Krister Stendahl, *The Bible and the Role of Women* (Philadelphia: Fortress Press, 1966), p. 32.

13. Rom. 8:33–34.

1971: *The Rising Woman Consciousness in a Male Language Structure*

1. "The Rising Woman Consciousness in a Male Language Structure" was first published in *Andover Newton Quarterly* 12 (March 1972), pp. 117ff.

2. Rom. 7:24

3. Jon. 2.

4. From a Religious News item entitled "Program Envy," *Newsweek,* December 6, 1971, p. 58.

5. Otto Jesperson, *Growth and Structure of the English Language* (Oxford, England: Basil Blackwell, 1935), p. 2.

6. Ibid., p. 5.

7. On the invitation to the noon meeting at Interchurch Center, August 26, 1970, prior to the National Women's Liberation March.

8. Extensive research project conducted by Princeton chapter of National Organization for Women. (Write to NOW chapter in Princeton, New Jersey, for information.)

9. Preliminary report published in the appendix to Sarah Bentley Doely, ed., *Women's Liberation and the Church* (New York: Association Press, 1970), p. 119.

10. News report from *New York Times*, October 10, 1970.

11. Germaine Greer on NBC's *Today* program, May 18, 1971, in which she accused psychologists for blaming sex discord and conflict on biology, sociology, and religion but never tackling the "sex of the mind."

12. Jean Piaget, *Structuralism* (New York: Basic Books, 1970), pp. 5, 14.

13. Cf. Piaget, *Language and Thought of the Child* (London: Routledge & Kegan Paul, 1926; revised and enlarged 1959).

14. Cf. Piaget, *The Child's Conception of the World* (London: Routledge & Kegan Paul, 1951), and *The Origins of Intelligence in Children* (New York: International Universities Press, 1952).

15. Antonin Artaud as quoted by Anais Nïn in the preface to Bettina Knapp, *Antonin Artaud* (New York: David Lewis, 1969), p. xii. Since the first publication of this essay, Susan Sontag has edited and published *Antonin Artaud, Selected Writings* (New York: Farrar, Straus & Giroux, 1976). She writes that "Antonin Artaud is one of the great, daring mapmakers of consciousness."

16. Antonin Artaud (1896–1948), French artist, poet, director, and writer founded a new theater called the Theater of Cruelty in which he sought to make theater language so elemental, meaningful, and forceful that it would evoke the creative unconscious in the audience so as to produce a living, personal experience.

17. Samuel Beckett (b. 1906), originally from Ireland, is now living in France. His novels, poems, and plays reflect an inner search for an authentic language that has to do as much with a way of hearing as with a way of speaking. Hearing, for Beckett, is not a matter of going to a certain place but a matter of where one finds oneself. It is not a matter of listening with the ears but listening with the whole body.

18. Authentic language for Beckett is that language which participates in reality with one's whole self—not just with the intellect, not just with the feeling—to the extent that speaking, hearing, and

gesture become shorn of the superfluous in order to affirm that which basically is.

19. Cf. Knapp, *Antonin Artaud*, pp. 23–29.

20. Cf. Antonin Artaud, *The Theatre and Its Double*, trans. Mary C. Richards (New York: Grove Press, 1958).

21. Nelle Morton, "Drama of Social Protest," *Social Action*, December 1965, p. 14.

22. Cf. John Mood, "Descent into Self: An Interpretation of the Prose Fiction of Samuel Beckett" (Ph.D. diss., Graduate School, Drew University, 1969); Raymond Federman, *Journey to Chaos* (Los Angeles: University of California Press, 1965); Ihab H. Hassan, *Into the Silence* (New York: Knopf, 1968).

23. Cf. Knapp, *Antonin Artaud*, p. 23.

24. Quoted from *New York Times* article, "Moody Man of Letters,' by Israel Shenker, May 6, 1956 sec. 2, p. 3; Samuel Beckett, *The Unnameable*, quoted from Hassan, *Into the Silence*, p. 139.

25. Samuel Beckett, *The Unnameable* (New York: Grove Press, 1958), p. 29.

26. Knapp, *Antonin Artaud*, p. 200.

27. Ibid., pp. xiii and 201.

28. *Beckett at Sixty* (London: Calder and Boyars, 1967).

29. Rom. 8:22–25.

1972: How Images Function

1. This essay on images was prepared originally for an official committee on abortion set up by the United Presbyterian Church, USA. The committee found it unacceptable. It was later published in an abbreviated form in *Quest*, vol. III, no. 2 (Fall 1976).

2. Jean Piaget, *Play, Dreams, and Imitation in Childhood*, trans. G. Gattegno and F. M. Hodgson (New York: Norton, 1962).

3. James Hillman, *Archetypal Psychology* (Dallas: Spring Publications, 1983).

4. Amos Wilder, *Language of the Gospels* (Philadelphia: Fortress Press, 1964), and *Theopoetic* (Philadelphia: Fortress Press, 1976). See also his essay "Symbol and Meaning" in *Children's Religion*, May 1964, published by the United Church of Christ, 132 W. 31st Street, New York. Since this journal is out of print, I quote a paragraph on image:

One can persuade a man [sic] to change his [sic] ideas without too much trouble, unless his [sic] ideas are rooted in unrecognized, nonrational assumptions (that is, an inveterate obsession or world picture). But one can only get a man [sic] to change his [sic] images by shock, by exorcism, by repentance, by rebirth. This is hard and requires potent persuasions. It takes a good reason to prevail over a false one, and that only through a war of images or a mythoclasm.

5. Cf. Ronald Goldman, *Religious Thinking from Childhood to Adolescence* (London: Routledge & Kegan Paul, 1964), and *Readiness for Religion* (New York: Seabury, 1973).

6. Piaget, *Play*, note 2.

7. Jean Piaget, *Etudes d'epistemologie genetique* (Paris: Presses Univer. France, 1957).

8. Laurens van der Post, *Patterns of Renewal* (Pennsylvania: Pendle Hill, 1962).

9. Wilder, *Language*, note 4.

10. Dorothy Lee, *Freedom and Culture*, A Spectrum Book (New Jersey: Prentice Hall, 1959), p. 162f.

11. See Boston's Women's Health Collective, *Our Bodies, Ourselves* (New York: Simon & Schuster, 1978).

12. See Una Stannard's essay "Adam's Rib, or the Woman Within," *Transaction*, November/December 1970, p. 25.

13. Seed is another false image out of the natural world which men made synonymous with sperm, in that seed contained all properties for sprouting. Note the myriad Biblical references to this false image as "Your seed shall inherit the earth."

14. Stannard, "Adam's Rib," p. 25, note 12.

15. Ibid., p. 30.

16. Ibid., p. 26f.

17. See Rosemary Ruether, *New Woman, New Earth* (New York: Seabury Press, 1975); and Susan Griffin, *Woman and Nature, The Roaring Inside Her* (San Francisco: Harper & Row, 1978).

18. Philip Roth, *Our Gang* (New York: Random House, 1973), p. 5.

19. Hugh M. Riley, *Christian Initiation* (Washington, D.C.: The Catholic University of America Press, Consortium Press, 1974), pp. 338–340.

20. Paul Kevin Meagher, O.P., S.T.M., Thomas C. O'Brien, Sister Consuelo Maria Aherse, S.O., eds., *Encyclopedia Dictionary of Religion* (Washington: Corpus Publishers, 1979). See also Marina Warner, *Alone of All Her Sex* (New York: Knopf, 1976), for theological interpretation of the meaning of the Assumption. However, my point in the essay is not the theological meaning but the image projected. If one is permitted a feminist reading of Warner when she says time belongs to the earth, so she (Mary) had to be taken out of it, one could read, patriarchal time belongs to a patriarchal reading of history. To affirm ourselves, as women, we would have to find ways of breaking out of patriarchy.

1973: Preaching the Word

1. "Preaching the Word" was published, along with the other Harvard lectures in the series, under the title *Sexist Religion and Women of the Church—No More Silence!* ed. Alice Hageman (New York: Association Press, 1974). The last four paragraphs of the essay as it appears in *Sexist Religion* were not in my original lecture and were printed in that 1974 volume by the editor's error; they are omitted in this edition.

2. The idea for this experiment came from Theo Wells, "Woman—Which Includes Man, of Course: An Experience in Awareness," *Newsletter for Humanistic Psychology* (San Francisco), December 1970. Paraphrased by permission.

3. Joan Chamberlain Engelsman, *The Feminine Dimension of the Divine* (Philadelphia: Westminster, 1979), ch. 5; Elisabeth Schüssler Fiorenza, *In Memory of Her* (New York: Crossroads, 1983), chs. 4, 7, 8; James Robinson, ed., *The Nag Hammadi Library* (New York: Harper & Row, 1977), pp. 117–130.

4. Mabel K. Howell, *Women and the Kingdom: Fifty Years of Kingdom Building by Women of the Methodist Episcopal Church South, 1878–1928* (Nashville: Cokesbury, 1928), pp. 24–25.

5. John Money and Anke A. Ehrhardt, *Man and Woman: Boy and Girl—Differentiation and Dimorphism of Gender Identity* (Baltimore: Johns Hopkins University Press, 1972), pp. 12–16, and Chapter 7.

6. Elaine Magalis, *Conduct Becoming to a Woman* (New York: Women's Division/Board of Global Ministries/The United Methodist Church, 1973), pp. 112–113.

7. *New York Times,* October 1, 1972.

8. Ibid.

9. From a conversation with Mary Daly.

10. Rom. 8:22-23.

11. Quoted from paper "The Coming of Woman," copyright Betty Farians, April 1971.

1974: Toward a Whole Theology

1. This is the first time the full text of "Toward a Whole Theology" has been in print. An abbreviated version appeared in *The Lutheran World,* January 1975, and in *Frau und Religion,* ed. Elisabeth Moltmann-Wendel (Frankfurt, Germany: Fischer Taschenbuch Verlag, 1983). The notes of my lecture were published in a garbled version in *Risk* (a World Council of Churches publication) 10 (no. 2). Erika Wisselinck, the editor of a woman's journal and also on the staff of the Lay Academy in Tutzing, Germany, after hearing my lecture in Berlin, set up a weekend at the academy in the summer of 1975 so that I could discuss at length its theological implications with women theologians.

2. Betty Thompson, *A Chance to Change* (Geneva and Philadelphia: The World Council of Churches and Fortress Press, 1982).

3. From the address of Philip Potter at the opening of the International Consultation on the Community of Women and Men in the Church, Sheffield, England, July 10-19, 1981.

4. Ibid.

5. Ibid.

6. Ibid.

7. Thompson, *A Chance to Change,* pp. 22-23.

8. See Marga Buhrig, "Discrimination Against Women," in *Technology and Social Justice* (Philadelphia: Judson Press, Student Christian Movement Press, 1971), for one of the finest critiques of the World Council of Churches.

9. Martin Luther (1531) as quoted by Karl Barth, *Church Dogmatics,* vol. I (Edinburgh: T & T Clark), p. 149.

10. Owen Barfield, *History in English Word* (Grand Rapids, Mich.: William B. Eerdmans), p. 170.

11. Cf. C. Kilmer Myers, "Should Women Be Ordained? No," *The Episcopalian,* February 1972, pp. 8-9.

12. See Mary Daly, *Beyond God the Father* (Boston: Beacon Press, 1973).

13. In conversation with Dr. James Sanders, professor of Old Testament at School of Theology at Claremont. See also Anne Bennett, "Women in the New Society," *Journal of Current Social Issues,* Winter 1972/73. Note her references.

14. Gal. 3:27.

15. Elizabeth Gould Davis, *The First Sex* (New York: Putnam, 1971) p. 67.

16. Amos Wilder, "Theology and Theopoetic I," "...II," "...III," *The Christian Century,* May 23, 1973, and March 3, 1972.

17. Daly, *Beyond God the Father,* p. 7.

18. J. J. Bachofen, *Mutterrecht und Urreligion* (Stuttgart: Alfred Kroner Verlag, 1926), p. 16; English trans., *Myth, Religion and Mother Right* (Princeton, N.J.: Princeton University Press,1967).

19. Eva Figes, *Patriarchal Attitudes* (New York: Stein and Day, 1970).

20. Cf. Bachofen, *Myth,* pp. 69-121; Davis, *The First Sex,* chs. 2-10; Figes, *Patriarchal Attitudes,* pp. 9-65; E.O. James, *The Ancient Gods* (New York: Putnam, 1960); Fustel de Coulanges, *The Ancient City* (Boston: Lee and Shepherd, 1889).

21. Cf. Krister Stendahl, *The Bible and the Role of Women* (Philadelphia: Fortress Press, 1966). First appeared as an essay in *Kvinnan and Samhallet Kyrkan* (Stockholm: Svenska Kyrkans Diakonstyrelses Bokforlag, 1958), pp. 138-67, under the title "Bibelsynen och kvinnan."

22. Etienne Gilson, *Etudes de Philosophie Medievale* (Strasbourg: Commission des Publications de la Faculté des Lettres, 1921). English translation, *The Spirit in Medieval Philosophy,* trans. by A. C. H. Downes (New York: Charles Scribner and Son, 1940), p. 51.

23. Corpus of Wisdom literature, especially Prov. 8-9.

24. Cf. Richard Tholin, "The Holy Spirit and Liberation Movements: The Response of the Church" (speech presented at Oxford Institute of Methodist Theological Studies, July 23-August 2, 1973).

25. Luke 4:14–30.

26. Cf. Professor Laurel Richardson Walum, "The Changing Door Ceremony: Notes on the Operation of Sex-Roles in Everyday Life" (paper presented at the Annual Meeting of the American Sociological Association, 1973).

27. Cf. United Nations official reports from the Commission on the Status of Women, Twenty-fifth Session, 1973. Also Anne Tucker-

man, "Women's Cause at the U.N.," *The Nation,* March 23, 1974.

28. Cf. Lillian Smith, *Killers of the Dream* (New York: Norton, 1949), and *Now Is the Time* (New York: Dell, 1955).

29. See "Church Investments, Corporations and Southern Africa," published for the Corporate Social Responsibility Challenges, 475 Riverside Drive, New York 10027, Spring 1974.

30. John Kenneth Galbraith, "How the Economy Hangs on Her Apron Springs," *Ms.,* May 1974.

31. Amos Wilder, "Symbol and Meaning," *Children's Religion* 25 (May 1964).

32. Rev. 21:1-4, 22-27.

1975: A Word We Cannot Yet Speak

1. "A Word We Cannot Yet Speak" was published (considerably cut by the editor) in *New Conversations* 2 (Winter 1977). When Judith Plaskow read the essay, she quickly commented: "You've convinced me that spirituality is a word we cannot give up. It has a fine history." Charlene Spretnak (editor of *The Politics of Women's Spirituality*), who has not read the entire essay, reminded me that just because a word has been distorted by patriarchy is no reason women have to turn it over to them and lose what history and potential it may contain for us.

I guess I am trying to question whether the naming of the new religious dimension of our struggle out of the old patriarchal religious language fully communicates what women are about.

2. Susanne Langer, *Philosophy in a New Key* (New York: Pelican Press, 1943), p. 5.

3. The Einstein/Bohr findings are from Owen Barfield, "Language and Discovery" (unpublished paper delivered at Drew University, Madison, N.J., 1974).

4. See Erich Fromm, *The Forgotten Language* (New York: Grove Press, 1951), ch. VII. Also J.J. Bachofen, *Myth, Religion and Mother Right* (Princeton, N.J.: Princeton University Press 1967). Also my address "Toward a Whole Theology" delivered in Berlin at the 1974 World Council of Churches' Consultation on Sexism in the 1970s.

5. Katharine Rogers, *The Troublesome Helpmate* (Seattle: University of Washington Press, 1966), pp. 3-4.

6. Joseph Campbell, *Masks of God: Occidental Mythology* (New York: Viking, 1975), p. 9, 29f.

7. Helen Lynd, *Shame and the Search for Identity* (New York: Harcourt, Brace and Co., 1958), comments on T.S. Eliot and quotes from Patric Heron's review of Kahnweiler's *Juan Gris* in *The New Statesman* and *The Nation,* March 20, 1938.

8. Erich Neumann, *The Great Mother* (Princeton, N.J.: Princeton University Press, 1963), pp. 40, 42.

9. See Cuthbert A. Simpson in *Interpreters' Bible,* vol. 1 (New York: Vintage, 1972), p. 466.

10. Story and photograph from *National Catholic Reporter,* January 1976.

11. Richard L. Vittitow, "Changing Men and Their Movement Toward Intimacy" (unpublished paper).

12. Richard Tholin, "The Holy Spirit and Liberation Movements," in *The Holy Spirit,* ed. Dow Kirkpatrick (Nashville: Tidings, 1974), pp. 40–75.

13. Cited by Elisabeth Schüssler Fiorenza, "Feminist Theology," in *Theological Studies* , 25, (December 1975), p. 625.

14. *Webster's Third International Dictionary of the English Language,* unabridged (Springfield, Mass.: Merriam, 1971). *Webster's Third World Dictionary of the American Language,* college edition (New York: World, 1966).

15. *Webster's Third World Dictionary of the American Language.*

1976: Educating for Wholeness

1. The full quotation of Goulet from his article "World Hunger; Putting Development Ethics to the Test," *Christianity and Crisis,* May 26, 1975, follows:

> Modern communication renders isolation among human societies impossible. More than forty years ago Lewis Mumford wrote that "the joint stock of knowledge and technical skill transcends the boundaries of individual or national egos, and to forget that fact is not merely to enthrone superstitions but to undermine the essential planetary basis of technology itself" *(Technics and Civilization).* And French economist François Perroux adds that "technical conditions for the establishment of a planetary economy now exist" *(La Coexistence Pacifique,* p. 126).

2. Robert L. Heilbroner, *An Inquiry into the Human Prospect* (New York: Norton, 1974).

3. Ibid., ch. 2.

4. Ibid., p. 144.

5. *The Limits to Growth*, a report for the Club of Rome's Project on the Predicament of Mankind (New York: Universe Books, 1972). From an unpublished lecture by Dr. Mensendiek," Asia After the Vietnam War—What Role for the U.S.?" delivered in Claremont, California, April 14, 1976.

6. Germaine Greer, *The Female Eunuch* (New York: McGraw-Hill, 1971).

7. Carter Heyward, *A Priest Forever* (New York: Harper & Row, 1976).

> *I see women as the single most creative force* . . . We are asked to bring something new to the world around us—as workers, wives, daughters, mothers, scholars, artists, politicians, priests. *We are called to tell our stories*, and in telling our stories we manifest a new reality (p. 3).

Professor Hans Kung, a Jesuit-trained theologian of Tübingen, under the title, "Feminism: A New Reformation," outlines sixteen theses for women's liberation, *New York Times Magazine*, May 23, 1976.

8. Luke 4:1–19; Matt. 25:31–46.

9. Laurens van der Post, *Race Prejudice as Self-Rejection* (New York: The Workshop for Cultural Democracy, 1956). Out of print.

10. John Kenneth Galbraith, "How the Economy Hangs on Her Apron Strings," *Ms.*, May 1974, pp. 52, 74–77.

11. Dorothy Berkley Phillips, Elizabeth Boyden Howes, and Lucile M. Nixon, eds., *The Choice Is Always Ours* (Wheaton, Ill.: Theosophical Publishing House, a Re-Quest Book, by arrangement with Harper & Row, 1975).

12. Story by Kay Mills, Star-Ledger Washington Bureau, in the *Newark* (N.J.) Star-Ledger, June 22, 1976.

13. Susanne Gowan, George Lakey, William Moyer, Richard Taylor, *Moving Toward a New Society* (Philadelphia: New Society Press, 1976), p. 252.

14. Conversation with Elizabeth Verdesi from what became her doctoral thesis, later revised and published under the title *In But Still Out* (Philadelphia: Westminster, 1973 and 1976).

15. Mariarosa Dalla Costa and Selma James, "Women and the Subversion of the Community," *The Power of Women and the Subversion of the Community* (N.Y.: Falling Wall Press, 1981).

16. Lorraine Masterson, "Feminist Leaders Can't Walk on Water," *Quest,* 2 (Fall 1976).

17. Anne McGrew Bennett, unpublished paper entitled "The Hidden History of Women."

18. Richard Tholin, "The Holy Spirit and Liberation Movements: The Response of the Church" (speech given at Oxford Institute of Methodist Theological Studies, July 23–August 2, 1973).

19. This does not mean redeeming the church nor suggest using patriarchal tools to create a new patriarchal religious order.

20. "Sister, I hear your pain!" is a refrain from an original rape ritual written by a small group of women including Nancy Bahmueller, Diane Bennecamper, and Josy Catoggio and presented at a women's counseling conference held in New York, November 30–December 2, 1973.

1977: Beloved Image

1. "Beloved Image" was published along with six other essays under the title *La sfida del femminismo alla teologia,* eds. Mary Hunt and Rosino Gibellini, translated into Italian by E. Liliana Lanzarini, Cherubino Guzzetti, Enrico ten Kortenaar (Editrice Queriniana, Brescia, in 1980).

2. Anne McGrew Bennett, ".... a part of me is missing," in *Women in a Strange Land,* eds. Clare Benedicks Fischer, Betsy Brenneman, and Anne McGrew Bennett (Philadelphia: Fortress Press, 1975), p. 7.

3. The methodology and theology reflected in this paper have grown out of various conversations and work session seminars with women theologians. The conversations and stories of women in small groups are from tapes of various workshops with women held across the country from 1969 to 1974. The nature of the subject of the paper and its purpose appear to demand a polemical style for its development.

4. Elizabeth Janeway, "Images of Women," *Arts in Society,* special issue on Women and the Arts (Spring–Summer 1974). Published

by Research and Statewide Programs in the Arts, University of Wisconsin Extension.

5. Robert McAfee Brown, "Context Affects Content, the Rootedness of All Theology," *Christianity and Crisis* 37 (July 18, 1977).

6. The added interpretation of *empowerment* was given me by Dr. Winsome Munro, Luther College, Decorah, Ia.

7. Reminiscent of Samuel Beckett's "I have no voice and I must speak. That is all I know," from *The Unnameable* (New York: Grove Press, 1955), p. 9.

8. Cf. W. H. Auden's "Ruffle the perfect manners of the frozen heart/And once again compel it to be awkward and alive." From a longer poem, "Commentary," in *The Collected Poems of W. H. Auden* (New York: Random House, 1945), p. 346.

9. Robert Coles, *Children of Crisis: A Study of Courage and Fear* (Boston: Little, Brown, 1967).

10. Judy Chicago, *Through the Flower, My Struggle as a Woman Artist* (Garden City, N.J.: Doubleday, 1975).

11. Cf. special issue on Women and the Arts, *Arts in Society* 11 (Spring–Summer 1974).

12. Arlene Raven, "Women's Art: The Development of a Theoretical Perspective," *Womanspace Journal 1* (February/March 1973), pp. 14–20.

13. Ruth Iskin, "Judy Chicago in Conversation with Ruth Iskin," *Visual Dialog* (Special Issue: "Women in the Visual Arts"; Spring 1977), p. 16.

14. Grace Glueck, "The Woman As Artist," *New York Times Magazine*, September 25, 1977, Section 6, p. 66.

15. Iskin, "Judy Chicago," pp. 16–17.

16. Adrienne Rich, *Of Woman Born* (New York: Norton, 1976).

17. Otto Jesperson, *Growth and Structure of the English Language* (Oxford, Eng.: Basil Blackwell, 1955), p. 2.

18. Helen Lynd, *On Shame and the Search for Identity* (New York: Harcourt, Brace, 1958), pp. 176–177.

19. Julia Stanley (now Julia Penelope), "The Rhetoric of Denial: Delusion, Distortion, and Deception," *Sinister Wisdom*, Spring 1977, p. 80.

20. Andrea Dworkin, *Woman Hating* (New York: Dutton, 1974), p. 200.

21. Conversations with Mary Daly, paraphrases and quotes from her address delivered at the Woman's Building, Los Angeles, September 23, 1977. *Be-ing* has been greatly misinterpreted by some feminists who have read Daly carelessly. Her intent in hyphenating the two syllables is to show *being* and *doing* combined into one dynamic action.

22. *Chrysalis* is out of print, but a fine new journal, *Trivia*, is now being published out of Amherst, Massachusetts. Also, *Woman-Spirit* has ceased publication.

23. Virginia Woolf, *A Room of One's Own* (New York and Burlingame: Harcourt, Brace & World, 1929), pp. 117, 118.

24. See Kaufmann's introduction to the original German and a new translation edition Goethe's *Faust* (New York: Anchor Books, 1961) when he speaks of the way Goethe wrote, "...the exegesis of symbols, the pursuit of images are possibly indispensable," p. 12.

25. Cf. Dorothy Lee, *Freedom and Culture* (Englewood Cliffs, N.J.: Prentice-Hall, 1959), p. 162f.

26. Brita and Krister Stendahl, review of *Beyond God the Father: Toward a Philosophy of Women's Liberation*, in *Boston Sunday Globe*, January 13, 1974. The review is pertinent to the theme of this paper, excerpts of it are included below:

> For a long time our society has been insecure about the term "God."...most of us have not paid much attention to our use of symbols, underestimating their potentially dangerous nature....A terrible revenge has been taken because of this lack of vigilance. Superstition has crept into our most real creation....We receive messages but we do not examine the language...Mary Daly...has understood the risk the church runs by using a language that for the initiated few is transformed and translated into something else than what it signifies to most people....She has been moved by the "non-being" of women, the phenomenal training that women go through in order to conform with the standards of patriarchal society, demanding them to identify with the fathers, husbands, company and country, rather than identifying themselves, becoming persons in themselves...This book is a contribution to the movement, helping women to question the values of patriarchal society...Theologians say that God transcends anthropomorphic symbolization

but she knows that society reads otherwise...Only women, themselves victims of patriarchy, can make all the other victims, air, earth and water included, visible, in order that we can come closer to the "sacred cosmos." Women must begin to obey their own commandments....She moves with her sisters into the radical experience where No-thing and No-noun can be allowed to stand in God's place.

27. See James Hillman, "An Inquiry Into Image," *Spring*, An Annual of Archetypal Psychology and Jungian Thought, 1977, for an intriguing comparison of symbol and image. See also Hillman, *Archetypal Psychology, A Brief Account* (Zurich: Spring Publications, 1983).

28. Gerhard von Rad, *Old Testament Theology*, vol. 1 (New York: Harper & Row, 1957), p. 146.

29. Elaine Pagels, "Did Man Make God in His Image? Politics and Religion in Early Christianity," Colwell Lecture for Claremont School of Theology, October 25, 1977, projects the theory that the feminine images in the Gnostic Gospels and the threat of women's leadership in the early Christian Community combined, had much to do with branding Gnosticism as heresy and restricting women's participation in the church.

30. Robert L. Heilbroner, *An Inquiry into the Human Prospect* (New York: Norton, 1974), esp. pp. 142–144.

1978: The Goddess as Metaphoric Image

1. A somewhat abbreviated copy of this essay was published in *WomanSpirit*, spring 1984.

2. For an excellent treatment of androgyny see Janice Raymond's "The Illusion of Androgyny," *Quest* 11 (Summer 1975).

3. See Erich Fromm, *Forgotten Language: An Introduction to the Understanding of Dreams, Fairy Tales, and Myths* (New York: Reinhart, 1951), and J. J. Bachofen, *Myth, Religion and Mother Right* (Princeton, N.J.: Princeton University Press, 1967).

4. Edward Whitmont, *The Return of the Goddess* (New York: Crossroads, 1983).

5. Grailville is a Catholic Women's Community located near Cincinnati, Ohio, the entire structure of which allows for full and mutual participation of all its members.

6. The image is of Isis with great, outstretched wings as if to enfold all who approach her. A silver replica of her was given to me by Carole Etzler.

7. Pilgrim Place, a retirement community in Claremont, California.

8. The Seminary Quarter for Women held at Grailville was a six-week course open to women enrolled in accredited seminaries. Academic credit was available. It dealt with feminist theory, theology, and practice.

9. Z Budapest, a Dianic High Priestess, held her meetings in her own goddess shop in Los Angeles. She has now moved to Oakland.

10. Taken from Ntozake Shange's musical, *For Colored Girls Who Have Considered Suicide, When the Rainbow Is Enuf* (New York: Macmillan, 1976), p. 63.

11. Sideroblastic anemia is a disease of the bone marrow in which the excess iron forms a ring around young red blood cells and does not allow them to mature. No known cure. Certain medications and blood transfusions are required at frequent intervals.

12. See Susan Griffin, *Women and Nature* (New York: Harper & Row, 1978).

13. Julia Kristeva, *Desire in Language* (New York: Columbia University Press, 1980). See entire first essay, "The Ethics of Linguistics," p. 23ff.

14. See G. M. Mullet, *Spider Woman, Stories of the Hopi Indians* (Tucson: University of Arizona Press, 1979), p. 15.

15. Erich Neumann, *The Great Mother*, The Bollingen Series XL, VII (Princeton, N.J.: Princeton University Press, 1972), pp. 184–185.

16. Ibid., p. 177.

17. Ibid., pp. 305–308.

18. Adrienne Rich, *A Wild Patience Has Taken Me This Far* (New York: Norton, 1981), p. 9.

19. Adrienne Rich, *Of Woman Born, Motherhood as Experience and Institution* (New York: Norton, 1976), pp. 93–94.

20. Conversation with John Maguire, president, Claremont Graduate School.

21. I am more indebted to Robert Funk than anyone for my interest in and knowledge of metaphor. He first got me involved with metaphor in his work with parables, which he called extended metaphors.

22. See Boston Women's Health Collective, *Our Bodies, Ourselves,* rev. ed. (New York: Simon & Schuster, 1979).

23. Robin Morgan, *Anatomy of Feminism: Feminism, Physics, and Global Politics* (New York: Doubleday, 1982).

24. Owen Barfield, *Poetic Diction: A Study in Meaning* (New York: McGraw-Hill, 1964), p. 63.

25. Ibid., See chapter III on metaphor.

26. See Susan Sontag, *Antonin Artaud, Selected Writings* (New York: Farrar, Straus & Giroux, 1976).

27. Rubem Alves, *A Theology of Human Hope* (Washington, D.C.: Corpus Books, 1969).

28. Helen Lynd, *On Shame and the Search for Identity* (New York: Harcourt, Brace, 1958) pp. 176-177.

29. Mary Daly, *Gyn/Ecology* (Boston: Beacon Press, 1978).

30. Owen Barfield, *Speaker's Meaning* (Middletown, Conn.: Wesleyan University Press, 1967).

31. Ibid., p. 98.

32. Ibid., p. 112. But all of chapters 3 and 4 are relevant.

33. Prov. 8.

1979 and into the 1980s: Unfinished Business

1. "Hearing to speech" is a phrase that came out of a workshop in Elgin, Illinois, in 1970. See Appendix.

2. "Transcending," the verb, came out of a discussion with a prominent male theologian who said "women can't have it both ways—transcendent and organic." I confronted him because he was conceiving "transcendent" as static, "down from above." Women do not separate the "transcending," which we conceive as a verb and not a noun, from the organic "up from down under," thus avoiding patriarchal, dualistic thinking.

3. Anne Wilson Schaef, *Women's Reality* (Philadelphia: Winston Press, 1981).

4. See Susan Griffin, *Woman and Nature* (New York: Harper & Row, 1978); Mary Daly, *Gyn/Ecology* (Boston: Beacon Press, 1978); Rosemary Ruether, *New Woman, New Earth* (New York: Seabury Press, 1975).

5. Catharine B. Stimpson interview, "Gerda Lerner on the Future of Our Past," *Ms.,* September 1981, p. 50.

6. Schaef, *Women's Reality,* ch. 7.

7. Amos Wilder in *Children's Religion*, May 1964. Ceased publication. See note 4 in 1972 essay.

8. Robert McAfee Brown, "Context Affects Content, the Rootedness of All Theology," *Christianity and Crisis* 37 (July 18, 1977).

9. Nelle Morton, "The Word We Cannot Yet Speak," *New Conversations* 2 (Winter 1977). Also in this collection.

10. Hispanic Ecumenical Theological Conference held at the Mexican American Cultural Center, San Antonio, October 1978.

11. Justo Gonzales, quoted in *JASAC Grapevine* 10 (February 1979).

12. See Audre Lorde, "The Master's Tools Will Never Dismantle the Master's House," in *This Bridge Called My Back* (Watertown, Mass.: Persephone Press, 1981), p. 98. Reissued in 1984 and now distributed by Kitchen Table Press (New York).

13. *Historic Sites of Sullivan County*, published by the Sullivan County Historical Society Commission and Associates under auspices of the Sullivan County Court by Kingsport Press (Blountville, Tennessee), 1976.

14. See "The Spread of Chemical Disease in Kingsport," published in *The Elements*, April 1979, by the Public Resource Center at 1947 Connecticut Ave., N.W., Washington, D.C. 20009. Especially prepared for a citizen's forum on occupational and environmental health held in Kingsport and supported by a grant from the National Science Foundation.

15. The young woman drowning herself in Lake Susan became inseparable in my mind from an experience I had three years earlier in Brooklyn, N.Y., when I was dismissed from my first church position.

I was employed as parish assistant, which put me in touch with many immigrant families moving into the formerly elite area. It was at the height of the Depression. We had the privilege of sending indigent children to the Herald Tribune, Arbuckle Farms, and Brooklyn Sunday School Union fresh air camps.

One spring I had twenty children at the pier to board a boat up the Hudson to a Brooklyn Sunday School Union camp at Bear Mountain. An official sat at the dock to check each one in. When she came to Verna Perkins, she turned her around saying, "If you weren't quite so black, we could get you by."

It was I who had to take Verna and her neatly ironed and packed camp clothes back to her Jamaican family in Brooklyn. I don't know who sobbed the loudest. Fortunately my sobs were stifled by anger.

The church refused to protest or withdraw support from the Brooklyn Sunday School Union for discrimination. The organist resigned. The associate minister resigned. I was persuaded to remain through confirmation class when the pastor said that the church would make up to Verna for what had happened to her and her family. But when it came to a showdown, the board refused to admit her into church membership, saying she would be happier "with her own kind." I raised such a howl I was fired.

I still have Verna's picture. She would be around forty years old if she is alive. But always, she will be to me ten years old, with her family seeking justice and freedom in a household of faith in a new land.

16. It appears that Howard Zinn in *SNCC: The New Abolitionists* (Boston: Beacon Press, 1964) may have confused the First Freedom Ride (1947), called the Journey of Reconciliation, with the first of several freedom rides into the Deep South some ten or fifteen years later (1961). Certainly Anthony Dunbar in *Against the Grain* (Charlottesville: University Press of Virginia, 1981), p. 231, confused the two or accepted rumors as facts.

When the Fellowship of Southern Churchmen cooperated with the Fellowship of Reconciliation (FOR) through George Hauser and Bayard Rustin in setting up the First Freedom Ride of 1947, I was not aware that CORE (Congress of Racial Equality) participated in the preparation and execution of the journey (not that it would have made any difference!). Certainly, neither CORE nor FOR was available to pick up the pieces after the ride blew up in Chapel Hill, North Carolina, or follow through with the data Bayard Rustin gathered on prison conditions while riders served time in Raleigh, North Carolina, jail. It is important to note that the trouble in Chapel Hill was not caused by the bus driver nor the passengers. It was caused by local taxi drivers incensed at the riders using station facilities and trying to ride integrated in taxis. It is also worth noting that by the time of the second freedom ride in 1961 the law banning segregation in interstate travel had broadened to cover station facilities. There was no mob, as Dunbar reported. The rumors that fed Dunbar's story grew as time passed until it became difficult to discover the actual facts. The Zinn book was published in 1964; Dunbar's in 1981. Dunbar's account of the Fellowship of Southern Churchmen, beginning page 225 to the end, was greatly garbled and some data completely inaccurate.

However, pages 1 to 224, relating to the story of the Southern

Tenant Farmers Union, taken directly from the recorded accounts of Howard Kester, executive secretary of the Fellowship of Southern Churchmen, and H. L. Mitchell, founder of STFU who served on the board of FSC, is a remarkable and moving historical document and should have been published as a book in itself.

Incidentally, the 1961 freedom ride and all successive rides complied with the FSC's original conditions for the first ride in 1947: briefing sessions on nonviolence and inclusion of southern riders were carefully observed. Perhaps this was due to James Farmer's becoming CORE's national director.

17. Amos Wilder, *Theopoetic and the Religious Imagination* (Philadelphia: Fortress Press, 1976).

18. Gayraud Wilmore, "From an Editor at Large," in *Christian Century*, April 11, 1979.

19. It is the two languages that have forced Robin Morgan and Mary Daly to refuse questions from men in their audiences. The drain of energy is almost too much when a feminist speaker entertains a question from a male. By the time she translates it into her language, words the answer, translates it back into the male language, she is exhausted. Even then the answer may not be completely understood by the questioner.

20. Many feminists have misunderstood Mary Daly's use of "Be-ing" to hark back to an old Thomas dualism. Daly's intent was to indicate that God could be known only in being-in-movement—in act in the human arena. Daly was at my house in Madison, N.J., when we discussed this idea in depth. Reference was made at the time to Ernest Wright's *God Who Acts* and also to Goethe's contention that "in the beginning was not the Word. In the beginning was the Act." She intended to combine Being and Doing into one dynamic movement. At the same time she came out with "God is a Verb," an essay published in the December 1970 issue of *Ms.*

21. For this idea I am indebted to my close friend and former colleague Dr. George Kelsey, Professor Emeritus, the Theological School, Drew University, Madison, N.J., in conversation. See also Janice Raymond, *The Transsexual Empire* (Boston: Beacon Press, 1979).

22. Basil Moore, ed., *Black Theology: The African Voice* (London: Hurst, 1973).

23. In conversation with Joan Martin of Temple University and Judy Mintier, a public school teacher in Philadelphia.

Index

Nelle Morton was born in 1905 in Sullivan County, Tennessee. She received her formal training from the New York Theological Seminary and the University of Geneva. She has had a rich and varied career working for civil rights in the South, teaching at the Theological School of Drew University and lecturing throughout the U.S. and the world. The first theologian to teach a university course on women, theology, and language, she has been awarded honorary degrees from St. Andrews Presbyterian College and from Drew University for her early work in peace and human rights and more recently for her leadership in women's liberation and the church. Long in the vanguard of social and religious reform, Nelle Morton has been a mentor to many of the current generation of feminists writing on theology and language.